Mac OS X for Absolute Beginners

Wallace Wang

Apress®

Mac OS X for Absolute Beginners

Wallace Wang
San Diego, California, USA

ISBN-13 (pbk): 978-1-4842-1912-6   ISBN-13 (electronic): 978-1-4842-1913-3
DOI 10.1007/978-1-4842-1913-3

Library of Congress Control Number: 2016943053

Managing Director: Welmoed Spahr
Lead Editor: Louise Corrigan
Development Editor: James Markham
Technical Reviewer: Brandon Scott
Editorial Board: Steve Anglin, Pramila Balen, Louise Corrigan, James DeWolf, Jonathan Gennick, Robert Hutchinson, Celestin Suresh John, Nikhil Karkal, James Markham, Susan McDermott, Matthew Moodie, Douglas Pundick, Ben Renow-Clarke, Gwenan Spearing
Coordinating Editor: Nancy Chen
Copy Editor: Kim Burton-Weisman
Compositor: SPi Global
Indexer: SPi Global

Distributed to the book trade worldwide by Springer Science+Business Media New York, 233 Spring Street, 6th Floor, New York, NY 10013. Phone 1-800-SPRINGER, fax (201) 348-4505, e-mail orders-ny@springer-sbm.com, or visit www.springer.com. Apress Media, LLC is a California LLC and the sole member (owner) is Springer Science + Business Media Finance Inc (SSBM Finance Inc). SSBM Finance Inc is a Delaware corporation.

For information on translations, please e-mail rights@apress.com, or visit www.apress.com.

Apress and friends of ED books may be purchased in bulk for academic, corporate, or promotional use. eBook versions and licenses are also available for most titles. For more information, reference our Special Bulk Sales–eBook Licensing web page at www.apress.com/bulk-sales.

Any source code or other supplementary materials referenced by the author in this text is available to readers at www.apress.com. For detailed information about how to locate your book's source code, go to www.apress.com/source-code/.

Printed on acid-free paper

This is book is dedicated to everyone who has suffered through the complexity, confusion, and chaos of other types of computers and finally discovered the simplicity and ease of use that the Macintosh offers. Welcome to the future, where computers actually work to make the lives of people easier and more enjoyable.

Contents at a Glance

Contents

About the Author

Wallace Wang has written dozens of computer books over the years, beginning with ancient MS-DOS programs like WordPerfect and Turbo Pascal, and graduating up to Windows programs like Visual Basic and Microsoft Office. After taking one look at the incredible mess that Microsoft made with Vista, he decided to abandon the Windows world and shift toward the friendlier and less frustrating world of the Macintosh. (His decision was confirmed when Microsoft released Windows 8 to an unsuspecting public.)

After being a happy Macintosh user for nearly a decade, he's spent the last several years helping people make the transition from Windows to Macintosh as painless as possible. When he's not helping people discover the joys of personal computing with a computer that's actually fun to use, he performs stand-up comedy and appears on two radio shows on KNSJ in San Diego (http://knsj.org) called *Notes From the Underground* and *Laugh In Your Face Radio* (www.laughinyourfaceradio.com).

He also writes a screenwriting blog called *The 15 Minute Movie Method* (http://15minutemoviemethod.com), a blog about the latest cat news on the Internet called *Cat Daily News* (http://catdailynews.com), and a blog about the latest technology related to Apple products called *Top Bananas* (www.topbananas.com).

About the Technical Reviewer

 **Brandon Scott** specializes in software engineering for desktop applications, software development kits, and distributed systems. He currently leads development efforts for AspiraCloud Ltd., focusing on Microsoft SharePoint and Azure work streams. Additionally, Brandon also partners with Razer Inc., aiding with the design of SDK products and open source libraries. He experience comes from working for a variety of companies in different industries, including JP Morgan Chase & Co. and Microsoft.

Acknowledgments

Thanks go to all the wonderful people at Apress for giving me a chance to write about OS X and the Macintosh.

Additional thanks go to Dane Henderson and Elizabeth Lee (www.echoludo.com), who share the airwaves with me on our radio show *Notes From the Underground* on KNSJ.org. More thanks go to Chris Clobber, Diane Jean, Ikaika Patria, and Robert Weems for letting me share their friendship and lunacy every week on another KNSJ radio show called *Laugh In Your Face Radio* (www.laughinyourfaceradio.com), where we combine comedy with political activism and commentary.

A special mention goes to Michael Montijo and his indomitable spirit that has him driving from Phoenix to Los Angeles at least once a month for the past 20 years to meet with Hollywood executives. One day when you hear about his cartoon series *Life of Mikey* and *Pachuko Boy*, you'll know how they finally appeared on television because he never gave up on his dream, despite all the obstacles in his way.

Thanks also go to my wife, Cassandra, and my son, Jordan, for putting up with a house filled with more gadgets than actual living people. Final thanks go to my cats, Oscar and Mayer, for walking over the keyboard, stepping on the trackpad and mouse, and chewing on power cords at the most inconvenient times of the day.

Introduction

Most people don't buy a Macintosh because they want to use Photos, iTunes, or Pages. Instead, most people buy a Macintosh because they want to accomplish a specific result, such as saving and viewing photographs, playing music, or typing and printing a letter. That's why thick books explaining how to use the Macintosh operating system, called OS X, can be so intimidating. These thick books assume readers want to become computer experts by learning how OS X works.

As a result, most computer books exhaustively explain every possible feature of OS X without telling you why you might want to use that particular feature. That's like forcing you to learn how a six-cylinder internal combustion engine works before you learn how to drive.

This book is different because it teaches you the most common tasks you'll need to be productive on your Macintosh. You won't learn every possible feature of iTunes or Mail. Instead, you'll just learn enough so you can feel comfortable using a Macintosh.

A computer is nothing more than a tool. What you do with that tool is entirely up to you.

A paintbrush is also a tool, but if you give a paintbrush to the average person, they might be able to scribble some blobs of pretty colors on a canvas. Yet if you give a paintbrush to an artist like Michelangelo, you get a work of art painted on the ceiling of the Sistine Chapel.

The co-founder of Apple, Steve Jobs, once described computers as "bicycles for the mind." Jobs said this after reading a *Scientific American* article that showed that condors used the least amount of energy to move a kilometer. In comparison, humans were extremely inefficient in moving that same distance by walking or running. However, when humans used a bicycle to travel a kilometer, they expended far less energy than even a condor. Just as a bicycle is a tool to make humans more efficient in getting from one place to another, computers are a tool to make humans more efficient in tapping their creativity.

So this book won't waste your time by teaching you what different tools can do. Instead, this book focuses on teaching you how to use different tools so that you can create useful results on your Macintosh.

Whether you need to write a letter, jot down some notes, edit a picture, or play music, this book will show you the fastest, simplest, and easiest way to achieve a given task—so that your Macintosh becomes a bicycle for your mind.

Understanding How a Macintosh Works

Whether you have an iMac or Mac mini that sits on a desk, or a MacBook laptop that you can take with you, every Macintosh is nothing more than a chunk of hardware. What makes that chunk of hardware work is a special program called an *operating system*.

If you've used a PC before, you're probably already familiar with an operating system called Microsoft Windows. With a Macintosh, the operating system is called OS X.

Don't worry. You don't have to know anything about OS X to use your Macintosh. All you need to know is that any time you want to do something, you need to find the right program that works with OS X to accomplish it. On OS X, you can do such things as

- Play music
- Write letters
- Edit video
- Browse web pages on the Internet
- Send and receive e-mail
- And many other tasks

While OS X makes your Macintosh work, individual programs stored on your Macintosh let you perform specific tasks. For example, your Macintosh might have a word processor that lets you type and print letters from it, an e-book viewer that allows you to read books on it, or a game that lets you to play chess with it.

Each time you install a new program, you make your Macintosh more versatile and capable of performing different tasks. With the right program, your Macintosh can do almost anything. However, this book focuses solely on the programs that come free with every Macintosh.

So whether you've used a computer before or you're a complete novice, don't worry. This book won't bog you down with technical details. Instead, you'll learn what to do, how to do it, and more importantly, why to do it.

There's a reason why more people are buying and using Macintosh computers. It's because a Macintosh is easier, more reliable, and maybe more fun to use than most other types of computers. So get ready to learn shortcuts, tips, and basic instructions for getting the most out of your Macintosh today.

What to Expect from this Book

Don't expect to learn every possible feature available on a Macintosh. Also, don't expect dense explanations that show how to do something without telling you why you might want to do it in the first place.

What you can expect from this book is a chance to learn how to use your Macintosh as quickly, easily, and painlessly as possible.

This book doesn't have all the answers to using a Macintosh, but it does have lots of tips and tricks for helping you work faster and more efficiently than ever before.

Once you learn just enough to get started, you'll feel more comfortable—until you're able to figure out how to use your Macintosh all by yourself. Fair enough? If so, then turn the page and let's get started.

Part I

Basic Training

One of the biggest problems with learning anything new is knowing where to get started. In this part of the book, you'll learn the most common commands for using the Macintosh-no matter what program you need to use.

You'll learn how to

- give commands using a mouse, trackpad, and keyboard

- start and stop programs

- write and edit text

- save your data in files that you can organize in different ways

By the time you've completed reading this part of the book, you should feel confident that you can use your Macintosh all by yourself.

Chapter 1

Understanding OS X

Most computers tend to work in similar ways. By understanding how computers work in general, you can quickly learn how to use any particular type of computer now and in the future.

The monitor can show useful information such as stock quotes or news stories displayed on a web page.

The keyboard, mouse, or trackpad let you control the computer by typing text or manipulating items on the screen, such as editing a photograph.

Once you give commands to the computer, the processor calculates a new result and displays those changed results on the screen.

Using a computer is essentially a back and forth conversation where the computer shows information on the monitor and then waits for you to do something about it. You can use the keyboard, mouse, or trackpad to manipulate data on the screen, such as editing text or modifying a picture. Once you've given a command to the computer, it changes the data on the screen and shows the result so that you can do something else.

What makes every computer do something useful is software. By installing different programs, you can literally make the computer do practically anything you want.

People can use a computer to write letters, play games, draw cartoons, plot stock market prices, or edit movies. Software turns your computer into a versatile tool customized for your particular needs.

However, the most important software every computer needs is called an *operating system* because it literally controls how the entire computer works. If you have a Mac, you use an operating system called *OS X*.

OS X controls the physical parts of your Mac, such as sending data to a printer or accepting characters typed from the keyboard. To use a Mac, you need to learn how to use OS X.

© Wallace Wang 2016
W. Wang, *Mac OS X for Absolute Beginners*, DOI 10.1007/978-1-4842-1913-3_1

Don't worry. You don't need to learn technical details about OS X. Neither do you need to learn every possible feature of OS X. All you really need to know are the basics to using OS X so that you can do something useful with your Mac.

> **Note**   If you've used another type of computer before, you probably used an operating system called Microsoft Windows. OS X works much the same way as Microsoft Windows, but it doesn't work exactly like Microsoft Windows. If you're used to the way Windows works, you need to relearn how to perform specific tasks using OS X.

Why Computers Are So Difficult to Understand

In the early days of computers, you had to be a computer expert just to turn on a computer, let alone use it. Fortunately, computers have gotten much easier to use, thanks to the Mac, but in case you still feel computers are too hard to use, the reason is simple.

Computer programmers and engineers created and designed computers for themselves.

Think about how every field has its own jargon and way of thinking. Accountants know the meaning of terms like balance sheets, cash flow, and equity, while plumbers can easily understand terms like auger, closet bend, and dip tube.

If you're not an accountant, you won't understand common accounting terms. Likewise, if you're not a plumber, you won't understand common plumbing terms.

If you're not a computer expert, you won't understand common computer terms, and that's why computers have always seemed so confusing and difficult to use. Most computer manuals are written by programmers for other programmers, using terms that they already understand. If you don't understand common computer terms, you probably won't be able to understand most computer manuals, help files, or other types of documentation that are supposed to help you but only tend to confuse and frustrate you even more.

Even worse, programmers already know how to use a computer, so they readily skip over steps, assume too much, and gloss over explanations. The actual steps to using a computer are often based on earlier, more primitive ways of using a computer. If you aren't familiar with these earlier, more primitive ways of using a computer, you probably won't completely understand why today's computers work the way they do.

For example, the first IBM PC came with a keyboard that combined a numeric keypad with cursor keys is shown in Figure 1-1. If you wanted to use the numeric keypad, you had to press a special Num Lock key. If you wanted to move the cursor on the screen, you had to press the Num Lock key a second time to turn off the numeric keypad.

Figure 1-1. The keyboard of the original IBM PC combined cursor keys with a numeric keypad

How could you tell if the Num Lock key was on or off on the original IBM PC keyboard? You couldn't. You had to press a key on the numeric keypad, and if it typed a number, then you knew the Num Lock key was turned on. If it moved the cursor, then you knew the Num Lock key was turned off.

IBM later redesigned the keyboard to offer separate cursor keys and numeric keys. Inexplicably, the separate numeric keypad retained the Num Lock key, so it could double up as a cursor keypad as well. This meant you now had one dedicated cursor keypad and a second cursor/numeric keypad, as shown in Figure 1-2.

Figure 1-2. IBM modified the keyboard to include a separate cursor keypad along with a second cursor/numeric keypad

Why would anyone ever turn off the Num Lock key to have two separate cursor key pads? No one would do this. Yet you can still see this horrible design in many PC keyboards even today.

Computer manufacturers often retain old features out of inertia and familiarity. Rather than question why certain features exist and eliminating outdated ones, computer people tend to keep old features and pile on new ones to create a confusing mess that only they can understand.

Just as computer people have retained obsolete hardware designs, so have they also retained obsolete software designs.

In the old days, people used floppy disks, which were circular disks coated with magnetic material. These early floppy disks were 8 inches in size, but later shrank down to 5.25 inches and eventually to 3.5 inches in size, as shown in Figure 1-3. They were called *floppy disks* because they were disks and would flop up and down if they weren't enclosed in a protective plastic case.

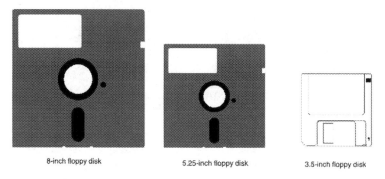

8-inch floppy disk   5.25-inch floppy disk   3.5-inch floppy disk

Figure 1-3. Early computers stored data on 8-, 5.25-, and 3.5-inch floppy disks

A 3.5-inch floppy disk could only hold a maximum of 1.44 megabytes of data. Today, a single audio file of a popular song takes up more than 3 megabytes. Since floppy disks weren't able to store today's larger files, they quickly fell out of popularity. That's why you never see floppy disk drives used in any modern computer.

Yet if you look at the user interface of Microsoft Word 2016, you can still see that Microsoft uses a floppy disk icon to represent the Save command, as shown in Figure 1-4.

Figure 1-4. Microsoft Word 2016 uses a floppy disk icon to represent the Save command

Even though people haven't used a floppy disk in over a decade, and many newer computer users have never seen a floppy disk in their life, Microsoft and many other companies still use the floppy disk icon to represent the Save command.

None of this makes sense unless you understand the historical origins. Even when you do understand the historical origins, it still doesn't make any sense to cling to antiquated features and icons that no longer have any meaning.

That's why computers have traditionally been so hard to understand—they force people to decipher obsolete ideas that increase confusion for no good reason.

Fortunately, OS X sheds many of these obsolete vestiges of computer history to make a Mac easier to use. OS X may not be perfect, but it eliminates much of the confusion that still clutters other operating systems.

Computers Are Designed for Experts, Not Beginners

Programmers create and design computers, so to better understand how any computer works, you need to understand how programmers think. Programmers tend to create multiple ways to perform the exact same command. For example, to save a file in almost any program, you typically have the following three ways to choose the same Save command:

- Click the File menu and choose Save
- Click the Save icon
- Press Command+S

Why do computers offer so many ways to perform the exact same command? It's because programmers like shortcuts and options so that they can choose the way that they like best.

The drawback of so many options is that they tend to confuse beginners. Car manufacturers never give you three different ways to signal a left turn because that would just confuse drivers. Instead, car manufacturers give you one simple way to signal a left turn. Once you learn this one, simple way, you never have to relearn anything different or new to signal left turns.

Rather than simplifying computers, multiple options clutter the screen and get in the way, while at the same time making computers harder to use. Computer novices just want to learn one way to perform a task. Only computer experts care about using multiple shortcuts to perform the same task, so ultimately computers are designed to satisfy experts, not beginners.

Understanding the Mac Philosophy

When Apple introduced the original Mac back in 1984, the goal was to make a powerful computer that was easy for non-computer experts to use. The Mac philosophy has always been about maximizing the user experience to make it as effortless as possible. That's not always the case with other operating systems.

On Windows PC laptops, the trackpad displays a left and right mouse button so that you can give commands to the computer. On Mac laptops, pressing the trackpad lets you give commands to the computer. By eliminating extra buttons, Apple's trackpads are not only more elegant in appearance, but also easier and simpler to use.

As a result of this design philosophy, the Mac hardware and its OS X operating system shields you from the technical complexity of using a computer. On a Windows PC, a single program often consists of dozens of files. If you accidentally delete one of these critical files, your program won't work. Despite this danger, Windows displays all program files by default, increasing the chance that a novice will move, rename, or delete a file by mistake.

On a Mac, program files are hidden from view; so unless you specifically ask to see all the files that make up a single program, you'll never see anything but a single icon that represents that entire program. This ensures that you can't accidentally delete or move a program file by mistake.

Attention to details that protect the user makes the Mac and OS X much easier and safer to use. The goal of the Mac is to free you from maintaining and caring for a computer so that you can spend more time actually getting useful work done.

With a Windows 8 PC, scrolling the mouse button up and down moves the Windows 8 tiles left and right. If this sounds disorienting, confusing, and illogical, you're right. In all versions of Windows, sliding your finger up on a trackpad moves the content of a window down, and sliding your finger down on a trackpad moves the content of a window up. This is like turning your left turn signal in a car to signal right and turning your right turn signal on to signal left.

On a Mac, sliding your finger up a trackpad moves the content of a window up, and sliding your finger down a trackpad moves the content of a window down. This more natural movement helps you better associate how the motion of your finger correlates to the motion of data displayed on the screen.

If you've never used a Mac before, you'll find using OS X can feel natural and intuitive. If you've used a Windows PC before, you'll find that a Mac running OS X can be more logical to understand and much simpler to use.

Just remember that when you learn anything for the first time, you'll be clumsy and awkward. With a little practice, you become more proficient—until the day that you find yourself performing tasks without thinking.

Using a computer is a skill that anyone can learn and develop. The more you use a Mac, the more comfortable you become. The more comfortable you become, the more adventurous you become, and you'll start exploring on your own.

Best of all, once you run into problems and learn how to fix them yourself, your confidence level starts increasing until the day comes that you won't have any problems using a Mac at all.

Understanding the OS X Desktop

As you learned earlier, OS X is an operating system that controls the computer. OS X acts like an interpreter between you and your Mac.

First, OS X gets data from the computer and displays this information on the screen. If you select a command to manipulate the data on the screen, OS X obeys and then displays new information on the screen. Based on this new information, you can choose more commands.

OS X displays information on the screen and shows a list of commands that you can choose from; this is called the *user interface*. The main OS X user interface is called the *desktop*, which consists of the following three areas (also see Figure 1-5):

- Menu bar: Displays pull-down menus at the top of the screen
- Desktop: Displays an image to fill the screen
- Dock: Displays icons at the bottom of the screen

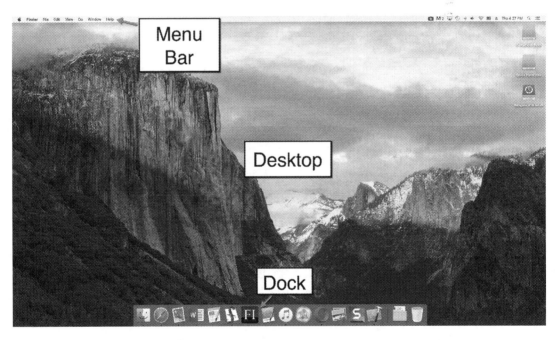

Figure 1-5. The three areas of the OS X desktop

The menu bar always appears at the very top of the screen. By clicking the different titles in the menu bar, you see a list of the available commands that you can choose, as shown in Figure 1-6.

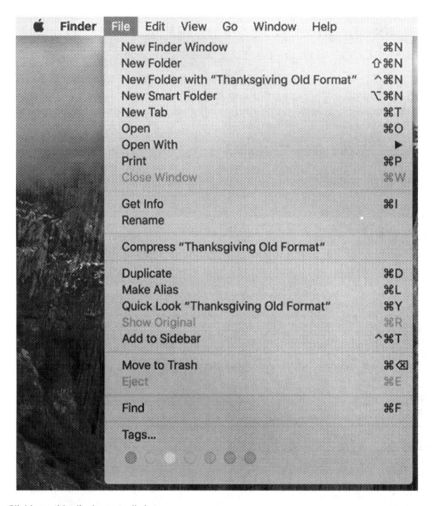

Figure 1-6. Clicking a title displays a pull-down menu

Directly underneath the menu bar is the desktop wallpaper. The wallpaper fills most of the screen. The wallpaper can be any image that you like so that you can customize the appearance of your Mac. The desktop is also a place to store icons that represent data or programs. Placing icons on the desktop lets you find them easily. When you open a program, it opens and displays one or more windows that appear on the desktop.

At the bottom of the screen is the Dock, which offers an organized way to store icons. The Dock normally appears at the bottom of the screen, but you can make it appear on the left or right sides instead.

Typically, you can use the Dock to store your most frequently used programs; that way, you can find and run your favorite programs.

Every time that you use a Mac, you see the desktop, although the menu bar at the top of the screen may change, depending on which program you are running at the time.

Using a Keyboard

The whole purpose of the desktop is to give you access to any programs installed on your Mac. By itself, the desktop does nothing but display information on the screen and wait for you to choose a command. To choose a command displayed on the desktop, you have to use the keyboard and a mouse or trackpad.

The keyboard contains letters, numbers, and symbols (such as $, &, @, and #) that you can type. Besides these character keys, keyboards also contain the following additional sets of keys (also see Figure 1-7):

- Function keys
- Cursor keys
- Modifier keys

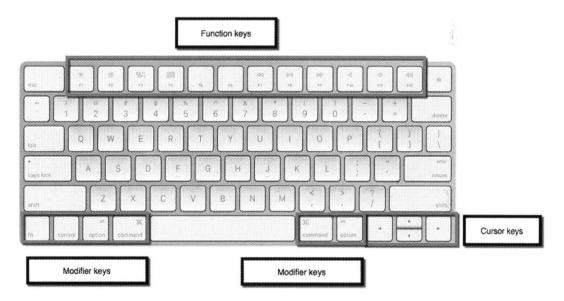

Figure 1-7. The types of keys on a keyboard

Function keys (located at the top of the keyboard) are another throwback to earlier computers. In the old days, many programs allowed you to give a command by pressing a function key. Pressing the F1 function key might display help, whereas pressing F10 might print data.

Nowadays, hardly any programs let you give commands by pressing a function key. That's why most computers, including the Mac, now assign hardware controls to the function keys, as follows:

- F1: Reduce (or dim) screen brightness

- F2: Increase screen brightness

- F7: Rewind

- F8: Play/Pause

- F9: Fast-forward

- F10: Mute

- F11: Decrease volume

- F12: Increase volume

> **Note**   In the rare event that you need a function key, you need to hold down the Fn key (normally located at the bottom-left corner of the keyboard) and then press a function key. The Fn key tells your Mac to ignore any hardware controls assigned to a function key.

Why do function keys still exist even though most programs completely ignore them? It's because function keys can be used to create custom shortcuts in addition to maintaining compatibility with the handful of older programs that may still use function keys.

In general, most people never use function keys, but they exist for more advanced users.

The cursor keys consist of four arrows, which point up, down, left, or right. Cursor keys are most often used when typing and editing text. The cursor appears on the screen as a vertical line that blinks on and off to make it easy to find on the screen.

Whenever you type any keyboard characters, they appear wherever the cursor currently appears, as shown in Figure 1-8.

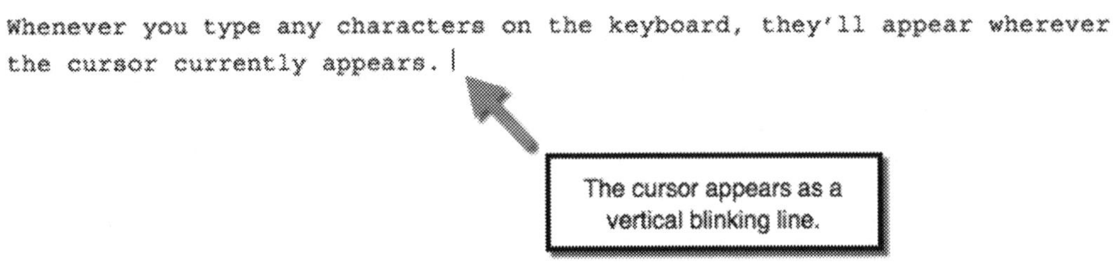

Whenever you type any characters on the keyboard, they'll appear wherever the cursor currently appears. |

The cursor appears as a
vertical blinking line.

Figure 1-8. The cursor lets you point where you want to edit text

Modifier keys allow you to use ordinary keys in different ways. The most obvious modifier key is the Shift key. Holding down the Shift key while pressing a letter key creates an uppercase letter. Holding down the Shift key while pressing a number key on the top row creates a symbol, such as $ or #.

Three other modifier keys include Control, Option, and Command, which are often represented by symbols, as shown in Figure 1-9.

⌃	Control
⌥	Option
⇧	Shift
⌘	Command

Figure 1-9. *Modifier keys let you change the behavior of other keys*

Modifier keys are only used to change the behavior of other keys. In most programs, you can hold down the Command key, tap the S key, and let go of both to choose the Save command, which is often abbreviated as Command+S.

You can also use two modifier keys along with a third key to choose a command, such as holding down the Shift key, holding down the Command key, and tapping the N key, which is abbreviated as Shift+Command+N.

Modifier keys let you choose commands through the keyboard. The most commonly used modifier key is the Command key. Beyond the Shift key, the other three modifier keys (Control, Option, and Command) are completely optional. It's possible to use a Mac without ever touching any of these three modifier keys.

Using a Mouse or Trackpad

Back in the early days of computers, all you could create on a computer was text, so a keyboard worked just fine. Of course, that meant computer-savvy people kept adding new features to the standard keyboard. That's why you see function keys and modifier keys on computer keyboards.

When Apple introduced the Mac in 1984, it was the first personal computer that allowed people to create and edit graphics as well as text. How can you edit and manipulate graphics using cursor keys on a keyboard? You can't.

That's why the Mac comes with a mouse: so you can point on the screen. The screen always displays a pointer that lets you point and click on the screen. By moving the mouse on a flat surface, you can move the pointer on the screen.

A trackpad works exactly like a mouse. A trackpad lets you move the pointer on the screen by sliding your finger across the surface of the trackpad.

Laptops use a trackpad to save space, whereas desktops typically use a mouse. However, you can always add a trackpad to a desktop computer or a mouse to a laptop. Some people prefer a mouse, others prefer a trackpad, and some people even use both.

When you point to something on the screen, nothing happens until you click the mouse/trackpad. Older mice had physical buttons that you could press. However, on Apple's mouse, there are no physical buttons.

Instead of clicking a physical button, an Apple mouse lets you press down on the top-left or top-right corners of the mouse with your finger. Pressing the top-left corner of an Apple mouse represents the left button and pressing the top-right corner of an Apple mouse represents the right button, as shown in Figure 1-10.

Figure 1-10. The top corners of the Apple mouse represent the left and right buttons

Pressing the left button on a mouse is known as a *click* or a *left-click*. When you use a mouse, you typically use the left mouse button by pressing the top-left corner of the mouse and letting go.

Pressing the right button is known as a *right-click* or a *secondary click*. This action often displays a menu of options that pop up wherever the pointer happens to be, as shown in Figure 1-11.

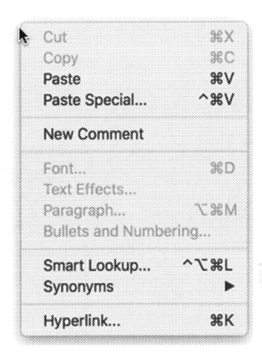

Figure 1-11. *Right-clicking often displays a pop-up menu of commands*

Since right-clicking is a shortcut, it's possible to use a computer and never press the right button. Often times, you must specifically turn on this right-click/secondary click feature before you can use it, which you'll learn to do later in this chapter.

With a trackpad, the entire surface acts like a button. To perform a left-click on a trackpad, just press your finger on the trackpad surface and lift up your finger. To perform a right-click/secondary click on a trackpad, press two fingers on the trackpad surface and lift up both fingers.

Pointing at something on the screen and then clicking it is the most common mouse/ trackpad task. To help you learn how to use a mouse or trackpad, try the following exercise:

1. Turn on your Mac by pressing its power button. (On an iMac or Mac mini, the power button is located on the back of the computer. On a laptop Mac, the power button is located in the upper-right corner of the keyboard.)

2. Using the mouse or trackpad, move the mouse pointer over the Apple icon on the left side of the menu bar and then left-click (press the top-left corner of the mouse or press one finger on the trackpad). If you clicked the mouse/trackpad successfully, the Apple menu appears, as shown in Figure 1-12.

Figure 1-12. *The Apple menu lets you customize your Mac*

3. Move the mouse pointer over System Preferences and click the left
    mouse button or press one finger on the trackpad. If you clicked
    System Preferences correctly, a System Preferences window
    appears, as shown in Figure 1-13.

Figure 1-13. *The System Preferences window*

4. Point and click the Mouse or Trackpad icon in the second row from the top. Clicking the Mouse icon displays the Mouse window, as shown in Figure 1-14. Clicking the Trackpad icon displays the Trackpad icon, as shown in Figure 1-15.

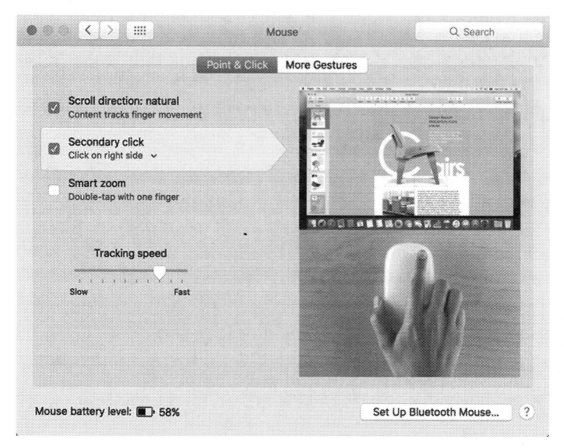

Figure 1-14. The Mouse window

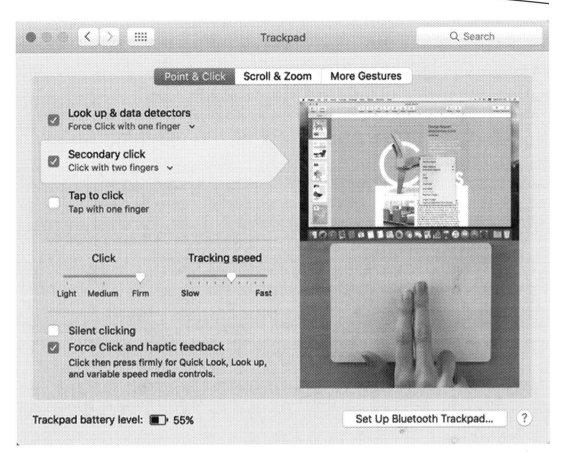

Figure 1-15. The Trackpad window

5.   Make sure that a check mark appears in the "Secondary click" check box. If not, click in the "Secondary click" check box to select it. (A check mark tells you that secondary click is turned on. An empty check box means that it is turned off.)

6.   Click the red dot in the upper corner of the Mouse or Trackpad window. This red dot represents the Close window command.

Congratulations! By using the mouse or trackpad in the preceding exercise, you've learned to customize your mouse or trackpad to allow secondary or right-clicking.

You also learned how to use the menu bar at the top of the screen and choose commands by pointing and clicking them with the mouse/trackpad.

To use OS X, you must learn how to point and click using a mouse/trackpad. Since pointing and clicking is such a crucial part of using OS X, the next chapter goes into more details on how to use a mouse/trackpad.

Note   If you don't turn on the secondary-click option, you can simulate a right-click by holding down the Control key and clicking the left mouse button or pressing one finger on the trackpad; then release both the mouse/trackpad and the Control key.

How to Turn a Mac On and Off

The most crucial lesson to learn is how to turn a Mac on and off. One reason why computers seem so confusing is that they don't work the way you'd expect them to. When you have a blender, you turn it on by flicking a switch to the On position. Then to turn it off, you flick that same switch to the Off position. The same switch turns a blender on and off.

That's not how computers work, which is part of the reason why computers can be so frustrating and confusing. To turn a Mac on, you press a button. On an iMac or Mac mini, the power button is in the back of the computer. That's to keep you from pressing it by mistake and turning your computer off.

On a Mac laptop, the On switch is in the upper-right corner above the keyboard. This out-of-the-way location is also designed to keep you from pressing the button and turning your computer off by mistake.

If you want to use the power button to turn off your Mac, hold the power button for a few seconds until a message appears, asking if you want to shut the computer down. When this message appears, click the Shut Down button.

A more common way to turn a Mac off is to shut down OS X. When you shut down OS X, the operating system first checks if you have any unsaved data. If you do, OS X displays a message on the screen that asks if you want to save your data or not. Regardless of how you answer, OS X then makes sure that all files on your computer are closed before shutting off your Mac. This helps to avoid your data getting lost or scrambled.

Any time you want to turn off your Mac, you must first shut down OS X. To shut down OS X, follow these steps:

1.   Click the Apple icon on the menu bar. A pull-down menu appears, as shown in Figure 1-16.

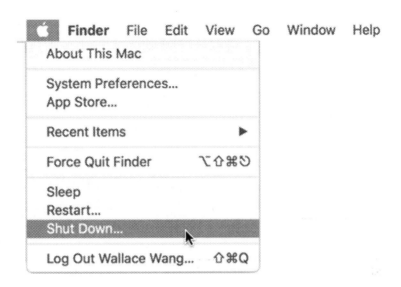

Figure 1-16. The Shut Down command in the Apple pull-down menu

2. Click Shut Down. If you have any unsaved data, OS X asks if you
    want to save it or not.

Always (yes, always) turn off your Mac using the Shut Down command. If you fail to use the
Shut Down command, you could lose data.

Summary

Computers display information on the screen and wait for the user to choose a command to
modify the information. To give commands to a computer, you have to use the keyboard and
the mouse. Instead of a mouse, you may have a trackpad that mimics a mouse.

By moving the mouse or sliding your finger on the surface of a trackpad, you can move a
pointer on the screen. Left-clicking (pressing down and letting go of the top-left corner of a
mouse, or pressing one finger on a trackpad surface and letting go) selects something on
the screen, such as a pull-down menu command.

A menu bar always appears at the top of the screen and allows you to point and click on a
command. As a shortcut, you can often choose common commands by using modifier keys
on the keyboard instead, such as the Shift, Control, Option, or Command keys.

OS X is an operating system that controls how your Mac works. Although OS X and the Mac
try to make computers easier to use, you may still find some confusing features that don't
make any sense until you understand the original reason why they were used.

Most importantly, always (yes, always) turn your Mac off by clicking the Apple icon on the menu bar and then choosing the Shut Down command. The Shut Down command can help you avoid losing data, such as important business reports.

Remember, using a computer is a skill that you can always improve through practice. Don't be afraid to experiment and play around with your Mac. The best way to learn anything is through constant practice and experimentation, until you feel more and more comfortable using your Mac.

Chapter 2

Giving Commands with the Mouse, Trackpad, and Keyboard

To use OS X, you need to know how to point and click to choose commands. In addition, you need to know how to type and edit text. That means you need to know how to use keyboard and a mouse or a trackpad.

The mouse/trackpad is the main way to control a Mac. Once you understand how to move the pointer on the screen by moving the mouse (or sliding your finger across the trackpad surface), you need to know how to give commands to OS X. The following are the four basic tasks needed to perform commands through the mouse or trackpad:

- Hover
- Click (also known as *left-click* because you use the left mouse button)
- Drag
- Right-click (also known as *secondary click*)

Hovering

To *hover*, or *hovering*, means to move the pointer over something that appears on the screen. A common example of hovering is when you place the pointer over an icon and then wait a few seconds until a brief explanation of the icon's purpose pops up.

By hovering the pointer over the icons in any program's user interface, you can often learn the command that each icon represents.

© Wallace Wang 2016

W. Wang, *Mac OS X for Absolute Beginners*, DOI 10.1007/978-1-4842-1913-3_2

Hovering lets you tell OS X this: "Do you see where the pointer is? Whatever appears underneath the pointer is what I want to choose."

> **Note**   If you can't see the pointer, jiggle the mouse (or slide your finger erratically across the trackpad surface). This temporarily enlarges the pointer so you can easily find it on the screen.

Pointing and Clicking

The most common use for clicking is to choose a command. For example, if you move the pointer over the Apple icon on the menu bar and then click, you're telling OS X, "I want to open the Apple menu."

When the Apple menu appears, you can move the pointer over the System Preferences command and click again, which tells OS X, "Choose the System Preferences command." When you choose the System Preferences command, the System Preferences window appears.

When you move the pointer over the Mouse or Trackpad icon in the System Preferences window and click, you tell OS X, "Show me the options that I can use to modify the mouse or trackpad."

Within the Mouse or Trackpad window, you could point and click check boxes to select or disable features such as secondary click.

When you finish changing options for the mouse or trackpad, you can then point at the red button (the close button) in the upper-left corner of the Mouse or Trackpad window and click to close the window.

This point-and-click procedure is something that you use every time you use a Mac. The most common use for point-and-click is to choose a command from a menu or to choose an option in a window, such as clicking a button or a check box.

> **Note**   Always make sure that you point at the correct item that you want to choose before clicking the mouse or trackpad. If you point at the wrong item and click, you won't get the expected result, which will likely confuse and frustrate you.

Pointing at something on the screen and then clicking it is the most common task that you'll do with a mouse/trackpad. To practice pointing and clicking, try the following exercise to discover the type of Mac that you have and which version of OS X you are using:

1. Click the Apple icon on the menu bar to display a pull-down menu.

2. Point and click About This Mac. A window appears, as shown in Figure 2-1.

Figure 2-1. The Overview tab tells you the OS X version and the type of Mac that you're using

3. Click the Displays tab (see Figure 2-2). The window now lists the resolution of your monitor and the type of graphics processor inside your Mac.

Figure 2-2. The Displays tab identifies information about your monitor and graphics processor

4. Click the Storage tab (see Figure 2-3). The window now lists the storage capacity of your hard disk and any external hard disks connected to your Mac.

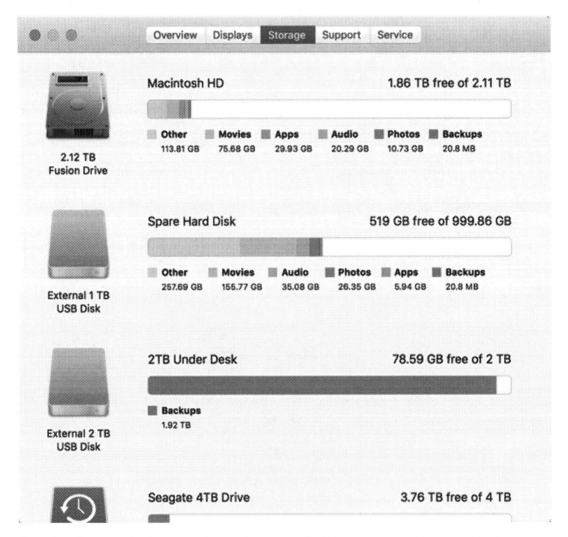

Figure 2-3. The Storage tab lets you see how much room your Mac has available on hard disk or solid-state storage

Note   If the memory in your Mac can be upgraded, you also see a Memory tab that lists which types of memory chips are plugged into the memory slots in your Mac.

5. Click the red close button (the red dot in the upper-left corner of the window) to close the window.

Notice that by pointing and clicking with the mouse or trackpad, you can perform common tasks like choosing menu commands, opening and closing a window, and choosing options inside that window.

In this case, you learned how to open the About This Mac window to identify the different features of your Mac.

Dragging

The mouse and trackpad are most commonly used for pointing and clicking to select commands and options. The second-most common use for the mouse and trackpad is *dragging*.

Dragging involves the following three steps:

1. Move the pointer over the object that you want to manipulate.

2. Hold down the left mouse button (or keep your finger pressed on the trackpad).

3. Move the mouse (or hold your finger down on the trackpad and slide it around).

Dragging is most often used to move something on the screen such as a window, a picture, or a chunk of text. For novices, dragging might initially feel awkward since you need to hold down the left mouse button while moving the mouse (or keep your finger pressed down while moving your fingertip across the trackpad surface), so here's a simple exercise to let you practice dragging.

> **Note**   To move anything on the screen with the mouse or trackpad, make sure that you select it first. That means positioning the pointer exactly over the object that you want to move. If the pointer isn't over the object that you want to move, then dragging won't do anything but move the pointer.

1. Click the Apple icon on the menu bar to display a pull-down menu.

2. Choose (point and click) About This Mac. The About This Mac window appears.

3. Move the pointer over the gray area (called the *title bar*) near the top of the window, as shown in Figure 2-4.

Figure 2-4. *The title bar of a window appears as a gray band near the top*

4.   Hold down the left mouse button and move the mouse (or press the trackpad surface and move your finger). Holding down the left mouse button or pressing the trackpad surface while moving the mouse or your finger at the same time is called *dragging*. Notice that the window moves wherever you move the pointer.

5.   Release the left mouse button, or lift your finger off the trackpad, when you're happy with the position of the About This Mac window.

6.   Click the red button (the close button) in the upper-left corner of the About This Mac window to make it disappear.

Remember, when dragging the mouse (or trackpad), keep the left mouse button or finger pressed down on the trackpad. If you lift up your finger too soon, OS X stops moving your selected object on the screen.

Right-Clicking (or Secondary Clicking)

Right-clicking (also known as *secondary clicking*) is used far less often. In fact, it's possible to use a Mac without ever using the right-click or secondary click command at all, which is why some Mac computers have secondary clicking turned off.

However, right-clicking offers shortcuts to common commands. To right-click, first move the pointer over the object that you want to manipulate. Then choose the right-click command in one of the following ways:

▓   (Mouse) Press and release the right mouse button

▓   (Trackpad) Press and release two fingers on the surface of the trackpad

▓   (Mouse or trackpad) Hold down the Control key and then press and release the left mouse button (or press and release one finger on the trackpad)

When you right-click over an item, a pop-up menu appears, showing you a list of commands for manipulating the object that the pointer currently appears on. So if you right-click a picture, you only see a pop-up menu of commands for manipulating pictures, as shown in Figure 2-5.

Figure 2-5. *Right-clicking over an image displays a pop-up menu of image manipulation commands*

If you right-click over selected text, you only see a pop-up menu of commands for manipulating text, as shown in Figure 2-6.

This is text that you can select. Notice that right-clicking only displays a list of commands for manipulating text, but if you right-click on a picture, you'll only see a list of commands for manipulati

Look Up "This is text that you ca..."
Cut
Copy
Paste
Phonetic Guide Text...
Remove Phonetic Guide Text
Add Link
Speech   ▶
Search With Google
New TextWrangler Document with Selection
Add to iTunes as a Spoken Track
Convert Text to Full Width

Figure 2-6. Right-clicking over selected text displays a pop-up menu of text manipulation commands

To see how right-clicking can display a pop-up menu of commands, try the following exercise:

1. Move the pointer anywhere over the desktop wallpaper image.

2. Click the right mouse button (or press two fingers on the trackpad surface) and lift up your fingers. A pop-up menu appears, as shown in Figure 2-7.

Figure 2-7. Right-clicking over the desktop displays a pop-up menu of commands for manipulating the desktop

3. Click the Change Desktop Background command. The Desktop & Screen Saver window appears.

4. Click the red dot (the close button) in the upper-left corner of the Desktop & Screen Saver window to make it disappear.

Let's see how to find the Change Desktop Background command without right-clicking. It takes the same number of steps, but notice how you need to hunt around to finally find it.

1. Click the Apple icon on the menu bar at the top of the screen. A pull-down menu appears.

2. Click System Preferences. The System Preferences window appears.

3. Click the Desktop & Screen Saver icon. The Desktop & Screen Saver window appears.

4. Click the red dot (the close button) in the upper-left corner of the Desktop & Screen Saver window to make it disappear.

Both methods work, but right-clicking saves you the time of hunting around the screen, looking for the right commands to choose. Just remember that right-clicking may not always display a commands pop-up menu for everything that the pointer appears over.

Using the Keyboard

The keyboard is mostly used to create and edit text. Beyond the normal character keys that let you type letters, numbers, and symbols, the two other types of keys on the keyboard are the cursor keys and the modifier keys.

The cursor keys let you move the cursor up, down, left, or right within text. Occasionally, you can also use the cursor keys to move objects on the screen after you have selected them.

The modifier keys are used to change the behavior of another key, such as the S or O key. Pressing a modifier key along with another key lets you access keystroke shortcuts for common commands.

The most common modifier key is the Command key. The following are the most common keystroke shortcuts that work in nearly every OS X program:

▓ Command+N: The New command

▓ Command+O: The Open command

▓ Command+P: The Print command

▓ Command+S: The Save command

The advantage of keystroke shortcuts is that they let you choose a command quickly, without wasting time looking for the command in a pull-down menu. The disadvantage is that you must memorize the keystrokes to choose your favorite commands.

To help you find keystroke shortcuts for common commands, just look at the commands in any pull-down menu. The most common commands in each pull-down menu show the keystroke shortcuts to the right of the command, as shown in Figure 2-8.

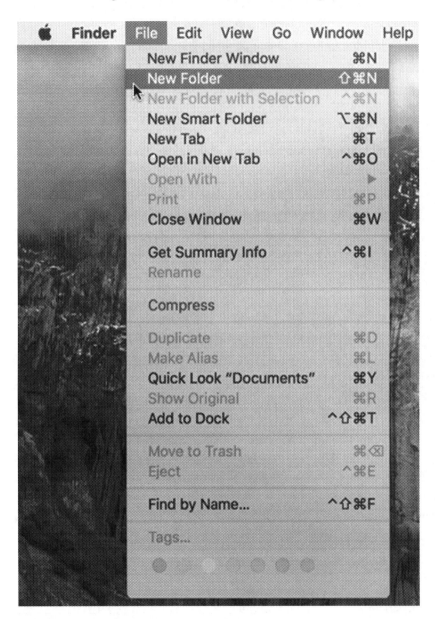

Figure 2-8. Almost every pull-down menu lists keystroke shortcuts

Keep in mind that the same keystroke shortcuts may not work the same in every program. In the Finder program shown in Figure 2-8, for example, you can press Shift+Command+N to choose the New Folder command, but if you press Shift+Command+N in another program, nothing at all may happen.

The most common keystroke shortcuts only use two keys, such as Command+S. The less common keystroke shortcuts use three or more keys, such as Control+Shift+Command+T.

To see how keystroke shortcuts work, try the following exercise:

1.   Click the Finder icon on the Dock, as shown in Figure 2-9.

Figure 2-9. The Finder icon appears on the left side of the Dock at the bottom of the screen

2.   Hold down the Command key and tap the N key (Command+N). Release both keys. This chooses the New Finder Window command, which opens another Finder window on the screen.

3.   Click the File menu and choose New Finder Window. Notice that this opens another Finder window on the screen.

4.   Click the red dot (the close button) in the upper-left corner of each Finder window to make it disappear.

For commonly used commands, it's much faster to memorize and use keystroke shortcuts. For less commonly used commands, it's easier to use pull-down menus rather than trying to memorize obscure keystroke combinations.

Summary

The three ways to control your computer involve the mouse, trackpad, and keyboard. Most desktops use the mouse, whereas most laptops use the trackpad, but it's possible to use both.

The four commands for using a mouse or trackpad are hover, click, drag, and right-click.

Hover means moving the pointer over something on the screen, such as an icon, which usually displays a brief explanation of the command that the icon represents.

Clicking means pressing and releasing the left mouse button once, or pressing and releasing your finger on the trackpad surface.

Dragging means holding down the left mouse button while moving the mouse, or pressing one finger on the trackpad while sliding your fingertip across the trackpad surface.

Right-clicking means pressing and releasing the right mouse button once, or pressing and releasing two fingers on the trackpad surface.

Right-clicking displays a pop-up menu of common commands for manipulating the object that the pointer currently appears on.

The keyboard offers modifier keys to choose shortcuts. The most common modifier key is the Command key.

Make sure that you feel comfortable using the mouse to click and drag. Right-clicking is optional but it can make using OS X much easier.

To find common keystroke shortcuts, look in the different pull-down menus of your favorite programs. Just remember that each program may use different keystroke shortcuts to choose the same commands.

Once you get comfortable giving commands to your Mac through the mouse/trackpad and keyboard, you're ready to start exploring and customizing the different features of OS X.

Chapter 3

Running Programs

The only reason to use OS X is to run programs (also called *applications* or *apps*) on your Mac. Some common types of applications include word processors, games, browsers, spreadsheets, databases, and painting or drawing programs. By installing different applications, you can make your Mac perform a variety of different tasks.

Most people really care about OS X running the applications they need. By just installing the right application, you can turn your Mac into the right tool for your needs.

Although you'll likely buy additional programs or applications to install on your Mac, you might be pleasantly surprised to find that every Mac comes with plenty of free apps that you can use right away. The following are some of the types of apps that come free with OS X:

- Office suite programs (word processor, spreadsheet, and presentation programs)
- Personal productivity programs (calendar, contacts, notes, reminders, and stickies)
- Utility programs

Office suite programs let you create letters, balance budgets, or make slide show presentations for work, school, or personal use.

Personal productivity programs let you save personal information such as appointments, short ideas you don't want to forget, and names and contact information of friends and business associates.

Utility programs let you examine and maintain your hard disk, capture screen images, record audio, and manage files.

You can run one or more programs at the same time, depending on how much memory your Mac has. The more memory it has, the more programs you can run simultaneously. The main reason to have two or more programs open at the same time is so that you can share data between them or quickly switch between programs. For example, you can copy text from a browser and paste it in a word processor document.

© Wallace Wang 2016
W. Wang, *Mac OS X for Absolute Beginners*, DOI 10.1007/978-1-4842-1913-3_3

Generally, you'll want to run a program as long as you need it and then shut it down when you're finished with it. So the main steps to using any program are as follows:

1. Launch the program.

2. Use the program.

3. Quit the program.

Remember that there are usually multiple ways of doing anything with a computer. So when you learn two or more ways to perform the same task, just choose the method you like best and feel free to ignore the other methods.

Finding a Program

Before you can use any program, you have to find it. Almost every program is stored in a special location called the *Applications folder* (see Figure 3-1). Each program appears as a colorful icon along with a descriptive name to help you identify it. You can find any program by looking for either its name or icon.

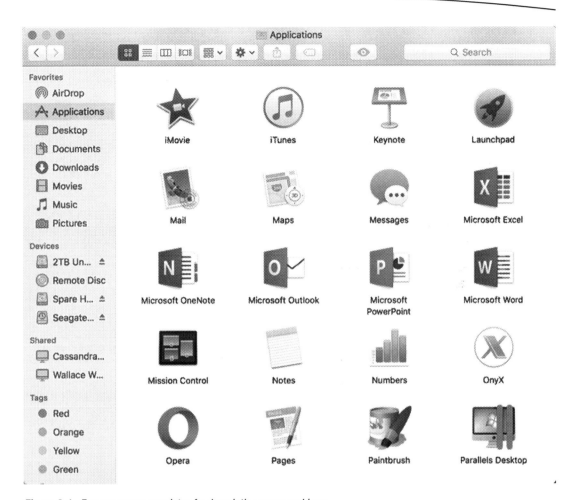

Figure 3-1. *Every program consists of a descriptive name and icon*

To see a list of programs stored on a Mac, you need to use a special program called the *Finder*.

Since the Finder is so important in helping you locate other programs, it always appears on the left side of the Dock, as shown in Figure 3-2.

Figure 3-2. *The Finder icon appears on the Dock*

To view the contents of the Applications folder, follow these steps:

1. Click the Finder icon on the Dock. The Finder menu bar appears at the top of the screen.

2. Do one of the following:

    *   Click the Go menu and click Applications (Go ➤ Applications).

    *   Press Shift+Command+A on the keyboard.

    *   Open a Finder window and click Applications in the left pane, as shown in Figure 3-3.

Figure 3-3. The Applications folder appears in the left pane of the Finder window

3. Move the pointer over the program icon that you want to run and use one of the following methods to start the program:

    *   Click to select the program icon and then choose File ➤ Open (click the File menu and then click Open).

    *   Click to select the program icon and then press Command+O.

    *   Left-click twice in rapid succession (known as *double-clicking*).

    *   Right-click the program icon and when a pop-up menu appears, choose Open, as shown in Figure 3-4.

Figure 3-4. *Right-clicking a program icon displays a pop-up menu*

Notice that when you launch a program, its program icon appears on the Dock. After you quit the program, its icon disappears from the Dock. When a program is running, OS X displays a dot underneath that program's icon. If a program isn't running, the dot won't appear at all, as shown in Figure 3-5.

Dots identify currently running programs

Figure 3-5. *Dots appear underneath the icons of currently running programs*

Double-clicking a program icon is the most common way to start a program. When double-clicking, make sure that you click the left mouse button (or press one finger on the trackpad surface) twice in rapid succession. If you click too slowly, your Mac interprets it as two single-clicks, which won't start the program.

Of course, constantly having to open the Applications folder, hunt around for the program icon that you want to load, and double-clicking the program icon can be annoying, so OS X offers another way to start a program. To give you one-click access to your favorite programs, you can put a program icon on the Dock.

Using the Dock

The Dock holds your most commonly used program icons in one place so that you can find and click them quickly and easily. The Dock can appear on the bottom, left, or right side of the screen. Once a program icon appears on the Dock, you can start that program just by clicking its icon once.

OS X automatically displays some program icons on the Dock, but you can always add your own program icons or remove any existing icons.

Just remember that the more program icons you add to the Dock, the smaller each icon will appear, so it's best to include only those program icons that you use most often.

Adding Program Icons to the Dock

The Dock likely won't include all of your favorite program icons, so you'll need to add them to the Dock manually. There are two ways to add a program icon to the Dock:

- Drag a program icon from the Applications folder to the Dock

- Start a program within the Applications folder so that it automatically appears on the Dock, and then lock the icon on the Dock

To drag a program icon to the Dock, follow these steps.

1. Open the Applications folder in the Finder window.

2. Move the pointer over a program icon and drag the icon on the Dock. As soon as you drag a program icon to the Dock, the existing program icons make room for it, as shown in Figure 3-6.

Figure 3-6. Dragging a program icon from the Applications folder to the Dock

3. Release the mouse or trackpad when the program icon is on the Dock. Your chosen program icon now appears on the Dock.

Dragging a program icon is handy, but if you've already started a program, its icon automatically appears on the Dock anyway. You can choose to keep a program icon on the Dock by following these steps:

1. Start a program by opening it from the Applications folder. When you start a program, its program icon appears on the Dock with a dot underneath it.

2. Right-click the program icon on the Dock. A pop-up menu appears.

3. Choose Options ➤ Keep in Dock, as shown in Figure 3-7 (in other words, click Options and then click Keep in Dock). Once a check mark appears in front of the Keep in Dock command, the program icon will always appear in the Dock. If a check mark does not appear in front of the Keep in Dock command, the program icon will disappear from the Dock when you quit running the program.

Figure 3-7. *Right-clicking a program icon that's currently running displays a pop-up menu*

Rearranging Icons on the Dock

You can move any icon on the Dock to a new location just by dragging it with the mouse or trackpad. To move an icon to a different location on the Dock, follow these steps:

1.   On the Dock, move the pointer over the program icon that you want to move.

2.   Hold down the left mouse button (or hold a finger down on the trackpad surface).

3.   Slide the mouse (or finger on the trackpad) to move the program icon. As you drag the program icon, you'll see the other program icons slide out of the way.

4.   Release the mouse (or trackpad) when the program icon is in the location that you want.

> **Note**   The Finder icon is the only program icon on the Dock that you can't remove or move to a different position. That makes it easy to find the Finder icon at all times.

Removing Icons from the Dock

Once you've added and arranged a program icon on the Dock, you can always remove it if you later find that you don't use that program often enough. To remove an icon from the Dock, follow these steps:

1.   On the Dock, move the pointer over the program icon that you want to remove.

2.   Hold down the left mouse button (or hold a finger down on the trackpad surface).

3. Slide the mouse (or finger on the trackpad) to move the program icon up and away from the Dock until you see a Remove label appear above the program icon, as shown in Figure 3-8.

Figure 3-8. Dragging an icon up from the Dock lets you remove it

4. Release the mouse (or trackpad). Your chosen program icon disappears.

Remember, once you remove a program icon from the Dock, you can still find and run that program in the Applications folder. Removing a program icon from the Dock does not physically delete a program from your Mac.

Think of the Dock as a shortcut to your favorite programs. If you can't find a particular program icon on the dock, look in the Applications folder. If you can't find a particular program in the Applications folder, it may be stored somewhere else on the Mac or it may not be installed at all.

Using a Program

Each time you run a program, three things happen:

■ The program icon appears on the Dock

■ A dot appears underneath the program icon on the Dock to let you know that the program is running

■ The program's menu bar appears at the top of the screen

Besides the dot appearing underneath the program icon on the Dock, a second way to identify the currently running program is to look on the menu bar.

To the right of the Apple icon on the menu bar, you'll always see the Application menu title, which displays the currently active program's name, as shown in Figure 3-9.

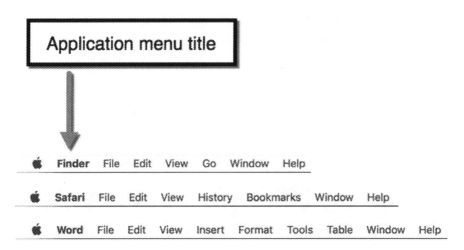

Figure 3-9. The Application menu title always changes to identify the currently active program

The currently active program is the one program that will accept anything you type on the keyboard. Remember, you can have multiple programs running at once, but you can only use one program at a time. No matter how many programs you may be running at the same time, you'll always have one program that's active, which you can identify by looking for its name in the Application menu title.

Most programs display a window that contains information. A word processor window might contain text, a game might contain animation, and a drawing program might contain lines and shapes. When you have multiple programs running, you'll often have multiple windows on the OS X desktop, as shown in Figure 3-10.

Figure 3-10. A typical Mac may have multiple windows on the desktop

Moving Windows

Program windows can fill either the entire screen or just part of the screen. When program windows only fill part of the screen, you can easily view data in multiple windows, side by side. For example, you can have a word processor window open so that you can write, while you have a browser window open so that you can look up and reference information as you write.

Many programs also let you open two or more windows. For example, you could open two windows in a word processor; that way, you could edit two documents at the same time, such as two chapters in a book.

When program windows fill only part of the screen, you can move them around as shown in Figure 3-11 by following these steps:

1. Move the pointer over the title bar of the window that you want to move. The title bar typically appears as a colored (often gray) area at the top of the window.

2. Hold down the left mouse button (or press a finger on the trackpad surface). Keep the left mouse button or trackpad pressed down.

3. Move the mouse or slide your fingertip across the trackpad surface. Steps 2 and 3 are known as *dragging*. As you drag the mouse or trackpad, the window moves with the pointer.

4. Release the left mouse button (or lift your finger off the trackpad) when you're happy with the new position of the window.

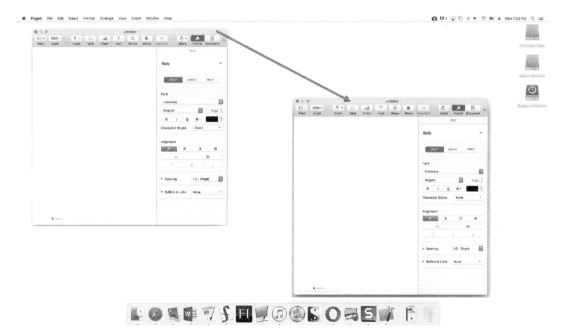

Figure 3-11. Dragging the title bar of a window moves it to a new location on the screen

When you only have a few windows on the screen, it can be easy to see what each window contains. However, having multiple windows on the screen can make everything look cluttered and confusing.

To avoid getting overwhelmed by seeing so many program windows on the screen, you have two options. First, you can resize a window to make it fill most of the screen. Second, you can hide windows so that you can focus only on the windows of one program.

By filling most of the screen or hiding the other windows, you can focus on the contents of the windows you want to see without distraction.

Resizing Windows

OS X provides several ways to resize a window:

■ Click the full size window button (the green dot in the upper-left corner of the window, as shown in Figure 3-12)

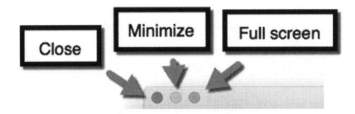

Figure 3-12. The full screen window button

■ Drag the sides or corners of a window to enlarge or shrink it

■ Choose Window ➤ Zoom (click the Window menu and then click Zoom)

In the upper-left corner of every window, you see the following three buttons:

■ Red: Closes the window

■ Yellow: Minimizes the window

■ Green: Displays the window to fill the entire screen

The red button closes the window. If you haven't saved the content of the program, OS X asks if you want to save the data. (Some programs, such as utility programs, don't create data, so you can close their windows without worrying about saving or losing data).

The yellow button temporarily hides a window. This is useful when you want to view certain windows without closing other windows.

The green button expands a window to full screen. Full screen mode even hides the menu bar from sight so that you have more space to see the actual contents of the window. If you need to access the menu bar, just move the pointer to the top of the screen with the mouse or trackpad.

Once a window completely fills a screen, you can shrink that window by moving the pointer to the top of screen to make the menu bar and the red, yellow, and green buttons appear in the upper-left corner. Click the green button again to shrink the window.

> **Note**   Each time that you click the green button, it toggles between expanding a window to full screen and shrinking a full screen window back to a smaller size.

To see how the full screen (green) button works, follow these steps:

1. Click the Finder icon on the Dock. A Finder window appears.

2. Click the green button in the upper-left corner of the Finder window. The Finder window expands to fill the entire screen.

3. Move the mouse pointer to the top of the screen so that the Finder menu bar and the red, yellow, and green buttons appear.

4. Click the green button in the upper-left corner. The Finder window shrinks back to fill part of the screen.

The ability to expand a window to full screen and then back to normal size works on every window. When you want to avoid distractions, expand a window to full size.

A second way to resize a window is to drag a corner or edge of the window with the mouse or trackpad. To do this, first move the pointer over the edge or corner of any window until the pointer turns into a two-way arrow, as shown in Figure 3-13.

Figure 3-13. When the two-way arrow appears, you can drag to resize the window

Second, hold down the left mouse button (or press a finger on the trackpad).

Third, as you move the mouse (or slide your finger across the trackpad surface), the window edge shrinks or enlarges the window.

The combination of moving and manually resizing a window with the mouse or trackpad can be convenient for aligning two or more windows next to each other.

For a faster way to resize a window, you can click the Window menu title and then choose Zoom (Window ➤ Zoom). This command toggles a window to enlarge or shrink it.

Switching Windows

When you have multiple programs open, you can switch from working in one program to another. If a single program displays two or more windows (such as a word processor displaying two or more documents), you can switch to different windows within the same program.

To switch windows, you can do one of the following:

- Click in another window visible on the screen
- Click another program icon that has a dot underneath it on the Dock

Remember, when you switch to another program's window, the menu bar changes to display that program's menu bar. So if you're using Microsoft Word, you'll see the Word menu bar at the top of the screen. Then if you switch to Safari, you'll see the Safari menu bar at the top of the screen.

If you have multiple windows open in the same program, you can switch to a different window in same program by doing one of the following:

- Click the Window menu and click the file name (this only switches to another window in the same program)

- Right-click the program icon on the Dock, and when the pop-up menu appears, click the file that you want, as shown in Figure 3-14

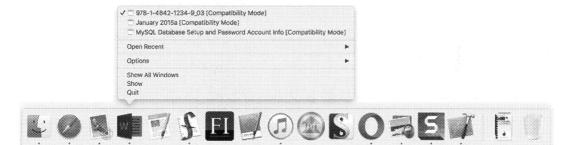

Figure 3-14. Right-clicking a program icon on the Dock displays a menu of all currently open files

Hiding Windows

Having multiple windows open in one or more programs lets you quickly switch from one file to another. The biggest problem is that the more windows you have open, the more cluttered your screen will look.

One option is to close a window, but if you just want to tuck it temporarily out of sight, it's easier to hide the window instead. OS X gives you three ways to hide windows:

- Click the Application menu title on the menu bar and choose Hide (program name), or press Command+H to hide all windows in the currently active program

- Right-click any program icon on the Dock that has a dot under it, and when a pop-up menu appears, choose Hide to hide all windows in the currently active program

- Click the Application menu title on the menu bar and choose Hide Others, or press Option+Command+H to hide all windows except the currently active program

Once you hide a window, you'll eventually want to make it visible again. To unhide or show a hidden window, you have two options:

▓   Right-click the program icon on the Dock that has a dot under it, and when a pop-up menu appears, choose Show (to show any hidden windows from that program icon)

▓   Click the Application menu title on the menu bar and choose Show All (to show all hidden windows from all programs)

Hiding windows is one way to ease the clutter of multiple open windows. To see how hiding windows can work, follow these steps:

1.   Click the Finder icon on the Dock. A Finder window appears.

2.   Click the Safari icon on the Dock to open a window in Safari.

3.   Manually move and resize the open windows so that you can see both of them on the screen.

4.   Click in one window. Notice that the title bar of the active window (the window currently displaying the cursor) appears darker, while the title bar of the other window appears dimmed. Also notice that the active window's program name appears in the menu bar, such as Finder or Safari.

5.   Click in the other program window. Notice that the title bar of this window now appears darker, while the title bar of the other window appears dimmed. Also notice that a different program name now appears in the menu bar.

6.   Click the Finder icon on the Dock. Notice that the Finder window title bar now appears darker and the menu bar now displays Finder next to the Apple icon.

7.   Click the Safari icon on the Dock. Notice that the Safari window title bar now appears darker and the menu bar now displays Safari next to the Apple icon.

8.   Right-click the Finder icon on the Dock to display a pop-up menu.

9.   Click Hide. Notice that this hides the Finder window. If you had multiple Finder windows open, all of them would be hidden.

10.   Right-click the Safari icon on the Dock to display a pop-up menu.

11.   Click Hide. Notice that this hides the Safari window. If you had multiple Safari windows open, all of them would be hidden.

12.   Click the Finder icon on the Dock. The Finder name appears next to the Apple icon on the menu bar.

13.   Click Finder on the menu bar and then click Show All (Finder ➤ Show All). OS X displays all program windows on the screen again.

14. Click Finder on the menu bar and then click Hide Others (Finder ➤ Hide Others). Notice that only the Finder window remains visible, whereas the Safari window is hidden.

15. Click Finder on the menu bar and then click Show All (Finder ➤ Show All). Notice that the Safari window appears again.

Minimizing Windows

Hiding windows makes them disappear, but it's not easy knowing which windows are hidden. The only way you can find a hidden window is to choose the Show All command from any application title menu, such as Finder ➤ Show All or Safari ➤ Show All. As an alternative to completely hiding a window, OS X gives you the option to minimize a window instead.

When you minimize a window, it appears on the Dock next to the Trash icon, as shown in Figure 3-15.

Figure 3-15. A minimized window appears on the Dock

Each time that you minimize a window, it appears as an icon on the Dock. To minimize a window, you have three options:

▓ Click the yellow button (the minimize button) in the upper-left corner of the window that you want to minimize

▓ Click the window that you want to minimize and press Command+M

▓ Click the window that you want to minimize, click the Window menu, and choose Minimize (Window ➤ Minimize)

Once you've minimized a window, you can open it again by clicking its icon on the Dock. To see how this works, try the following:

1. Click the Finder icon on the Dock. A Finder window appears.

2. Choose a way to minimize the Finder window, such as pressing Command+M, choosing Window ➤ Minimize, or clicking the yellow minimize button in the upper-left corner of the Finder window. Notice that the window shrinks to appear as an icon on the Dock.

3. Click the minimized window icon on the Dock. Notice that the window now appears back on the screen again.

Minimizing windows can be handy for temporarily tucking one or two windows out of sight, but if you minimize too many windows, their icons will take up room on the Dock.

Closing Windows

Hiding or minimizing windows tucks them out of sight but keeps them ready to view again. However, if you don't need a window any more, it's best to close it completely.

OS X offers three ways to close a window:

- Click the red button (the close button) in the upper-left corner of the window

- Click the window that you want to close and press Command+W

- Click the window that you want to minimize, click the File menu, and choose Close (File ➤ Close)

If you haven't saved the data in the window you want to close, you'll see a dialog message asking if you want to save the data or not.

Using Mission Control

If you have multiple programs running at the same time, you'll likely have numerous windows open on the desktop. Unfortunately, opening too many windows will likely bury some open windows underneath other open windows. Even though a window may be open, you may not see it on the screen.

To solve this problem, OS X offers a feature called Mission Control, which helps display open windows in one of two ways:

- Displays all open program windows as miniature windows on the screen, as shown in Figure 3-16

- Displays only open windows belonging to a single program

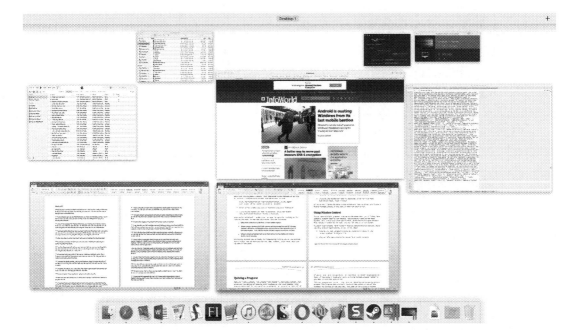

Figure 3-16. Mission Control shows you all the currently open windows

To display all open program windows, hold down the Control key and press the Up arrow key (Control+Up arrow). (If you have a trackpad, swipe three fingers up to display all open program windows.)

At this point, you can click any window to switch to that particular window. If you just want to go back to the window that you previously were using, do one of the following to exit out of Mission Control:

- Press Control+Up arrow
- Press Esc

The more open windows you have, the more cluttered your Mission Control display will look. To reduce the number of windows Mission Control displays, you can choose to only display windows from one program at a time.

For example, if you have three open windows in Microsoft Word, Mission Control can display just those three Microsoft Word windows. If you have two open windows in the Finder, Mission Control can display just those two Finder windows, as shown in Figure 3-17.

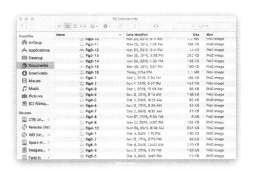
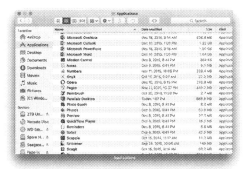

Figure 3-17. Mission Control can show only a program's currently open windows

To use Mission Control to open the windows of one particular program, follow these steps:

1. Click a program icon on the Dock.

2. Press Control+Down arrow. Mission Control only displays the open windows for the program you selected in step 1.

3. Click any open window to select it, or press Esc or Control+Down arrow to exit out of Mission Control.

By using Mission Control, you can easily select a different open window no matter how many open windows you have. As a general rule, close any window if you don't need it right away. This helps reduce the number of windows on the screen and keeps your screen from looking cluttered and confusing.

Quitting a Program

When you close a window, the program that opened it continues running. That gives you the option to open other windows in that program. When you no longer want to use a particular program, you can exit or quit out of that program.

To quit any program, you have three options:

- Click the application menu title (such as Safari) and choose Quit (such as Safari ➤ Quit Safari)
- Press Command+Q
- Right-click the program icon on the Dock, and when the pop-up menu appears, choose Quit

Because it's a part of OS X that's always running, the Finder is the only program that you cannot quit.

> **Note** If you haven't saved data in any open program windows that you try to quit, a dialog message will ask if you want to save your data or not.

Summary

The Mac operating system, OS X, runs all the time. To run other programs, you can double-click (click twice in rapid succession) a program icon in the Applications folder. As a shortcut, you can place program icons on the Dock so that you can get quick access to your favorite programs in one click.

You can open as many programs as you wish. Each time that you open a program, it displays a window with data that you can manipulate. A single program can open multiple windows.

You can manually move and resize windows, or choose various commands to make a window fill the screen, hide from view, or appear as a minimized icon on the Dock. Hiding and minimizing windows makes it easy to keep too many windows from cluttering the screen.

If you're done with certain data, you can close the window displaying that data. If you haven't saved your data, a dialog message will ask if you want to save the data or not.

Only one program can run at a time. You can identify the currently active program (the program that currently displays the cursor in one of its windows) by looking at the menu bar. The name of the currently active program appears to the right of the Apple icon on the menu bar, such as Safari or Finder.

When you have multiple windows open, you can switch between multiple programs by clicking a window belonging to another program, or by clicking a program icon displayed on the Dock. Any program icon on the Dock that has a dot underneath it is currently running.

By using Mission Control, you can view and select any currently open window. The Control+Up arrow command displays all open windows, whereas the Control+Down arrow command only displays the currently selected program's open windows.

To quit a program, you can choose the application menu title (such as Safari) and then choose Quit, or press Command+Q. If you haven't saved any data, you'll see a dialog message asking if you want to save your data or not.

By letting you run multiple programs at the same time and display multiple windows from each program, OS X lets you share data between programs or view data from two or more different programs so that you can work more effectively, no matter what you need to do with your Mac.

Chapter 4

Typing and Editing Text

Most people use a computer to type text to write letters, reports, blog posts, or messages. Since typing text (letters, numbers, and symbols) is so common, you need to know how to type and edit text no matter what type of program you use.

The basics of typing and editing text include knowing the following:

- How to type text, including unusual symbols such as foreign language characters

- How to select text

- How to copy, move, and delete text

Before you can type text, you need to move the cursor where you want that text to appear. The cursor shows you exactly where the text will appear the moment that you start typing.

To move the cursor to a new location, you can press the up, down, left, or right cursor keys on the keyboard, or you can move the pointer and click the mouse or trackpad.

Typing creates text such as letters, numbers, or symbols. Once you've typed text, you can modify it. To modify text, you must first select the text that you want to modify by using the keyboard or the mouse or trackpad.

Once you've selected text to modify, you can then choose a way to modify it, such as deleting the text or moving it to a new location.

Moving the Cursor

The fastest way to move the cursor is to use the mouse or trackpad by pointing and clicking. The problem with the mouse and trackpad is that they're not always precise. Trying to position the pointer in the exact spot that you want the cursor to appear can be difficult, so that's why you may also want to use the keyboard.

© Wallace Wang 2016
W. Wang, *Mac OS X for Absolute Beginners*, DOI 10.1007/978-1-4842-1913-3_4

The keyboard's cursor keys slowly move the cursor one character to the left or right, or one line up or down. Although the cursor keys move the cursor slowly, they do move it more precisely.

It's often faster to use the mouse or trackpad to place the cursor near the area where you want to start typing. Once you place the cursor near the area where you want to type, you can use the cursor keys on the keyboard to move the cursor more precisely to the exact position.

To make the keyboard faster at moving the cursor, OS X offers the following shortcuts, which use the modifier keys in combination with the cursor keys:

- Command+Left arrow: Moves the cursor to the beginning of a line
- Command+Right arrow: Moves the cursor to the end of a line
- Command+Up arrow: Moves the cursor up to the front of the previous paragraph
- Command+Down arrow: Moves the cursor down to the front of the next paragraph
- Option+Left arrow: Moves the cursor one word to the left
- Option+Right arrow: Moves the cursor one word to the right

Note Not all programs may accept these keystroke shortcuts for moving the cursor. Some programs, such as Microsoft Word, offer shortcuts of their own, such as pressing the Home key to move the cursor to the beginning of a line, or the End key to move the cursor to the end of a line.

Selecting Text

After you've created text, you can manipulate it to do the following:

- Delete text
- Change the text size
- Change the text font
- Change the text color
- Copy text to paste in another location
- Move text to another location

Before you can manipulate text, you must first select the text that you want to modify. To select text, you can use the mouse, the keyboard, or a combination of both.

Selecting Text with the Mouse or Trackpad

The mouse and the trackpad offer different ways to select text. If you click the mouse or trackpad anywhere in text, you move the cursor where you clicked. However, if you double-click within a word, you can select just that word. If you triple-click, you can select an entire paragraph.

- Click: Places the cursor in text

- Double-click inside a word: Selects the word

- Triple-click inside a paragraph: Selects the entire paragraph

Note   Remember that double-clicking and triple-clicking mean that you click in rapid succession. If you allow too much time to pass between clicks, OS X interprets it as multiple single clicks.

If you want to select text within a paragraph or text that spans across multiple paragraphs, double- or triple-clicking won't work. That's when you need to drag the mouse or trackpad over the text that you want to select.

To select text by dragging, follow these steps:

1. Move the pointer to the beginning of the text that you want to select.

2. Hold down the left mouse button (or press down on the trackpad with one finger).

3. Move the mouse (or slide your fingertip across the trackpad while pressing down). As you move the mouse, or slide your finger across the trackpad, you select text (see Figure 4-1).

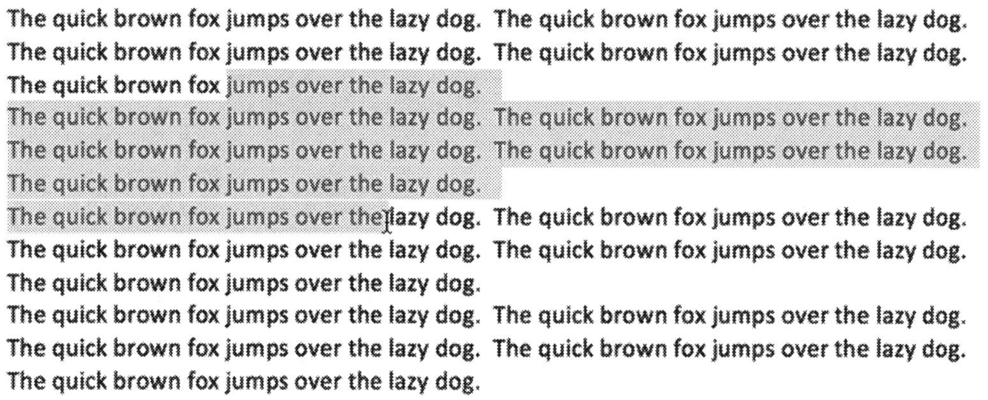

The quick brown fox jumps over the lazy dog. The quick brown fox jumps over the lazy dog.
The quick brown fox jumps over the lazy dog. The quick brown fox jumps over the lazy dog.
The quick brown fox jumps over the lazy dog.
The quick brown fox jumps over the lazy dog. The quick brown fox jumps over the lazy dog.
The quick brown fox jumps over the lazy dog. The quick brown fox jumps over the lazy dog.
The quick brown fox jumps over the lazy dog.
The quick brown fox jumps over the lazy dog. The quick brown fox jumps over the lazy dog.
The quick brown fox jumps over the lazy dog. The quick brown fox jumps over the lazy dog.
The quick brown fox jumps over the lazy dog.
The quick brown fox jumps over the lazy dog. The quick brown fox jumps over the lazy dog.
The quick brown fox jumps over the lazy dog. The quick brown fox jumps over the lazy dog.
The quick brown fox jumps over the lazy dog.

Figure 4-1. Dragging the mouse or trackpad selects text

4. Release the left mouse button (or lift your finger off the trackpad) when you're done selecting text.

Double- or triple-clicking allow you to select entire words or paragraphs. Dragging is another way to select multiple lines of text. A third way to select text uses a combination of the Shift key and the mouse or trackpad; the following explains how to do this:

1.   Move the cursor to the beginning of the text that you want to select.

2.   Move the pointer to the end of the text you want to select.

3.   Hold down the Shift key and click the left mouse button (or press and let go of the trackpad surface) to select this text.

Selecting Text with the Keyboard

Using the mouse to select text can often be imprecise because you need to click exactly where you want to define the beginning or end of the text that you want to select. If you're one letter off, then your selected text won't be exactly what you wanted.

For more accuracy in selecting text, you can use the keyboard. To select text with the keyboard, follow these steps:

1.   Move the cursor to the beginning of the text that you want to select.

2.   Hold down the Shift key and press the up/down, left/right cursor keys. Each time you press a cursor key, you select text in the direction that you moved the cursor.

3.   Release the Shift key when you're done selecting text.

> **Note**   Don't forget that in addition to using the cursor keys, you can also use the shortcut keys for moving the cursor to the beginning of a line (Command+Left arrow) or to the end of a line (Command+Right arrow).

If you ever select text and then change your mind about it, you can deselect text in one of two ways:

▪   Tap any of the cursor keys

▪   Click anywhere

Deleting Text

One of the simplest ways to modify selected text is to delete it. After you've selected text, just tap the Delete key on the keyboard.

> **Note**   Any time you modify text (such as deleting) and then suddenly change your mind, press Command+Z or click the Edit menu and choose Undo (Edit ➤ Undo). The Undo command reverses the last command that you performed. If you keep choosing the Undo command, you'll keep reversing the last commands that you chose.

Copying Text

Another common way to manipulate text is to copy it from one place and paste it into another. You can copy and paste text within the same document, or you can copy and paste text from one program to a completely different program. For example, you might want to copy text from a browser (e.g., Safari) window and paste it in a word processor (e.g., Pages or Microsoft Word) window.

To copy text, you must do the following:

1. Select the text that you want to copy.

2. Choose the Copy command.

3. Move the cursor to the new location where you want the place a second copy of the selected text.

4. Choose the Paste command.

To choose the Copy command, you have the following three options:

- Click the Edit menu and click Copy (Edit ➤ Copy)

- Press Command+C

- Right-click over the selected text, and when a pop-up menu appears, choose Copy, as shown in Figure 4-2

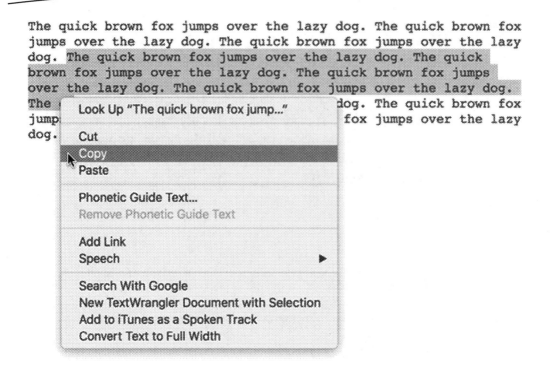

Figure 4-2. Right-clicking selected text displays a pop-up menu

Whenever you copy anything, OS X stores that selected item temporarily. If you select and copy something else, OS X forgets any previously copied item. That means that if you select and copy a paragraph, and then select and copy a second paragraph, OS X only remembers the last paragraph you selected and copied.

After you've selected and copied text, you'll eventually need to use the Paste command to place a copy of that text somewhere else. You have three ways to choose the Paste command:

- Click the Edit menu and click Paste (Edit ➤ Paste)

- Press Command+V

- Right-click over the selected text, and when a pop-up menu appears, choose Paste (see Figure 4-2)

Moving Text

When you copy text, you create a duplicate of any text you selected. However, if you want to move text from one location to another, you need to use the Cut command, as follows:

1. Select the text that you want to move.

2. Choose the Cut command (your selected text will disappear).

3. Move the cursor to the location that you want to place the selected text.

4. Choose the Paste command.

To choose the Cut command, you have the following three options:

- Click the Edit menu and click Cut (Edit ➤ Cut)

- Press Command+X

- Right-click over the selected text, and when a pop-up menu appears, choose Cut (see Figure 4-2)

Note   Remember, when you select text and choose the Cut command, make sure that you move the cursor to a new location and use the Paste command as soon as possible. The Paste command only works with the text that was last selected.

Copying and Moving Text by Dragging

If you find copying and cutting too slow, you can copy and cut text by using the mouse or trackpad instead. To copy or move text using the mouse or trackpad, you need to follow these steps:

1. Select the text that you want to move.

2. Move the pointer over the selected text using the mouse or trackpad.

3. Hold down the left mouse button (or press a finger on the trackpad surface).

4. Drag the mouse (or slide your finger on the trackpad surface). As you drag the mouse or slide your finger on the trackpad surface, the cursor moves to show where the text will appear when you let go of the mouse or trackpad.

5. Release the mouse or trackpad to move your text at the current cursor location.

These steps let you move selected text by dragging it to a new location. This is equivalent to choosing the Cut and Paste command.

If only want to copy text, hold down the Option key in step 3 before holding down the left mouse button or pressing a finger on the trackpad surface. Then in step 5, release the Option key along with the mouse or trackpad. When you copy text by holding down the Option key, you see a plus sign in a green circle, as shown in Figure 4-3.

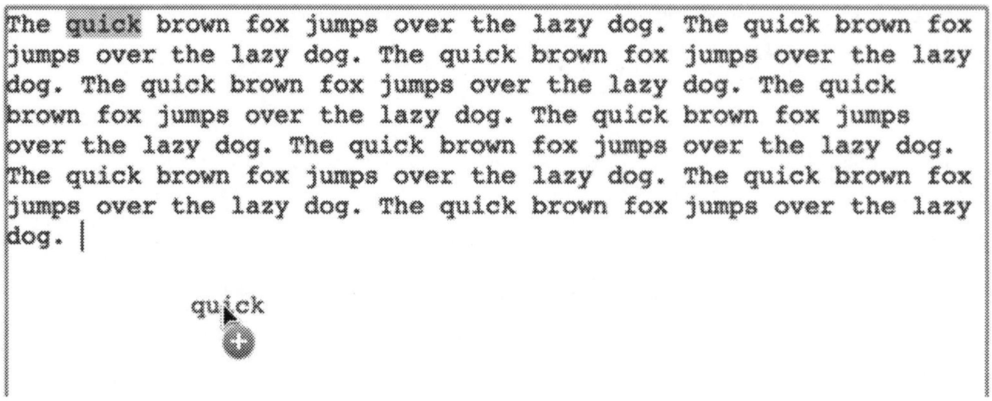

The quick brown fox jumps over the lazy dog. The quick brown fox
jumps over the lazy dog. The quick brown fox jumps over the lazy
dog. The quick brown fox jumps over the lazy dog. The quick
brown fox jumps over the lazy dog. The quick brown fox jumps
over the lazy dog. The quick brown fox jumps over the lazy dog.
The quick brown fox jumps over the lazy dog. The quick brown fox
jumps over the lazy dog. The quick brown fox jumps over the lazy
dog.

quick

Figure 4-3. Holding down the Option key while dragging displays a plus sign in a green circle to identify the Copy command

Formatting Text

The most visually interesting way to modify text is to format it. Formatting can mean one or
more of the following:

- Changing the text size (known as the font size)

- Changing the text font

- Changing the text color and/or background color

- Changing the text style (bold, underline, or italics)

The font size defines how big or small text might appear, measured in points, as shown in
Figure 4-4.

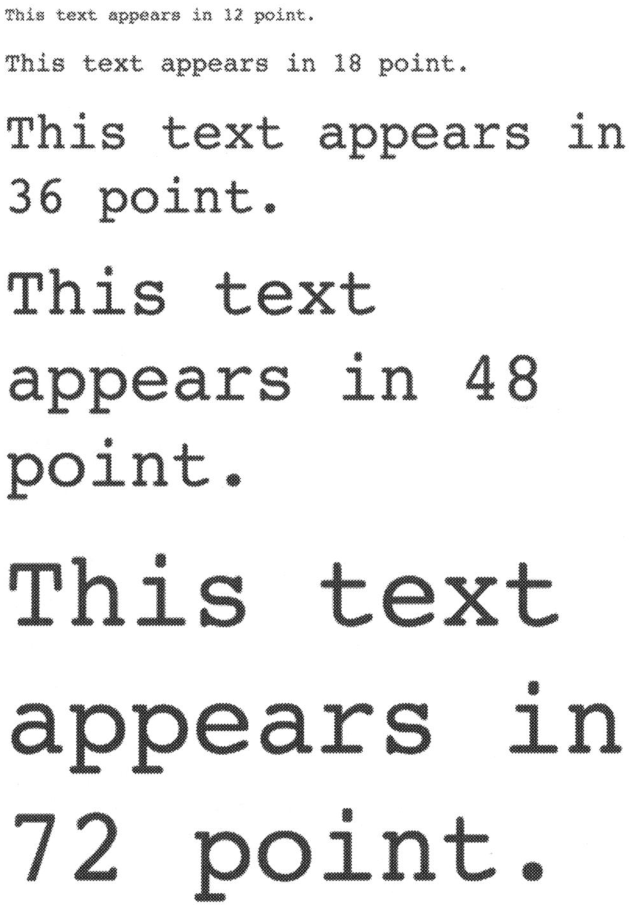

This text appears in 12 point.

This text appears in 18 point.

This text appears in 36 point.

This text appears in 48 point.

This text appears in 72 point.

Figure 4-4. *The different appearance of text displayed in various font sizes*

Fonts determine the appearance of each character. For example, fonts can make your text look like Old English, calligraphy, or even handwriting, as shown in Figure 4-5.

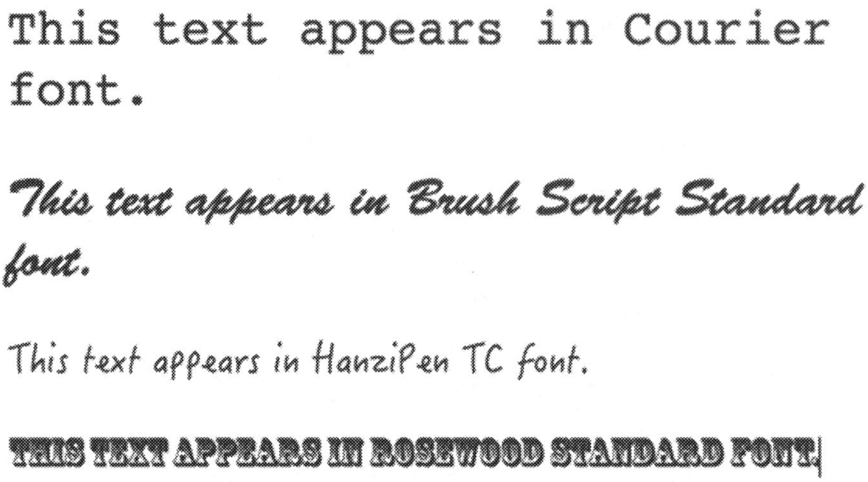

This text appears in Courier
font.

*This text appears in Brush Script Standard
font.*

This text appears in HanziPen TC font.

THIS TEXT APPEARS IN ROSEWOOD STANDARD FONT.

Figure 4-5. The different appearance of text displayed in various font sizes

> **Note**   Not all computers have the same fonts installed and not all programs support text
> formatting. If you need to share files with others, make sure that they have the same fonts installed
> or else your text will look different on another computer.

Text color defines the color of each character. In this book, every character is colored black.
The text background defines the color that appears behind each character. In this book, the
background color is white.

Changing the text background is like using a highlighting marker to emphasize text, such
as making the text background yellow or orange. When working with text colors and
background colors, always make sure that they contrast. For example, you don't want to
choose a light text color and a light background color because that would be hard to read.
Instead, you either want a darker text color and a lighter background color, or a lighter text
color and a darker background color, as shown in Figure 4-6.

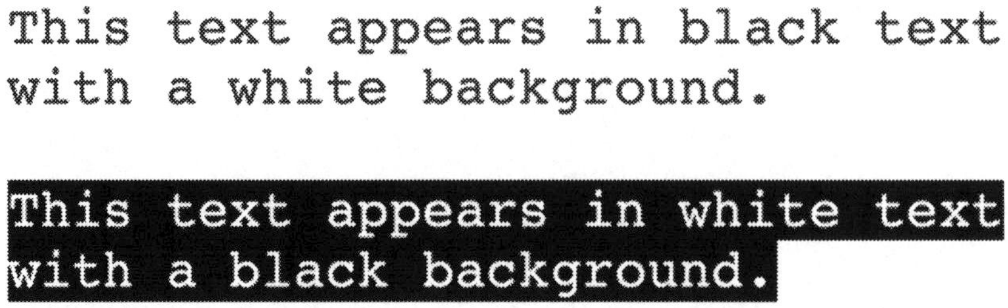

This text appears in black text
with a white background.

**This text appears in white text
with a black background.**

Figure 4-6. Changing the text color and background color can make text stand out

Yet another way to format text is to modify its style. The three most common styles are underline, bold, and italics, which you can also combine, as show in Figure 4-7.

<u>This text appears in underline.</u>

This text appears in bold.

This text appears in italics.

<u>*This text appears in italics and underline.*</u>

Figure 4-7.   Three common text formatting styles

To choose different styles for text, you can use keyboard shortcuts, as follows:

- ▓ Command+U to underline text
- ▓ Command+B to bold text
- ▓ Command+I to italicize text

To turn off a text style, simply select the text again and choose the same command. So if you formatted text by underlining it, you can select the underlined text and choose the underline command again (Command+U) to remove the underlining.

Typing Unusual Characters

Most keyboards display letters, numbers, and symbols such as #, *, and @, which you can type by pressing a key or holding down the Shift key and pressing another key. However, what happens if you need to type characters that don't appear on the keyboard? For example, many keyboards don't have keys for typing foreign language characters that use accent marks.

Fortunately, OS X offers a shortcut for typing foreign language characters. Just hold down the letter key that represents a letter with an accent mark in a non-English language, such as a, e, i, o, u, or c. When holding down one of these letter keys, OS X displays a list of common accent marks, as shown in Figure 4-8.

Figure 4-8. Holding down a letter key displays a menu of common accent marks

Then, type the number that corresponds to the character that you want and OS X will enter it in the program.

If you need to type more unusual characters or symbols, you have two options:

- Choose Edit ➤ Emoji & Symbols (click the Edit menu and click Emoji & Symbols)

- Press Control+Command+Spacebar

When you choose either of these two options, you get a Characters window that lets you choose from different categories of symbols, as shown in Figure 4-9.

Figure 4-9. The Characters window lets you create unusual characters

The Characters window lets you choose from several different categories of symbols, such as currency symbols, emoji, or math symbols. To choose a symbol from the Characters window, click a category in the left pane (such as Emoji or Currency Symbols). For the Emoji category, you also need to click a subcategory, such as Food & Drink or Smileys & People. Then double-click the unusual character that you want to insert where the cursor appears.

When you're done with the Characters window, you need to click the red button (the close button) in the upper-left corner of the Characters window to make it disappear.

To see how to add unusual characters, follow these steps:

1. Click the Finder icon on the Dock. The Finder window appears. If a Finder window does not appear, click the File menu and click New Finder Window (File ➤ New Finder Window).

2. Click Applications in the left pane of the Finder window. The Finder window now displays icons of all the programs installed on your Mac.

3. Double-click the Pages icon. Pages is a free word processor that comes with every new Mac. Notice that the Pages icon appears on the Dock and the Pages menu bar appears at the top of the screen, as shown in Figure 4-10.

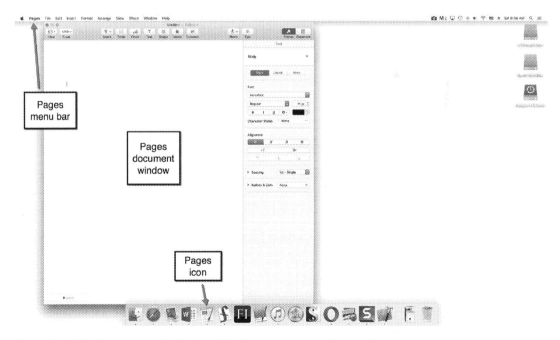

Figure 4-10. The Pages icon on the Dock and the Pages menu bar at the top of the screen

4. Click the Edit menu and click Emoji & Symbols (Edit ➤ Emoji & Symbols), or press Control+Command+Spacebar. The Characters window appears.

5.   Click the Emoji category and then click the Smileys & People subcategory to see the list of smiling faces that you can choose from (see Figure 4-9).

6.   Double-click a smiley face. Notice that your chosen smiley face now appears in the Pages document.

7.   Click the red button (the close button) in the upper-left corner of the Characters window.

8.   Click the Pages menu title and then click Quit Pages (Pages ➤ Quit Pages). Pages displays a dialog window asking if you want to save your document.

9.   Click Delete. Pages quits. It does not save your document.

By using the Characters window, you can type a variety of symbols and characters that you can't type on a keyboard.

Note   The Latin category in the Characters window also lets you choose common foreign language characters.

Summary

As you can see, there are multiple ways to modify the appearance of text in any program. With most programs, you can find different ways to emphasize and spice up the appearance of anything that you write.

Just remember that you can use the mouse and/or keyboard to select text. The mouse can be faster but the keyboard can be more precise.

Once you've selected text, you can modify it by changing its size, font, or style. One common way to manipulate text is to copy or move it. To copy selected text, use the Command+C command. To cut selected text, use the Command+X command.

After you've copied or cut text, you can paste it using the Command+V command. Just make sure that after you cut or copy selected text, you choose the Paste command as soon as possible, because if you choose the cut or copy command again, the Paste command will only work with the last text selected.

You can type foreign language characters by holding down a letter key and choosing the correct character from a menu.

If you want to create unusual symbols, you can do that through the Characters window, which opens by using the Control+Command+Space bar command.

With so many ways to create and manipulate text, you'll be able to make your text look good no matter which program you use.

Chapter 5

Understanding Files and Folders

When you use most programs, you need to save data. That way, the next time you need the data, you can use or modify it without having to retype everything all over again.

For example, if you're writing a letter or a report on a word processor, you want to save that letter or report so that you don't have to retype the entire letter or report. Whenever you save data in a program, the program saves it in a file.

A file acts like a box that holds your stuff. If you write a letter in a word processor, that file contains your letter. If you type a list of names and addresses in a database, that file contains your names and addresses. If you draw a picture in a graphics program, that file contains your picture.

Almost every program can save data in a file. When you save data in a file, you need to give the file a name. This file name can be anything you want, although it's best to choose a descriptive name that helps you remember what type of data the file contains.

For example, you might give one file a name like "Tax Returns 2018" and another file a name like "Birthday Picture in Hawaii". File names typically consist of letters, numbers, and spaces, and they can contain up to 255 characters. Descriptive file names are for your benefit only. OS X only cares that each file in the same folder has a different name. It's actually possible to use identical file names multiple times as long as you store each identically named file in a different folder, but this can easily confuse people and it is not recommended.

© Wallace Wang 2016
W. Wang, *Mac OS X for Absolute Beginners*, DOI 10.1007/978-1-4842-1913-3_5

How OS X Organizes Files

Every Mac stores files on a disk that holds everything needed to make your computer work, including the OS X operating system and programs such as a word processor or a browser.

One problem with storing everything on a single disk is that it's like tossing all of your clothes in one big pile in a closet. This makes finding anything slow, confusing, and time-consuming.

Just as you would organize a closet to store shoes on a shelf and hang clothes on hangars, you can organize your computer's disk into separate sections to hold different items. When you divide a computer's disk into parts, you use something called *folders*.

A folder on your Mac lets you organize related files together. The left pane of the Finder window, called the *sidebar*, shows some of the folders that your Mac has already created for storing similar types of files. These are described in the following list and shown in Figure 5-1:

- Applications: Contains programs installed on the Mac
- Documents: Contains files you create
- Downloads: Contains files downloaded from the Internet
- Movies: Contains video files
- Music: Contains audio files such as songs
- Pictures: Contains graphic images such as digital photographs

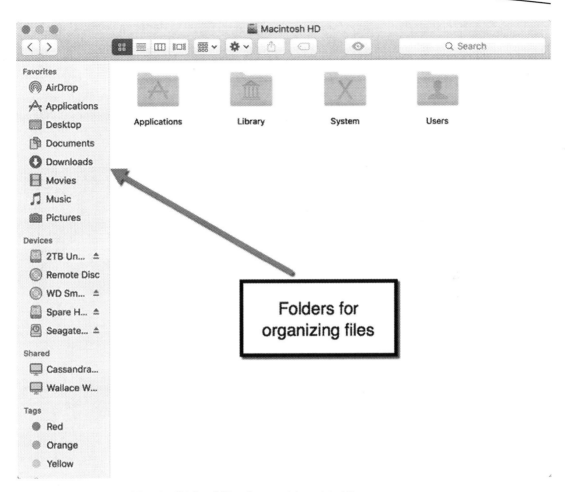

Figure 5-1. *Every Mac divides its disk into folders for organizing related files*

Note   You can actually store any type of file in any folder. However, it's best to store related files in the right folders, such as storing all programs in the Applications folder and all audio files in the Music folder, so that you can easily find them again.

Folders help keep all of your files organized. To avoid any single folder from getting too cluttered, you can create folders within folders (often called *subfolders*). Initially, every Mac divides its disk into four main folders:

- Applications
- Library
- System
- Users

The Applications folder contains all of your programs. The Library folder contains files used by OS X. The System folder contains the files that make up OS X. In most cases, you'll never need to open and view the Library or System folders.

The Users folder contains all the files that you create and save. Since multiple people can use the same Mac, OS X creates separate folders for each user. By creating separate folders (within the Users folder) for each person who uses the same Mac, OS X ensures that one person can't easily mess up files created by another person.

OS X organizes your disk in multiple folders, as described here and shown in Figure 5-2:

- The Users folder contains a Guest, Shared, and personal folder identified by your name, such as john smith or peggy norton.

- The personal folder (displaying your name) contains an Applications, Desktop, Documents, Downloads, Music, Movies, Pictures, and Public folder

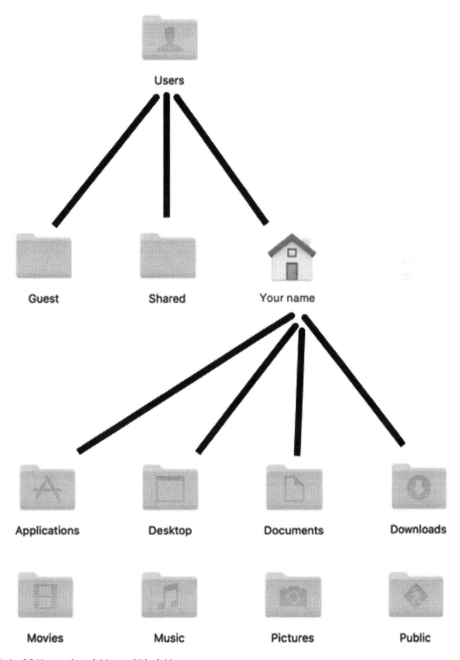

Figure 5-2. OS X organizes folders within folders

The most commonly used folders are Documents, Downloads, Movies, Music, and Pictures. The Documents folder stores most of your files. Most likely, you'll need to create additional folders within the Documents folder to keep everything organized.

For example, you might divide the Documents folder so that it contains a folder for your personal files and a second folder for your work files. Within your work folder, you might create a folder related to budgets, a folder related to travel expenses, and a third folder related to sales. By creating multiple folders within folders, you can keep your files organized.

Navigating Through Folders

Once you open the Finder window, you can view the contents of a folder in one of the following three ways (also see Figure 5-3):

▓ Double-click any folder displayed in the Finder window

▓ Click a folder name displayed in the left pane (sidebar) of the Finder window

▓ Click the Go menu and then click the folder that you want to view, such as Documents or Applications

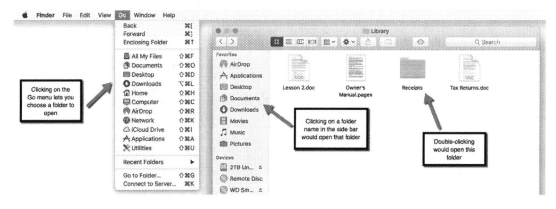

Figure 5-3. Three ways to open a folder

A limitation of both the sidebar on the left pane of the Finder window and the Go menu is that they only show a limited number of folders. If you create new folders, you won't be able to find them listed in the sidebar of the Finder window or on the Go menu.

To get around this limitation, you have two options:

▓ Click the Go menu and choose Recent Folders (Go ➤ Recent Folders)

▓ Click the Go menu and choose Go to Folder (Go ➤ Go to Folder) (or press Shift+Command+G)

The Go ➤ Recent Folders command displays a list of your recently viewed folders so that you can click the folder that you want to view, as shown in Figure 5-4.

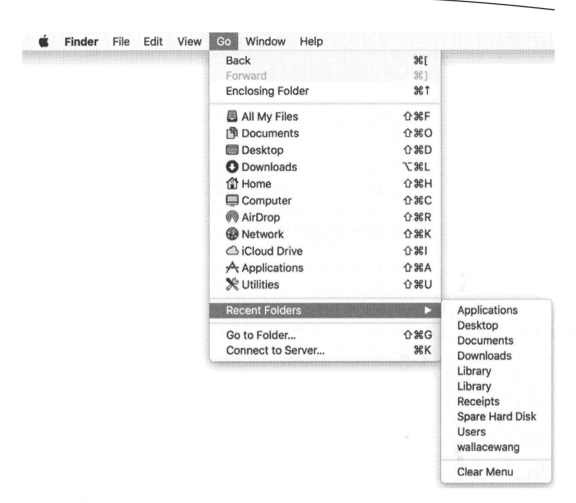

Figure 5-4. The Recent Folders list on the Go menu

If you want to view a folder that you haven't opened recently, you can choose the Go ➤ Go to Folder command. This opens a dialog that asks you to type the exact name of the folder that you want to view.

The main limitation of this Go ➤ Go to Folder command is that you may not know the exact spelling of the folder that you want to view. Misspell the folder name and the Finder won't know how to find the folder that you want.

Navigating Through Previously Viewed Folders

Another way to navigate through folders is to use the Back and Forward buttons that appear in the upper-left corner of the Finder window, as shown in Figure 5-5.

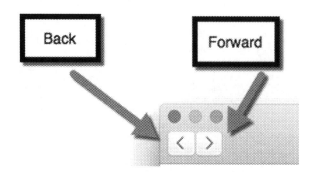

Figure 5-5. The Back and Forward buttons let you navigate through folders

The Back button takes you to the previous folder that you viewed. The Forward button normally appears dimmed until you click the Back button at least once. Then if you click the Forward button, you can move forward to the folder that you viewed before hitting the Back button.

To see how the Back and Forward buttons work, follow these steps:

1. Click the Finder icon on the Dock. The Finder window appears.

2. Click the Go menu and then click Documents (Go ➤ Documents). The Finder window displays the contents of your Documents folder. Notice that the Forward button appears dimmed.

3. Click the Go menu and then click Home (Go ➤ Home). The Finder window now displays the contents of the Home folder.

4. Click the Back button. The Finder window now takes you back to the Documents folder, because it is the folder that you viewed prior to the Home folder. Notice that now the Forward button no longer appears dimmed.

5. Click the Forward button. The Finder window now takes you forward to the Home folder, because it is the folder that you viewed before clicking the Back button.

If you click the Back button multiple times, you see the folders that you previously viewed. The Forward button simply reverses the order of the folders you viewed using the Back button.

Viewing the Contents of a Folder

Once you find a folder to view, you can view the contents of that folder in one of four ways:

- Icon view

- List view

- Column view

- Cover Flow view

To change the way a folder's content appears in the Finder window, you have the following two choices (also see Figure 5-6):

- Click the View menu and click an option, such as Icons or List

- Click an icon in the upper-left corner of the Finder window

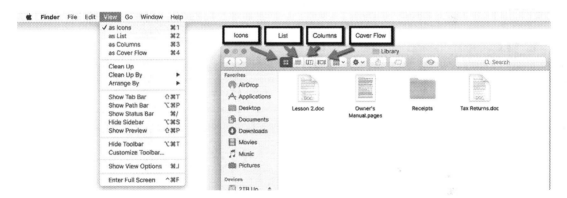

Figure 5-6. Changing how to view the contents of a folder

Icon view makes it easy to see each file or folder. File icons can also display thumbnail images of the file contents. These thumbnail images are especially handy for browsing through pictures or videos, as shown in Figure 5-7.

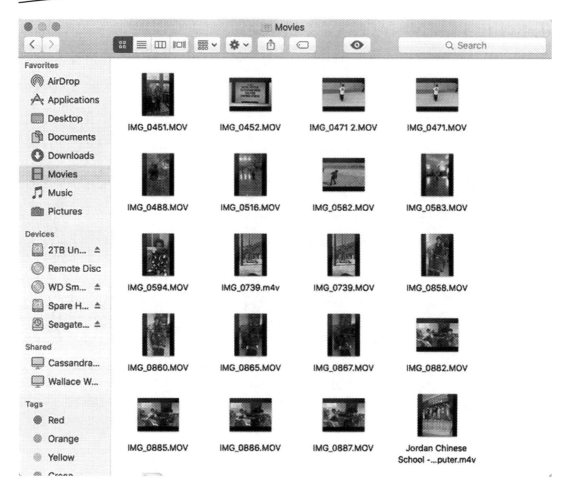

Figure 5-7. Icon view shows thumbnail images of picture or video files

The problem with Icon view is that when you're viewing a folder that contains many files and folders, you can't easily see everything at once. That's when you might prefer using List view instead.

List view lets you view the contents of multiple folders. This makes it easier to see the contents of a single folder and the contents of any folders inside that folder.

The drawback of List view is that everything appears as a much smaller icon. To view the contents of a folder, you need to click the gray disclosure triangle that appears to the left of a folder, as shown in Figure 5-8.

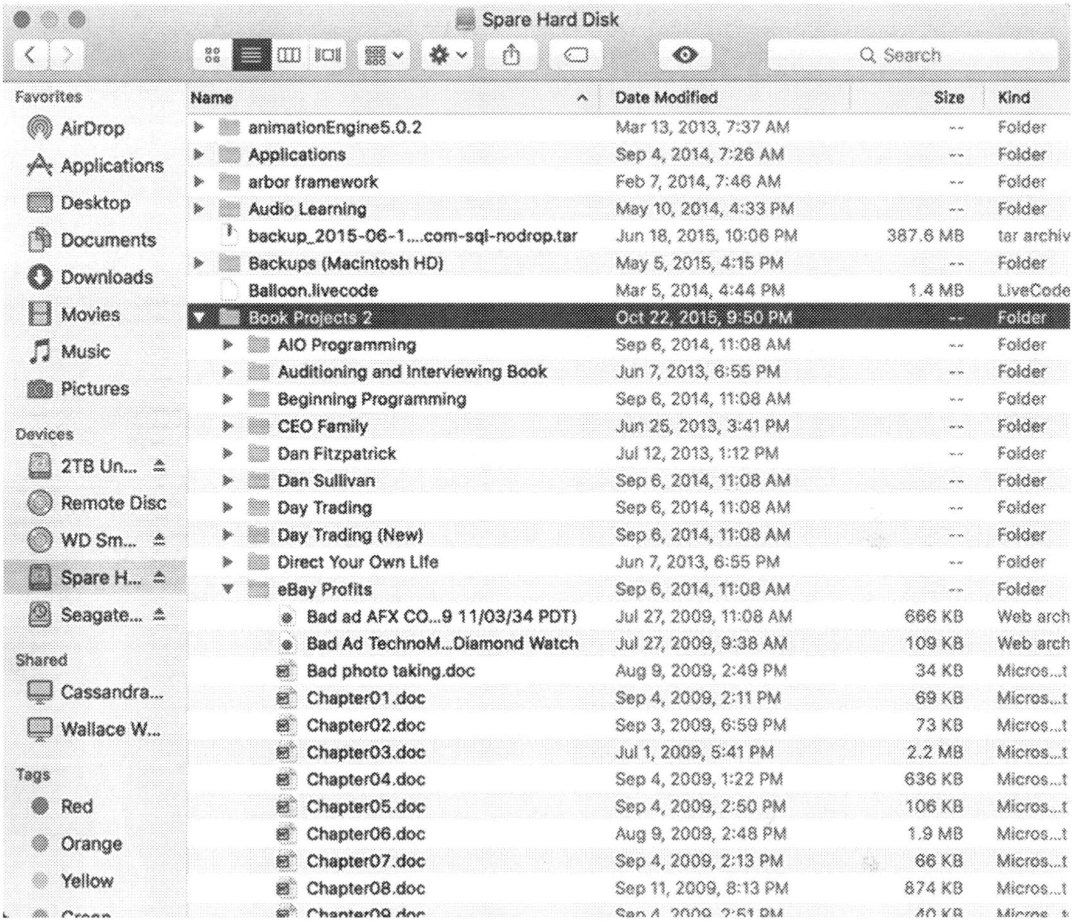

Figure 5-8. *List view shows the contents of folders within folders*

Column view is best at showing the contents of folders within folders because you can see the contents of each folder in a column. The leftmost column displays the folder that you're examining and each column to the right displays the contents of the currently selected folder, as shown in Figure 5-9.

Figure 5-9. *Column view displays the contents of folders in each column*

Cover Flow view is best at helping you browse through files so that you can view the contents without actually opening them, as shown in Figure 5-10. You can scroll left and right through Cover Flow view by swiping your finger left or right across the mouse or trackpad surface.

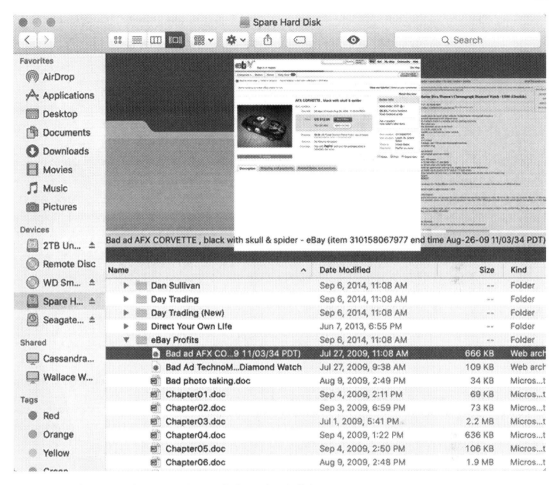

Figure 5-10. Cover Flow view shows thumbnail views of each file's contents

Creating Folders

Although OS X includes folders for storing different types of files, you'll likely need to create your own folder. You can create a folder in one of two ways:

- Click the File menu and click New Folder (File ➤ New Folder)
- Press Shift+Command+N

When you first create a folder, the Finder generically names it "untitled folder" (see Figure 5-11).

Figure 5-11. *A new folder has a generic folder name*

To rename a folder, follow these steps:

1. Click the folder that you want to rename. OS X highlights your selected folder.

2. Do one of the following:

   ▓ Click the File menu and click Rename (File ➤ Rename)

   ▓ Press Return

   ▓ Right-click the folder, and when a pop-up menu appears, click Rename

   No matter which method you choose, the Finder highlights the current folder name.

3. Type a new name for your folder or edit the existing name.

4. Press Return when you're done.

The Finder displays your folder with the new name that you typed. Remember, every folder needs a descriptive name, but two folders stored inside the same folder cannot have the same folder name.

While it's possible to give two or more folders identical names as long as they're stored in different folders, it's best to always give every folder a distinctive name. That way you'll avoid confusing yourself when trying to find a specific folder.

Summary

Every Mac has a disk for storing everything. To organize your files, your disk is divided into multiple folders, in which each folder stores related files. Some common folders that OS X has already created for you include Applications (for storing programs), Documents (for storing your files), Music (for storing your songs), and Pictures (for storing your digital photographs).

Folders often contain other folders. The Finder helps you find your way through these multiple hierarchies of folders within folders. You can view a folder's contents by doing one of the following:

- Double-click a folder

- Click a folder in the sidebar (left pane) of the Finder window

- Click the Go menu and then click the folder that you want to view

- Click the Go menu and click Recent Folders (Go ➤ Recent Folders) to view a list of your most recently viewed folders

- Click the Go menu and then click Go to Folder (Go ➤ Go to Folder) and type the exact name of the folder that you want to find

- Click the Back or Forward buttons in the upper-left corner of the Finder window

Once you've selected a folder to open, you can view that folder's contents as icons, as a list, in columns, or in a Cover Flow. Icon view and Cover Flow view provide thumbnail images of the file so that you can see the contents at a glance. List view and Column view are best for viewing folders within folders.

You can also create your own folders by choosing the New Folder command. When you create a new folder, it has the generic "untitled folder" name, so you'll need to rename to something more descriptive.

Ultimately, folders exist to help you stay organized. By giving your folders descriptive names, you'll more easily find the files stored in each folder.

Chapter 6

Manipulating Files

Files typically contain text and/or graphics. Once you save data in a file, you can always copy, modify, move, or delete the file. Since files contain personal or work data that's likely important to you, you need to know how to manipulate files stored on your Mac.

You can manipulate a file by modifying the contents or by changing the characteristics. To modify the contents of a file, you need to open the file in a program. If you have a word processor file, you need to use a word processor to edit the text stored in the file. If you have a graphics file, you need to use a graphics editor to change the picture stored in the file.

Beyond changing the contents of a file, you may also need to change the characteristics of the file, such as:

- Renaming a file

- Copying a file

- Moving a file to a new location

- Deleting a file

- Modifying information about the file, such as tags or comments

Think of files as boxes containing stuff. You can modify the stuff inside the box or you can mark up the outside of the box, move the box to a new location, or throw away the whole box (and everything inside it) altogether.

Opening a File

To open a file, you have two options. The first option is to start the program that created that file. If you want to open a file that you created using Microsoft Word, for example, you need to start Microsoft Word. (If you don't know or remember which program created the file that you want to open, the second option is best; this is explained later.)

© Wallace Wang 2016
W. Wang, *Mac OS X for Absolute Beginners*, DOI 10.1007/978-1-4842-1913-3_6

Once you start the program that created the file, click the File menu, and then click Open (File ➤ Open). When an Open window appears, click the file that you want to edit and then click the Open button in the bottom-right corner of the Open window, as shown in Figure 6-1.

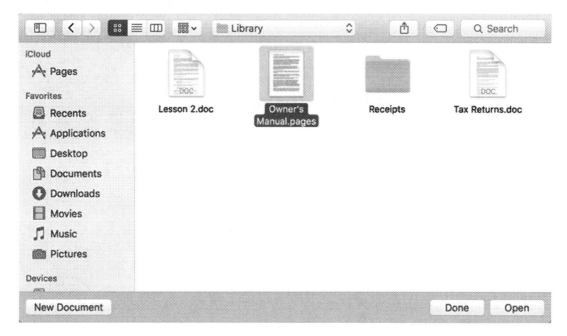

Figure 6-1. A typical Open window that lets you open a file within a program

A second and faster way to open a file is to do one of the following:

- Double-click the file

- Right-click the file, and when a pop-up menu appears, click Open

Both options open the file and load the program that created it at the same time. If you're ever in doubt which program created a file, just double-click that file (or right-click and choose Open).

There could come a time when you receive a file created by a program that you don't have on your Mac. Similarly, you may want to edit a file using a program different from the one that created it; for example, you have a file created in Microsoft Word but you want to edit it using Pages. When you want to edit a file using a program different from the one that originally created it, follow these steps:

1. Click the Finder icon on the Dock to open a Finder window.

2. Right-click the file that you want to edit. A pop-up menu appears.

3. Choose Open With. You see a submenu listing all the programs OS X thinks can open your chosen file, as shown in Figure 6-2.

Figure 6-2. The Open With command lets you choose which program to use to edit a file

Note   Even though the Open With submenu lists potential programs, there's no guarantee that any of these programs can actually open your file.

4. Click the program name that you want to open your chosen file. If it is able, OS X opens your file within the program that you just chose.

Although every file contains data, every program potentially stores data in a different way. The way that a program saves data in a file is called a *file format*. If you type the same letter in two different word processors, the first word processor would save the data in one file format and the second word processor would save that same data in an entirely different file format.

Fortunately, most programs can save files in multiple formats so that you can use the file format most convenient for you. For example, the Pages word processor can save files in its own Pages format or in Microsoft Word format. This lets you share Pages documents with anyone who might be using Microsoft Word.

To help identify the file format, programs typically add an identifying extension to the file name. This file extension helps you identify which programs created the file and how that data is stored. The following are some common file formats:

- Graphic files: .png, .jpg, .tiff, .gif, .psd

- Word processor files: .doc, .docx, .pages

- Spreadsheet files: .xls, .xlsx, .numbers

- Slide show presentation files: .ppt, .pptx, .keynote

The file extension appears after the file's name. So if you named a file "Letters to Grandma", it might have a file extension that makes the whole file name look like "Letters to Grandma. docx" or "Letters to Grandma.pages".

In general, all programs, such as Photoshop and Microsoft Word, are able to open a variety of different file formats.

If you use Apple's Pages word processor, you can open Microsoft Word .doc and .docx files, but Microsoft Word can't open .pages files. Likewise, Apple's Numbers spreadsheet can open Microsoft Excel .xls and .xslx files, and Apple's Keynote presentation program can open Microsoft PowerPoint .ppt and .pptx files, but the Microsoft programs can't open the Apple programs.

While file extensions can help you identify a file format, file extensions can be hidden. If a file extension isn't visible, you can still view the file extension by following these steps:

1. Click the Finder icon on the Dock to open a Finder window.

2. Right-click the file that you want to examine. A pop-up menu appears, as shown in Figure 6-3.

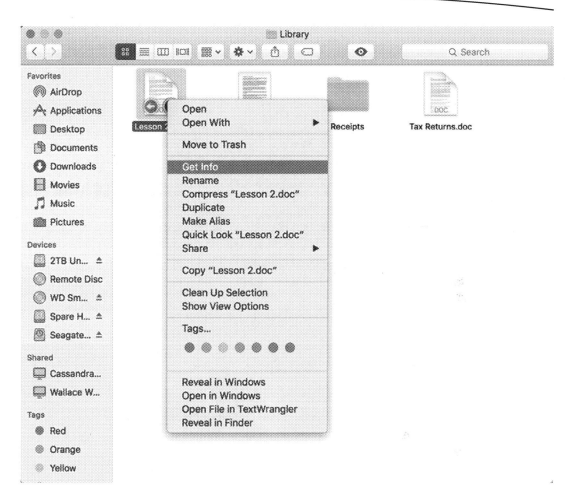

Figure 6-3. The Get Info command appears when you right-click a file

3. Click Get Info (or press Command+I). An Info window appears.

4. Click the red close button in the upper-left corner when you're done looking at the Info window.

As shown in Figure 6-4, the Info window clearly identifies the file name, the file extension, and the program that created the file. Look for the following in the figure:

▓ At the top of the window, you see the file name with the file extension and the icon of the program that created the file. In the example, Lesson 2.doc is a .doc file created by Microsoft Word.

▓ The Kind field includes the file format and file extension, stating the name of the program that created the file.

▓ The Name & Extension field also displays the file name and file extension. (If you clear the "Hide extension" check box, you can see the file extension in the Finder window.)

Program icon
and file
extension

File format
and file
extension

File extension

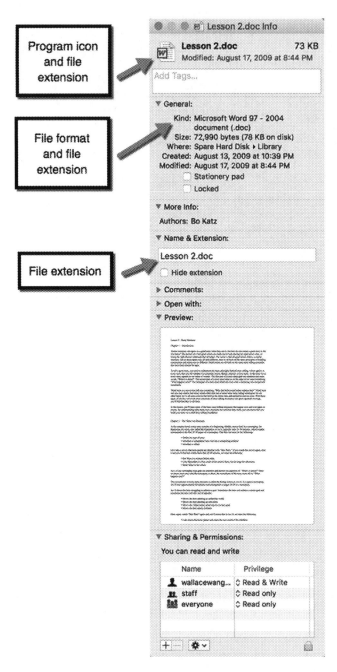

Figure 6-4. *The Info window identifies the file format and the program that created the file*

Previewing a File

Opening a file can be cumbersome because you have to load the program to see the file's contents. Instead of opening a file, it's often faster to preview a file.

Previewing simply shows you the contents of that file without having to start a program to open that particular file. The drawback is that OS X can only preview files stored in common formats such as graphics (.jpg, .png, .gif, .pdf), word processor documents (.doc, .docx, .pages), spreadsheets (.xls, .xlsx, .numbers), and presentation files (.ppt, .pptx, .keynote). If you try to preview a file created by a less commonly used program, you may not be able to use the preview feature.

To preview a file, follow these steps:

1. Click the Finder icon on the Dock. A Finder window appears.

2. Click the file that you want to preview.

3. Do one of the following to open a preview window like the one shown in Figure 6-5:

    a. Press the spacebar

    b. Press Command+Y

    c. Right-click the file, and when a pop-up menu appears, choose Quick Look

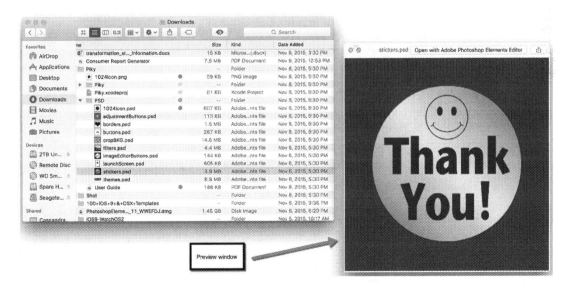

Figure 6-5. *The preview window displays the contents of a file without opening the file*

4. Click the close button in the upper-left corner of the preview window to make it disappear.

Creating and Saving a File

All files are created by programs. A word processor lets you type text, a paint program lets you draw pictures, a game lets you store high scores, and a video editor lets you modify video. Even OS X and Safari create files to store data for its own use, even though you may never know they exist.

With most programs, you have the option to create a new file. The following are two common ways to create a new file in any program:

- Click the File menu and click New (File ➤ New)
- Press Command+N

When you create a new file in a program, you see an empty window. Within this window, you create your data, such as typing a business report or drawing a picture.

Once you create a new file, you'll eventually want to save it. The following are two common ways to save a file:

- Click the File menu and click Save (File ➤ Save)
- Press Command+S

When you save a new file, you need to decide the following:

- The file name
- The location where you want to save the file

The file name can contain up to 255 characters but should be descriptive of the file's contents. For example, naming a file "Tax Returns" can help you find which file contains your tax return data.

The location of a file can be any folder, but most people usually save their files in the Documents folder. Of course, to further organize their files, people often create multiple folders inside the Documents folder.

The first time that you save a file, you always need to define a file name and location to save the file in. From that point on, saving that file simply saves the contents of that file so that you never need to worry about the file name or location again.

Identifying an Open File's Location

If you've opened an existing file in a program, here's a quick way to identify that file's location on your disk. At the top of every window, centered in the middle, you'll always see the title bar that displays the file name.

Right-click the file name on the title bar to make a pop-up menu appear. This menu lists a hierarchy of all the folders (folders tucked within other folders) in which you can find the file displayed in the current window, as shown in Figure 6-6.

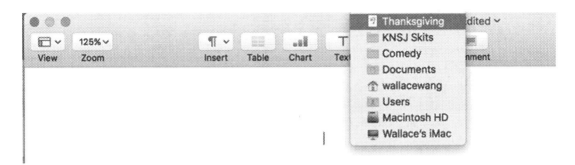

Figure 6-6. Right-clicking a window title bar displays the location of that file

In Figure 6-6, the current file in the window is named "Thanksgiving" and it's stored inside a folder called KNSJ Skits. This folder is stored inside a folder called Comedy, which is inside the Documents folder.

Your home folder is typically your name. Every home folder gets stored in the Users folder, which is stored on your Mac's hard disk. By simply following the hierarchy of folders, you can find the location of your file.

Renaming a File

When you first save a file, you should give it a descriptive and unique name. You can't give two files in the same folder the same name, but you can give two files the same name if they're stored in separate folders. However, this isn't recommended since it will likely confuse you.

You can always rename a file by either editing its existing name or giving it an entirely different name.

To rename a file, follow these steps:

1. Click the Finder icon on the Dock. A Finder window appears.

2. Click the file that you want to rename.

3. Do one of the following to select the existing file name:

   a. Press Return to highlight the current file name

   b. Right-click the file, and when a pop-up menu appears, choose Rename

4. Use the cursor keys to edit the existing name or type an entirely new name.

Copying a File

Copying a file makes a duplicate of that file. When you copy a file, you can store the copy of that file anywhere else, such as in a different folder on your Mac or on a separate device, such as a USB flash drive or an external hard drive.

Copying a file involves three steps: selecting, copying, and pasting.

Select the File

First, you need to select the file or files that you want to copy, as follows:

1. Click the Finder icon on the Dock. A Finder window appears.

2. Do one of the following:

   ▓ To select only one file in the Finder window, click the file that you want to copy. It becomes highlighted.

   ▓ To select two or more files in the Finder window, hold down the Command key and click each file that you want to select. This method lets you select two or more files that aren't necessarily next to each other.

To select a range of files that are next to each other, follow these steps:

1. Click the first file that you want to select in the Finder window.

2. Hold down the Shift key and click the last file that you want to select. The Finder selects the range of files, as shown in Figure 6-7.

Name		Date Modified	Size	Kind
	Fig4-2	Dec 1, 2015, 9:27 PM	147 KB	PNG image
	Fig4-3	Dec 1, 2015, 10:08 PM	98 KB	PNG image
	Fig4-4	Dec 2, 2015, 8:14 AM	136 KB	PNG image
	Fig4-5	Dec 2, 2015, 8:23 AM	82 KB	PNG image
	Fig4-6	Dec 2, 2015, 8:28 AM	67 KB	PNG image
	Fig4-7	Dec 2, 2015, 8:32 AM	73 KB	PNG image
	Fig4-8	Nov 27, 2015, 9:34 PM	8 KB	PNG image
	Fig4-9	Nov 27, 2015, 9:40 PM	125 KB	PNG image
	Fig4-10	Nov 28, 2015, 8:36 AM	331 KB	PNG image
	Fig5-1	Dec 3, 2015, 1:12 PM	130 KB	PNG image
	Fig5-2	Dec 3, 2015, 3:03 PM	93 KB	PNG image
	Fig5-3	Dec 4, 2015, 10:04 AM	210 KB	PNG image
	Fig5-4	Dec 3, 2015, 4:32 PM	126 KB	PNG image
	Fig5-5	Dec 3, 2015, 3:40 PM	15 KB	PNG image
	Fig5-6	Dec 3, 2015, 5:30 PM	174 KB	PNG image
	Fig5-7	Dec 3, 2015, 6:18 PM	291 KB	PNG image
	Fig5-8	Dec 3, 2015, 6:21 PM	391 KB	PNG image
	Fig5-9	Dec 3, 2015, 6:26 PM	398 KB	PNG image
	Fig5-10	Dec 3, 2015, 6:39 PM	343 KB	PNG image
	Fig5-11	Dec 3, 2015, 9:28 PM	7 KB	PNG image
	Fig5-12	Yesterday, 7:41 PM	102 KB	PNG image
	Fig5-13	Yesterday, 7:49 PM	59 KB	PNG image

Figure 6-7. Clicking once, holding down the Shift key, and clicking a second time selects the range of files

Copy the File

After you have selected one or more files, choose the Copy command in one of three ways:

- Click the Edit menu and click Copy (Edit ➤ Copy)
- Press Command+C
- Right-click the selected file and when a pop-up menu appears, choose Copy

Paste the File

Finally, open the folder where you want to store the copied file(s) and choose the Paste command in one of the following three ways:

- Click the Edit menu and click Paste (Edit ➤ Paste)
- Press Command+V
- Right-click the selected file, and when a pop-up menu appears, choose Paste

Moving a File

Unlike copying a file, moving a file physically moves it to a new location. To move a file, you can use the mouse or trackpad. However, keep in mind that moving a file works differently depending on whether you're moving a file to a new folder on the same storage device (such as the hard disk on your Mac) or whether you're moving a file from one device (such as your Mac) to a second device (such as a USB flash drive).

To move a file to another folder on the same storage device (such as a different folder on a Mac), follow these steps:

1. Click the Finder icon on the Dock. A Finder window appears. In this Finder window, find the folder in which you want to move a file to.

2. Click the File menu and choose New Finder Window (or press Command+N). This opens a second Finder window. You may want to move this second Finder window so that you can see both Finder windows side by side. (You can also drag a file to a different folder in the same Finder window if you can see the folder in which you want to store the file.)

3. In this second Finder window, move the pointer over the file that you want to move.

Note   If you hold down the Option key during steps 4 and 5, you can copy a file instead of moving it.

4. Hold down the left mouse button (or press your finger on the trackpad surface).

5. Drag the file icon to the folder where you want to move it to (such as the folder that you selected in step 1).

6. Release the mouse or trackpad. The Finder moves your selected file.

To move a file from one storage device (such as a hard disk on a Mac) to another storage device (such as an external hard disk or USB flash drive), follow these steps:

1. Click the Finder icon on the Dock. A Finder window appears. In this Finder window, find the folder on the storage device in which you want to move a file to.

2. Click the File menu and choose New Finder Window (or press Command+N). This opens a second Finder window. You may want to move this second Finder window so that you can see both Finder windows side by side.

3. In this second Finder window, move the pointer over the file that you want to move.

4. Hold down the Command key. (If you don't hold down the Command key, the Finder will copy your selected file instead of moving it.)

5. Hold down the left mouse button (or press your finger on the trackpad surface).

6. Drag the file icon to the folder where you want to move it to (such as the folder that you selected in step 1).

7. Release the mouse or trackpad. The Finder moves your selected file from one storage device to another.

Notice the differences when dragging and dropping a file from one folder to another. When you're dragging and dropping a file within the same storage device, the Finder defaults to moving the file unless you hold down the Option key to make it copy the file instead.

When you're dragging and dropping a file between two different storage devices, the Finder defaults to copying the file unless you hold down the Command key to make it move the file instead.

By defaulting to copying files between two different storage devices, OS X protects you from accidentally moving a file to a different storage device.

Deleting a File

No matter how important a file might be, you may eventually want to delete it. To delete a file, you need to move it to the Trash folder. There are several ways to delete a file after selecting it in the Finder window:

* Drag the file to the Trash icon on the right side of the Dock

* Right-click the selected file, and when a pop-up menu appears, choose Move to Trash

* Click the File menu and choose Move to Trash (File ➤ Move to Trash)

Remember, once you delete a file, you can still recover that file from the Trash if you change your mind. To retrieve a file from the Trash, follow these steps:

1. Click the Trash icon on the Dock. A Finder window appears, displaying all the files currently stored in the Trash.

2. Click the file that you want to retrieve and do one of the following:

   a. Click the File menu and choose Put Back (File ➤ Put Back)

   b. Right-click the file that you want to retrieve, and when a pop-up menu appears, choose Put Back, as shown in Figure 6-8

Figure 6-8. The Put Back command retrieves a file from the Trash

Note   The Put Back command moves a file from the Trash back to its original location when you deleted it.

If you're sure you want to delete any files stored in the Trash, you can permanently delete these files by emptying the Trash. To empty the Trash, do one of the following:

- Right-click the Trash icon on the Dock, and when a pop-up menu appears, choose Empty Trash

- Click the Finder menu and choose Empty Trash (Finder ➤ Empty Trash)

After you choose the Empty Trash command, OS X permanently deletes all files in the Trash. Always make sure that there aren't any files in the Trash that you actually need before you choose the Empty Trash command.

Searching for a File

Perhaps the biggest problem with files is trying to find them again. Storing files in folders with descriptive names is only part of the solution. No matter how carefully you name folders and store files in the appropriately named folder, chances are good you'll forget where you saved a particular file. When this happens, you need to search for that file by its name or contents.

To search for a file, follow these steps:

1. Click the Finder icon on the Dock. A Finder window appears.

2. Click in the Search field that appears in the upper-right corner of the Finder window, as shown in Figure 6-9.

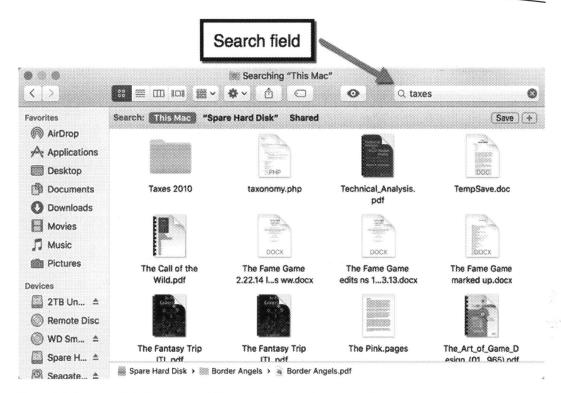

Figure 6-9. Searching finds file names and files that contain certain words or phrases

3. Type a word or phrase that you want to find in either the name of a file or in the contents of a file.

4. Press Enter to see a list of files that contain a match.

Searching for the word "taxes" helps you find files and folders that contain the word "taxes" in the file name. In addition, you'll find files that contain the word "taxes" somewhere in its data.

Note   When searching for the contents of a file, type phrases instead of single words. Searching for phrases minimizes finding files that contain irrelevant data.

Tagging Files

Most people forget where they stored files that they don't use that often. So no matter how disciplined you might be in making folders with descriptive names, chances are good that you'll forget where you stored a file.

Since you may not remember the name that you gave a file, and searches often results in too many files that you do not want, you can simplify searching by using tags.

Tags consist of two parts:

- A color

- A descriptive word or phrase

Tags let you mark files with a distinctive color and description. For example, you might tag some files with the color red and the word "taxes" and other files with the color yellow and the phrase "Vacation Photos 2017." The whole purpose of tags is to help you identify related files and provide another way to help you find a file later.

You can tag a file when you create it or you can tag a file that already exists. You can even place multiple tags on a single file. By placing two or more tags on a file, you'll be able to retrieve it by searching for any of the tags associated with it.

For example, you might tag a file with the phrase "Tax information" and a second tag called "Business expense". Then you can find that file by searching for either "Tax information" or "Business expense".

To tag a file that already exists, follow these steps:

1. Click the Finder icon on the Dock. A Finder window appears.

2. Click to select the file or folder that you want to tag. (If you hold down the Command key, you can click to select more than one file at a time.)

3. Click the File menu and click a tag at the bottom of the File menu. Alternatively, right-click the selected file and click a tag at the bottom of the pop-up menu, as shown in Figure 6-10.

Figure 6-10. Tagging a file through the File menu or the right-click pop-up menu

> **Note**   Tagging folders can be a faster and easier alternative than tagging multiple files individually.

After you have tagged a file, the Finder displays those tagged items with colors that appear to the right of the file or folder name, as shown in Figure 6-11.

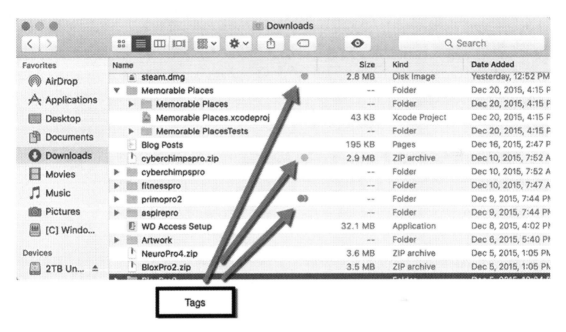

Figure 6-11. Tags appear to the right of a file or folder

To remove a tag from a file or folder, just repeat the preceding steps. So if a file has an orange tag, you can remove that orange tag by selecting it a second time, as shown in Figure 6-12.

Figure 6-12. *Selecting the same tag twice removes that tag from a file or folder*

Customizing Tags

By default, tags are simply colors, but you can add descriptive phrases to each color as well. To customize a tag with a descriptive name, you can either modify them within the Finder Preferences window or in the left pane of the Finder window.

To rename a tag in the Finder Preferences window, follow these steps:

1. Click the Finder icon on the Dock. The Finder window appears. If a Finder window does nots appear, click the File menu and click New Finder Window (File ➤ New Finder Window).

2. Click the Finder menu and choose Preferences (Finder ➤ Preferences). The Finder Preferences window appears.

3. Click the Tags icon. The Finder Preferences window displays all available tags.

4. Right-click the tag that you want to modify. A pop-up menu appears, as shown in Figure 6-13.

Figure 6-13. The Tags icon in the Finder Preferences window lets you add custom text to a tag

5.   Click the Rename command. The current tag name is selected.

6.   Edit the existing name or type a new name for your tag. Press Return when you're done.

7.   (Optional) If you want to change the color of a tag, right-click the tag that you want to modify. A pop-up menu appears (see Figure 6-13).

8.   Click the new color that you want to associate with your tag.

Searching with Tags

Once you've tagged one or more files and folders, you can easily search for those tagged items. You can use the sidebar (the left pane) of the Finder window to display a list of your most commonly used tags, as shown in Figure 6-14.

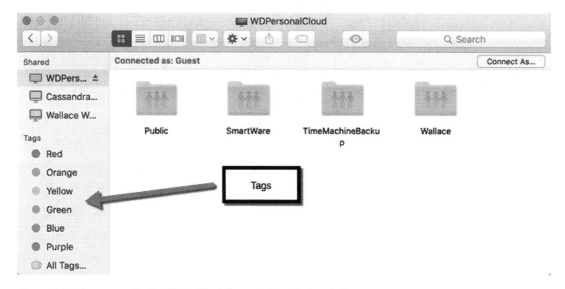

Figure 6-14. Tags appear in the sidebar (the left pane) of the Finder window

To define which tags appear in the sidebar of the Finder window, follow these steps:

1. Click the Finder icon on the Dock. The Finder window appears.

2. Click the Finder menu and choose Preferences (Finder ➤ Preferences). The Finder Preferences window appears.

3. Click the Tags icon. The Finder Preferences window displays all available tags.

4. Click the check box to the right of each tag that you want to appear in the Finder sidebar. A check mark means the tag will appear in the sidebar. An empty check mark means that the tag will not appear in the sidebar. By default, tags have an inactive mark in the check box, which means that OS X will only display the most common tags in the sidebar, such as Red, Orange, Yellow, Green, Blue, and Purple.

5. Click the close button in the upper-left corner of the Finder Preferences window.

Once you've defined one or more tags to appear in the sidebar of the Finder window, you can display only certain tagged files. To find all files with the same tag, follow these steps:

1. Click the Finder icon on the Dock. The Finder window appears.

2. Scroll through the sidebar of the Finder window until you see the list of available tags.

3. Click a tag. The Finder window displays all files and folders that have that particular tag, as shown in Figure 6-15.

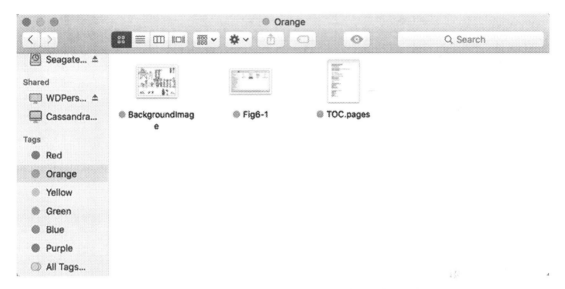

Figure 6-15. Clicking a tag in the sidebar displays only those tagged files in the Finder window

Another way to search for tagged files is to use the Search field in the upper-right corner of the Finder window. To use the Search field to look for specific tags, follow these steps:

1. Click the Finder icon on the Dock. The Finder window appears.

2. Click in the Search field in the upper-right corner of the Finder window.

3. Type part of the tag name, such as "taxes" or "orange". As you type, the Search field lists all matching tags, as shown in Figure 6-16.

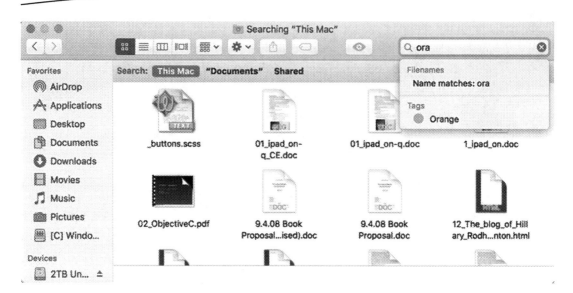

Figure 6-16. Searching for tags in the Search field

4.   Click the tag that you want, such as Orange. The Finder window
      displays all files and folders with that particular tag.

Using iCloud

Every Mac has a limited amount of built-in storage. If you need more storage, one option
is to use an external hard disk. However, if you're using a laptop, lugging an external hard
disk around isn't practical. That's why Apple offers another option, called iCloud, which only
relies on an Internet connection.

Think of iCloud as an external hard disk accessible over the Internet. The main advantage
of storing files on iCloud is that if your Mac is stolen, destroyed, or fails, all of your files are
still safely stored on iCloud. The disadvantage of iCloud is that you always need an Internet
connection to access it.

Another drawback of iCloud is that Apple only gives you a limited amount of free storage,
perhaps 5GB. If you want more storage space, you have to pay for it. From a privacy point of
view, any files stored on iCloud are physically out of your control, so there's always a small
chance that others could access those files without your knowledge or permission.

Before you can use iCloud, you need to create an Apple ID that uniquely identifies you.
To create a free Apple ID, visit Apple's web site at `https://appleid.apple.com`.

Once you've created an Apple ID, you can create an iCloud account by visiting Apple's web
site at `https://www.apple.com/icloud/setup`.

Besides providing a place to store backup copies of your critical files, iCloud also gives you
a place to store files that you want to access on different devices.

Without iCloud, you might modify a file on a Mac, and then copy that file to an iPad to
modify it some more. You might copy that file to a Windows PC to modify it yet again.

Copying a file from one device to another can be cumbersome, because now that you have multiple copies of the same file stored on different devices, if you make changes to the file, how do you know which is the most recent and up-to-date version?

iCloud eliminates this problem by letting you store a file on iCloud. There's always only a single copy of any file saved on iCloud. You can modify the file on a Mac and then switch to an iPhone to modify the file some more.

Each time that you modify a file on iCloud, you're only modifying one file, so you'll never have multiple copies of the same file. iCloud basically gives you a safe place to store files (unless you accidentally delete the files from iCloud).

Think of iCloud as a second disk on the Internet. Just as you can divide the disk in your Mac into folders, you can divide iCloud into folders to organize your files. You can view the contents of iCloud in the Finder.

To view your iCloud storage, first make sure that you have an Internet connection and that you have set up an iCloud account using your Apple ID. Then, follow these steps:

1. Click the Finder icon on the Dock. A Finder window appears.

2. Click the Go menu and click iCloud Drive, as shown in Figure 6-17.
    The Finder displays the contents of your iCloud drive.

Figure 6-17. Accessing iCloud Drive from the Finder

Once you open your iCloud Drive, you can store files on iCloud, create folders, and copy or move files between iCloud and your Mac.

Summary

File management is one of the most critical yet confusing elements of using any computer. Before creating files, it's best to develop a plan to keep all of your files organized.

Typically, you can store all of your critical files inside the Documents folder, but make sure that you create additional folders to keep your various files organized so that you can find them again.

Beyond using folders to organize files, consider tagging files with colors and descriptive phrases as well. Such tags can help you find a file quickly when you need it.

You can rename, copy, move, and delete any file. Just remember that if you delete a file, you can always retrieve it later from the Trash. However, if you empty the Trash, then all the files are gone for good.

Files contain your important data, so make sure that you know how to create files, save them, and find them again. Managing files might feel as exciting as organizing a closet, but when you take the time to do it, you'll be glad you did.

Chapter 7

Sharing Files

Most of the time, you create and modify files for your own use. However, sometimes you need to share files with other people. At times, you may want to let others see what you've created, and other times, you may need to let others edit your file and send it back to you. Since sharing files is often necessary, you need to know how to share files easily.

In a perfect world, you should be able to share files as easily as you can share a newspaper or a magazine. In reality, sharing files isn't as simple as you might expect.

Remember, programs often store data in a specific file format. That means that a file created in Microsoft Word can't be opened in iMovie, and a video edited in iMovie can't be opened in Microsoft Excel.

To share a file successfully, one or more of the following criteria must be met:

- Both the sender and the receiver of the file must have the same program that created the file

- The receiver must have a program that can import the file

- The sender must have a program that can export the file into another file format that the receiver can open

Files can contain the same data, but if the data is stored in different file formats, not everyone is able to access the data.

To simplify the problem with file formats, the Adobe company created a universal file format called a Portable Document File (PDF). Files stored in the PDF format have the .pdf file extension.

The advantage of .pdf files is that they preserve all text formatting and graphics displaying. Even better, you can share .pdf files across all types of computers, including Windows, Linux, OS X, and even iOS and Android devices.

The disadvantage of .pdf files is that they can be viewed but only partially edited and modified. Many government agencies and companies create .pdf files of forms that you can complete by entering data or by printing to fill out by hand.

© Wallace Wang 2016

W. Wang, *Mac OS X for Absolute Beginners*, DOI 10.1007/978-1-4842-1913-3_7

Creating a PDF File

With OS X, you can turn any file into a .pdf file just by using the Print command. Instead of printing the contents of a file to paper, you print your file to a .pdf file that displays your data exactly as if it were printed on paper. Since almost every program can print data, every program can create a .pdf file that you can share with others.

To create a .pdf file from most programs that can display text or graphics, follow these steps:

1. Open a file that you want to save as a .pdf file, such as a word processor document, spreadsheet, or slide show presentation.

2. Click the File menu and choose Print (File ➤ Print). A Print window appears, as shown in Figure 7-1.

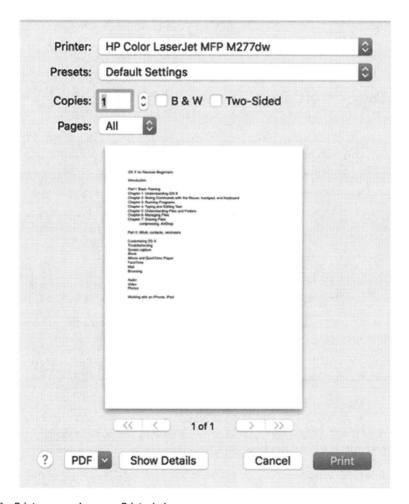

Figure 7-1. The Print command opens a Print window

3. Click the PDF pop-up menu in the bottom-left corner. A pop-up menu appears, as shown in Figure 7-2.

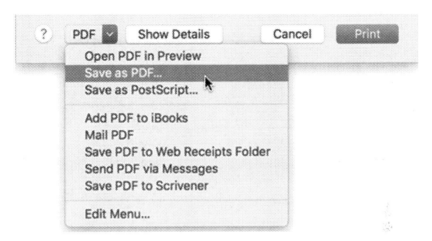

Figure 7-2. The PDF pop-up menu

4. Choose Save as PDF. A Save As window appears, letting you choose the folder to save your .pdf file and the name you want to give your .pdf file.

5. Click the folder where you want to save your .pdf file.

6. Type a descriptive file name for your .pdf file.

7. Click the Save button. Your .pdf file gets saved in the folder under the file name that you chose, as shown in Figure 7-3.

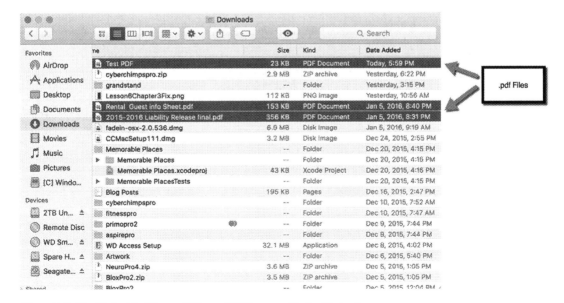

Figure 7-3. The Finder identifies .pdf files as PDF Document in the Kind column

Another way to create a .pdf file within most programs is to click the File menu and choose either Export (File ➤ Export) or Save As (File ➤ Save As). Then choose to export or save the file as a PDF file, as shown in Figure 7-4.

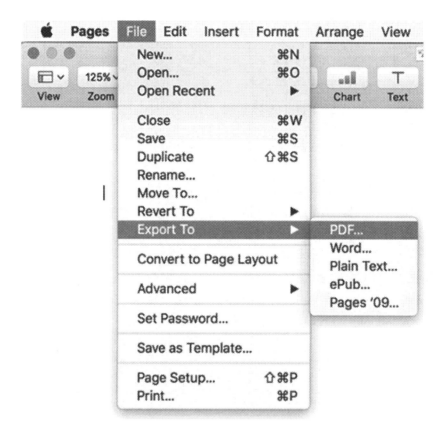

Figure 7-4. The File ➤ Export or File ➤ Save As command offers another way to create .pdf files

Opening a PDF File

To open and view the contents of a .pdf file on any computer, you would normally use a special PDF viewing program such as Adobe Reader. However, the Mac includes a program called Preview that can open and view .pdf files so that you don't need to download and install Adobe Reader on your Mac.

> **Note**   In addition to opening .pdf files, the Preview program can also open most common graphic files, such as .jpg, .png, and .gif.

To open a .pdf file on a Mac, you can double-click a .pdf file in the Finder window. You can also open the Preview program (in the Applications folder) and then choose File ➤ Open to select the .pdf file that you want to view.

Importing a File

If you want to share a file with another person, it's always easiest if the other person uses the same program as you do on a Mac. That way you can share your files without any problems.

Unfortunately, not everyone uses the same programs. Even different versions of the same program could save files in slightly different formats. When someone sends you a file created by another program, you need to know which type of program is able to open that file. When a program can open a file created by another program, that's called *importing*.

Some common types of files are shown in Table 7-1.

Table 7-1. *Commonly Shared File Formats*

File Type	Common File Extensions	Created by this Program	Can Be Imported by this Program
Word processor document	.doc, .docx	Microsoft Word	Pages
Graphics	.jpg, .png, .gif,	Any graphics program	Preview, Photos
Graphics	.psd	Adobe Photoshop and similar graphics editors	Preview
Spreadsheets	.xls, xlsx	Microsoft Excel	Numbers
Presentation slide shows	.ppt, .pptx	Microsoft PowerPoint	Keynote
Audio	.mp3, .wav, .aiff, .aac	Any audio player or editor	QuickTime Player, GarageBand
Video	.avi, .mov, .mpg, .mpeg, .mp4, .wmv	Any video player or editor	QuickTime Player, iMovie

Once you can identify the type of program that created the file, you can use a similar program to import and open that file. For example, if you wanted to import and open a .docx file, since you know it's a word processor file, you should be able to import and open that file using almost any word processor such as Pages.

Likewise, if you wanted to import and open an .xlsx file, you could use any spreadsheet such as Numbers. If you wanted to import and open a .pptx file, you could use a presentation program such as Keynote.

Note   When you import a file, you may lose the original formatting of the data.

Exporting a File

Because so many people use Microsoft Office on either Windows or the Mac, many people share word processor documents saved in Microsoft Word format, spreadsheets in Microsoft Excel format, and presentations in Microsoft PowerPoint format. Most modern programs can import Word, Excel, and PowerPoint files.

So if you need to share a file with someone who doesn't have the same program as you, save that file as a .pdf file—if the receiver doesn't need to edit the data in the file.

If others need to edit the data, then you should export the file as a Microsoft Word, Excel, or PowerPoint file.

All Word, Excel, and PowerPoint files come in two file formats. First, there's the old file format used in earlier versions of Word (.doc), Excel (.xls), and PowerPoint (.ppt).

Second, there's the new file format used in more recent versions of Word (.docx), Excel (.xlsx), and PowerPoint (.pptx).

For maximum compatibility, export files into the new file format of Word (.docx), Excel (.xlsx), or PowerPoint (.pptx). If you need to share files with someone using an older computer running any version of Word 2003, Excel 2003, PowerPoint 2003, or earlier versions, you may need to share files using the older file format of Word (.doc), Excel (.xls), and PowerPoint (.ppt).

To export a file from most programs, click the File menu and choose Export or Save As. Then choose the file format you want to use, such as Word or Excel.

If you need to share files with programs that won't accept a Word, an Excel, or a PowerPoint format, you may need to export your files in one of the following types of file formats that practically all programs and computers can import:

- Text (for word processor documents)
- CSV (comma-separated value) (for spreadsheets)

Text files contain nothing but text such as letters, punctuation marks, and symbols. Unlike a word processor file format, text files don't contain any formatting.

CSV files contain nothing but numbers and text separated by commas, tabs, or other symbols. Like text files, CSV files only contain data but no formatting or formulas.

Remember, when you export data to text or CSV file formats, you lose all formatting, such as bolding, fonts, or font sizes. To retain formatting, share your files as Microsoft Word, Excel, or PowerPoint files, if possible.

> **Note**   You can purchase special file conversion programs that are especially useful for converting files trapped in formats that are no longer popular, such as dBASE, Lotus 1-2-3, WordStar, or WordPerfect files.

Compressing Files

If a file is small, it is easy and fast to copy a file from one computer to another. Unfortunately, many graphics and video files can be extremely large. Even worse, if you want to share multiple files, you don't want to copy each file individually.

To solve both of these problems, you can compress files. Compressing a file offers two huge benefits:

- It can often shrink a file size up to half its original size
- It can combine multiple files into a single file

Compressing saves space and stuffs multiple files into a single compressed file called a *ZIP file*. ZIP files can be opened or unzipped by Windows, Linux, and Mac computers, so compressing is a way to make file sharing easier for everyone.

To compress one or more files, follow these steps:

1. Click the Finder icon on the left end of the Dock. A Finder window appears.

2. Do one of the following:

   a. Click one file to compress

   b. Hold down the Command key and click two or more files

   c. Click the first file to compress, hold down the Shift key, and click the last file to compress to select a range of files

> **Note** Rather than select two or more files to compress, you can also select one or more folders, which will compress all files within that folder.

3. Do one of the following:

   a. Click the File menu and choose Compress (File ➤ Compress)

   b. Right-click the selected file or files, and when a pop-up menu appears, choose Compress

Compressed files appear in the Finder window with .zip file extension and a ZIP icon as shown in Figure 7-5.

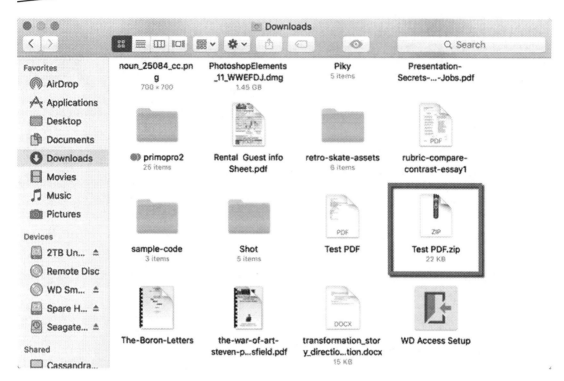

Figure 7-5. *You can identify a ZIP file by its icon and file extension*

Once you've compressed a file, you can share that file with others. If someone sends you a ZIP compressed file, you can unzip that file by following these steps:

1. Click the Finder icon on the left end of the Dock. A Finder window appears.

2. Double-click the ZIP file that you want to unzip. The Finder now displays your unzipped file or folder.

Using AirDrop

The simplest way to share a file is to copy it on to a USB flash drive, plug that flash drive in another computer, and then copy the file to the other computer. This method can be especially useful for sharing files between a Mac and a PC running Windows or Linux.

The main drawback with this method of sharing files is that you need a USB flash drive. Even if you have a flash drive, you can't use it to share files with an iPhone or an iPad. To solve this problem, you can share files wirelessly using AirDrop.

The main idea behind AirDrop is that you can share files just by dragging and dropping them to a special AirDrop window. This lets you share files between two Mac computers, two iOS devices, or a Mac and an iOS device such as an iPhone or iPad.

To use AirDrop, your two devices need to meet the following criteria:

- Be within 30 feet (9 meters) of each other

- The Mac must be running OS X Yosemite or later

- The Mac must have its "Block all incoming connections" option turned off in the Security & Privacy preferences window

- The iOS device must have Personal Hotspot turned off in Settings ➤ Cellular

Using AirDrop Between Two Mac Computers

When you want to share files between two Mac computers, both of them need to be capable of running AirDrop. To share a file using AirDrop between two Mac computers, follow these steps:

1. Click the Finder icon on the Dock on both Mac computers. A Finder window appears.

2. Click the Go menu and choose AirDrop (Go ➤ AirDrop) on both Mac computers. The AirDrop icon appears in both Finder windows. Wait a few seconds and an icon representing the other Mac appears in the Finder window, as shown in Figure 7-6.

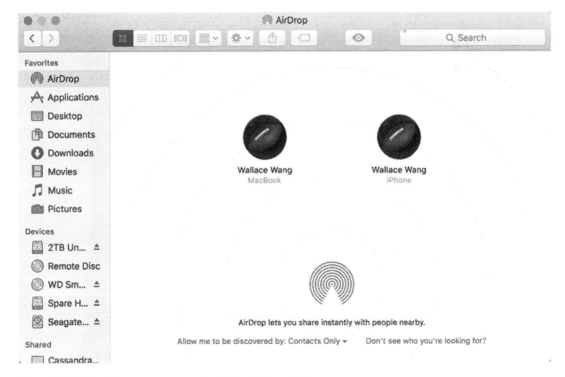

Figure 7-6. Each device appears as an icon in the AirDrop window

> **Note**   If you're trying to connect to a Mac model older than 2012, click the "Don't see who you're looking for?" link in the bottom-right corner of Figure 7-6.

3. On the Mac that has the file that you want to share, click the File menu and choose New Finder Window (File ➤ New Finder Window). This opens a second Finder window. You may want to rearrange the two Finder windows so that they appear side by side.

4. In this second Finder window, find the file that you want to share.

5. Using the mouse or trackpad, drag the file over the icon representing the other Mac computer.

6. Release the mouse or trackpad when the file appears directly over the other Mac computer icon. On the receiving Mac computer, the AirDropped file appears in the Downloads folder.

Using AirDrop Between a Mac and an iPhone/iPad

AirDrop can be a convenient way to share files between a Mac and an iPhone/iPad without physically connecting them with a cable.

> **Note**   If you send a file from a Mac to an iOS device, make sure that you have an iOS app that can open the file.

On the iOS device, make sure that you have both Wi-Fi and Bluetooth turned on. Then follow these steps to send a file from a Mac to an iOS device:

1. Click the Finder icon on the Dock on the Mac. A Finder window appears.

2. Click the Go menu and choose AirDrop (Go ➤ AirDrop) on the Mac. The AirDrop icon appears in the Finder window.

3. Turn on the iOS device. Wait a few seconds and an icon representing the iOS device appears in the Finder window (see Figure 7-6).

4. Click the File menu and choose New Finder Window (File ➤ New Finder Window). This opens a second Finder window. You may want to rearrange the two Finder windows so that they appear side by side.

5. Find the file that you want to share using this second Finder window.

6. Drag the file, using the mouse or trackpad, over the icon representing the iOS device.

At times, you may want to share a file from an iOS device to a Mac. To share a file on an iOS device and copy it to a Mac, follow these steps:

1. On the iOS device, open the file that you want to send to the Mac.

2. Tap the Share icon, as shown in Figure 7-7. Depending on the app that you use, the Share icon may appear near the top or bottom of the screen. Another screen lets you select how to share the file.

Figure 7-7. The Share icon lets you send a file to another computer

3. Tap the icon representing the Mac that you want to receive the file. This icon appears under the AirDrop category, as shown in Figure 7-8. The file gets stored in the Downloads folder of the Mac.

Figure 7-8. *The Mac appears as an icon under the AirDrop category*

Using File Attachments with E-mail

AirDrop works fine with new Mac and iOS devices. However, what if you want to share a file on a Mac with a Windows or Linux PC, or an Android device? In these cases, you can't use AirDrop, but you can use file attachments.

Since nearly all modern computers can send and receive e-mail, you can use e-mail to send files, which are known as *file attachments.* To send file attachments by e-mail, you need to set up an e-mail account on your Mac (see Chapter 18) and know the e-mail address on the other device.

To send a file attachment by e-mail, follow these steps:

1. Click the Finder icon on the Dock. A Finder window appears.

2. Click the Go menu and choose Applications (Go ➤ Applications), or just click the Applications folder in the sidebar of the Finder window. A list of all applications on your Mac appears.

3. Double-click the Mail icon to open the Mail program. (Make sure that you have an e-mail account in the Mail program.)

4. Click the File menu and choose New Message (File ➤ New Message). The New Message window appears.

5. Click the file attachment icon in the upper-right corner (it looks like a paperclip), as shown in Figure 7-9. A window appears, letting you click the file that you want to send.

Figure 7-9. The file attachment icon in the New Message window

Note   You may want to compress a file first before sending it by e-mail to make it smaller or to send multiple files at once.

6. Click a file to attach to your e-mail message. (If you hold down the Command key, you can click and select two or more files to attach to the e-mail message.)

7. Click the Choose File button to attach the selected files to your e-mail message, as shown in Figure 7-10. At this point, you need to type an e-mail address and a subject, and then click the Send icon, which looks like a paper airplane icon in the upper-left corner.

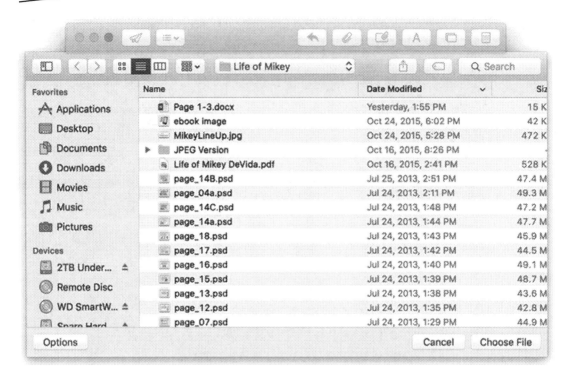

Figure 7-10. The Choose File button lets you attach one or more files to an e-mail message

Summary

Before you share files with another computer, make sure that other computer can open your file. You may need to export your file into another file format or make sure that another computer can import your file.

If you just want to share a file for someone to view but not edit, then you can save the file in the .pdf file format, which practically every computer can open. If you want to share a file for someone else to edit, save it in a commonly used file format.

For graphics, that means saving files in .jpg, .png, or .psd files that nearly every graphics program can import. For word processor documents, save files in .doc or .docx format. For spreadsheets, save files in .xls or .xlsx format. For presentations, save files in .ppt or .pptx format.

To make it easy to share files, compress files. Compressed files take up less space and let you combine multiple files into a single file.

If you need to share files within other Apple products, such as a Mac or an iPhone, use AirDrop. AirDrop can wirelessly transfer files. If you need to transfer files to non-Apple products, attach the file to an e-mail message.

Files contain important data so make sure that you know how to share files with others. After all, your data is only useful if someone else can use it.

Part II

Customizing OS X

When you first plug in a Macintosh and turn it on, it looks exactly like every other Macintosh in the world. While this is nice, you may want to spend a little time customizing the way that your Macintosh looks and works.

Such customization can make your Macintosh a unique expression of your own personality. For example, you might want to display personal pictures on your screen, or you may want to install certain programs, such as games or specialized software that helps you write novels or create animated cartoons.

By learning to customize your Macintosh for personal reasons or for productivity needs, you can turn your Macintosh into a specialized machine that's uniquely suited to help make your life easier.

Chapter 8

Using the Dock and the Launchpad

To find a program or file, you normally have to open a Finder window and then look for the program or file that you want to use. This means going through several steps just to start a program. If you use a program or file often, going through multiple steps can be annoying.

OS X offers the Dock as a place to store commonly used programs, files, and folders so that you can access them with one click. The Dock doesn't have room to store everything on your computer, just the programs, files, and folders that you use most often.

Think of the Dock as a shortcut to your favorite programs, files, and folders.

To customize the dock, you can add new icons that represent programs or files, rearrange icons, change the way the Dock appears, and even place the Dock on the left or right side of the screen instead of at the bottom.

The two main features of the Dock that are always visible are the Finder icon on the far left of the Dock and the Trash icon on the far right, as shown in Figure 8-1. Unlike other icons on the Dock, you can never move the Finder icon or the Trash icon to a new position on the Dock.

Figure 8-1. *The Finder and Trash icons appear on opposite ends of the Dock*

© Wallace Wang 2016
W. Wang, *Mac OS X for Absolute Beginners*, DOI 10.1007/978-1-4842-1913-3_8

Changing the Location of the Dock

The dock normally appears at the bottom of the screen. If you don't like this location, you can place the Dock in one of the following three locations:

- At the bottom of the screen (its default location)
- On the left of the screen, as shown in Figure 8-2
- On the right of the screen

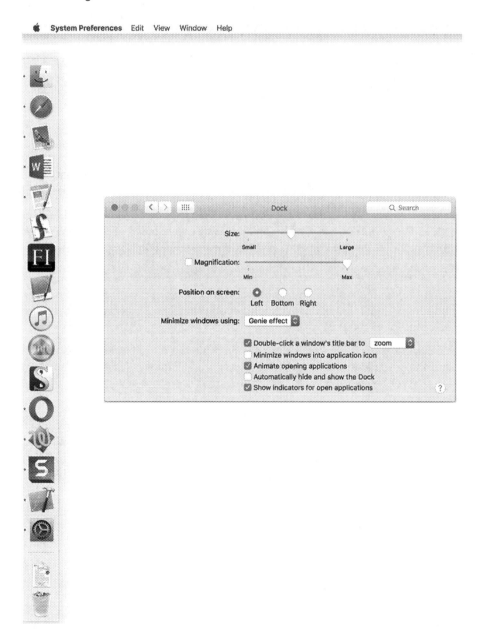

Figure 8-2. The Dock can appear on the left side of the screen

The location of the Dock is solely your personal preference. No matter where you place the Dock, it behaves the same way.

To change the location of the Dock, follow these steps:

1. Click the Apple icon in the upper-left corner of the menu bar.

2. Click System Preferences to open the System Preferences window, as shown in Figure 8-3.

Figure 8-3. The System Preferences window

3. Click the Dock icon in the top row. The Dock window appears (see Figure 8-2).

4. Click the Left, Bottom, or Right radio button in the "Position on screen" category.

5. Click the red close button in the upper-left corner to make the Dock window disappear.

Changing the Size of Dock Icons

The more icons you place on the Dock, the more crowded the Dock will appear. To help you find icons on the Dock, you can increase or decrease the size of the icons that appear on the Dock, as shown in Figure 8-4.

Figure 8-4. Changing the Dock icons makes them easier to see or allows you to add more of them to the Dock

Increasing the Dock icons makes them easier to see but gives you less room to display icons. Decreasing the Dock icons allows more icons to appear on the dock but makes all of them smaller and harder to see.

To change the size of the Dock icons, follow these steps:

1. Click the Apple icon in the upper-left corner of the menu bar.

2. Click System Preferences to open the System Preferences window (see Figure 8-3).

3. Click the Dock icon in the top row. The Dock window appears (see Figure 8-2).

4. Drag the Size slider left (to make Dock icons smaller) or right (to make dock icons larger).

Magnifying the Dock Icon

By shrinking Dock icons, you can display more of them on the screen. By increasing the size of Dock icons, you can see them easier. However, tiny Dock icons can be hard to see and larger Dock icons take up too much space.

For another way to modify the Dock icons, you can turn on magnification. With magnification turned on, all Dock icons remain the same size, but the moment you move the pointer over a Dock icon, magnification makes that icon temporarily expand in size. As soon as you move the pointer away from the Dock icon, all icons shrink back to their original size.

Magnification is a way to help make it easier to see your Dock icons, as shown in Figure 8-5.

Figure 8-5. *Magnification enlarges icons near the pointer to make them easier to see*

To turn on magnification of the Dock icons, follow these steps:

1. Click the Apple icon in the upper-left corner of the menu bar.

2. Click System Preferences to open the System Preferences window, as shown in Figure 8-3.

3. Click the Dock icon in the top row. The Dock window appears (see Figure 8-2).

4. Select the Magnification check box. (If the Magnification check box is clear, then magnification is turned off.)

5. Drag the Magnification slider left or right to change the size of the Dock icon when the pointer appears over it.

Temporarily Hiding the Dock

Having the Dock appear all the time may clutter the screen. To solve this problem, you can make the Dock temporarily disappear. When the Dock is hidden, you can make it appear by moving the pointer to the Dock's location.

So if the Dock appears at the bottom of the screen, you can make a hidden Dock appear by moving the pointer to the bottom of the screen. If the dock appears at the left side of the screen, you can make a hidden Dock appear by moving the pointer to the left side of the screen.

> **Note**   Make sure that you know the location of the Dock before you hide it. That way you'll know which edge of the screen to move the pointer to make the Dock appear again.

To temporarily hide the Dock, follow these steps:

1. Click the Apple icon in the upper-left corner of the menu bar.

2. Click System Preferences to open the System Preferences window as shown in Figure 8-3.

3. Click the Dock icon in the top row. The Dock window appears (see Figure 8-2).

4. Select (or clear) the "Automatically hide and show the Dock" check box.

Adding Folders to the Dock

In Chapter 3, you learned how to add program icons to the Dock, rearrange them, and remove them as well. Putting program icons on the Dock gives you one-click access to your favorite programs.

However, you can also add folders to the Dock. This gives you one-click access to your favorite folders containing the files that you use most often.

The Dock actually consists of two parts. On the left side, program icons appear on the left and folder icons appear on the right, as shown in Figure 8-6.

Figure 8-6. The Dock contains program and folder icons

To place a folder on the Dock, follow these steps:

1. Click the Finder icon on the Dock. A Finder window appears.

2. Find the folder that you want to place on the Dock.

3. Move the pointer over the folder that you want to place on the Dock. Hold down the left mouse button (or press your finger on the trackpad) and drag the folder anywhere on the right side of the Dock. The current icons on the Dock slide out of the way to make room for your folder icon, as shown in Figure 8-7.

Figure 8-7. Dragging a folder from the Finder window to the Dock

4.   Release the mouse or trackpad to place your folder on the Dock.

Displaying Folder Contents

Once you've placed a folder on the Dock, you can view its contents by clicking its icon on the Dock. You can display your folder contents as a fan, grid, or list. If you aren't sure which method to use, you can choose the Automatic option to let OS X choose for you based on the number of items in the folder.

The Fan view is best when folders contain a small number of files, so that you can easily see all of them at once, as shown in Figure 8-8.

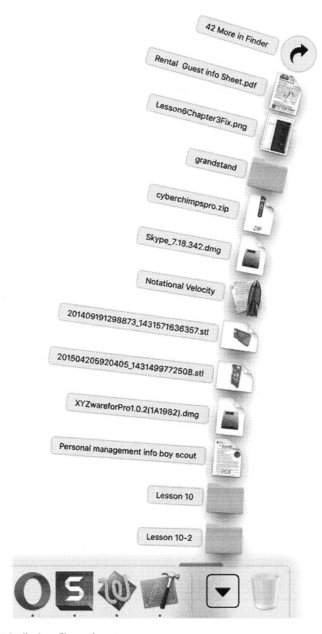

Figure 8-8. *The Fan style displays files as icons*

The Grid style displays files in rows, which are easier to see if the folder contains many files, as shown in Figure 8-9.

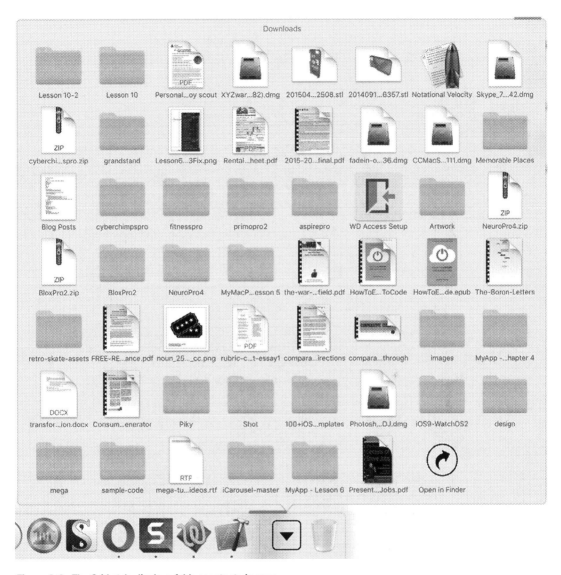

Figure 8-9. The Grid style displays folder contents in rows

The List style is best at showing all the contents of a folder in a condensed style, although it may be hard to read because the text is tiny, as shown in Figure 8-10.

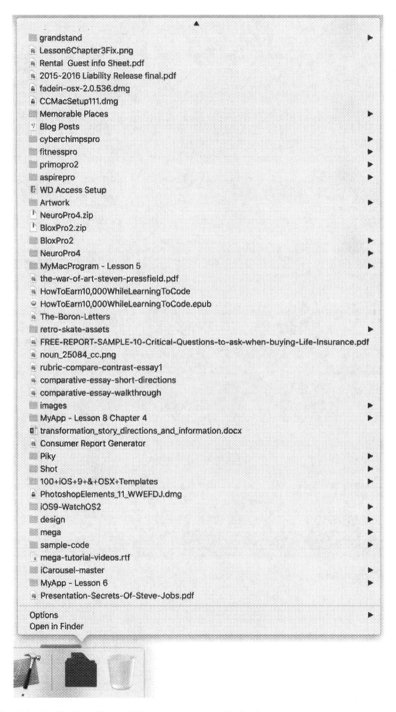

Figure 8-10. The List style displays file and folder names in a vertical column

To define how a folder displays its contents from the Dock, follow these steps:

1. Right-click the folder that you want to modify. A pop-up menu
    appears, as shown in Figure 8-11.

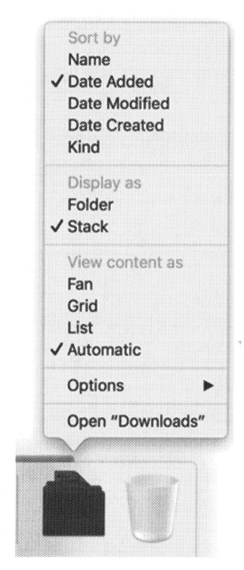

Figure 8-11. Right-clicking a folder icon displays a pop-up menu

2. Click Fan, Grid, List, or Automatic under the View content as
    category. If you choose Automatic, OS X will display a folder's
    contents based on how many items are stored inside.

Once you define how to display a folder's contents, you can click that folder to display the
contents of that folder in your chosen style (Fan, Grid, or List).

Displaying Folder Contents in the Finder Window

When you display folder contents in the Fan, Grid, or List view, you can open a file by double-clicking on that file icon.

The problem with the Fan, Grid, and List views is that you may prefer to view a folder's contents in the more familiar Finder window.

To display a folder's contents in the Finder window, follow these steps:

1. Right-click the folder that you want to open. A pop-up menu appears (see Figure 8-11).

2. Click Open.

Using the Launchpad

If you're more familiar with iOS, you might prefer displaying program icons as if they were on an iPhone or iPad screen. To do this, OS X provides a special program called Launchpad.

To run Launchpad, follow these steps:

1. Click the Finder icon on the Dock. A Finder window appears.

2. Click the Go menu and choose Applications (Go ➤ Applications). Look for the Launchpad icon, as shown in Figure 8-12.

Figure 8-12. The Launchpad icon

3. Double-click the Launchpad icon. Launchpad appears, displaying your program icons like an iPhone or iPad display, as shown in Figure 8-13.

Figure 8-13. Launchpad displays OS X programs like an iOS screen

4. Click any program that you want to run.

While in Launchpad, you still have access to the Dock. Launchpad just displays all of your program icons on the screen at once.

Note   If you have a trackpad, you can pinch four fingers on the trackpad surface as a shortcut to open Launchpad.

To exit out of Launchpad, press the Esc key on the keyboard, or click in the gray area on the right or left side of the screen, making sure that you don't click any program icons.

Summary

The Dock acts as a shortcut to your favorite programs or folders. You can place the Dock on the left, right, or bottom of the screen, or even temporarily hide it from sight until you move the pointer toward the screen edge to make it appear again.

To customize the Dock, you can shrink or enlarge the size of its icons. You can also magnify icons so that they appear enlarged only when the pointer appears over them.

To clear the screen, you can also make the Dock temporarily disappear. When you want the Dock to appear again, just move the pointer toward the edge of where the Dock is located (on the left, right, or bottom of the screen).

Besides placing program icons on the Dock, you can also place folders on the Dock. You can open a folder within the Finder window or by displaying icons on the screen as a fan, grid, or list.

Finally, if you're more comfortable using apps on iOS, you can make OS X display all of your programs as icons in a grid. To do this, you need to run a program called Launchpad.

The Dock and Launchpad act like shortcuts to help you find and run your favorite programs. By taking the time to learn how the Dock and Launchpad work, you can make your Mac even easier to use.

Chapter 9

Installing Software

Every Mac comes with plenty of free software, but it's likely you'll want to install additional programs on your Mac. Installing software on a Mac might seem straightforward, but you need to be aware of several issues.

First, most newer Mac computers don't have a DVD drive, which means you have to either get an external DVD drive or download a program from a web site.

Second, OS X tries to protect your Mac from malware (viruses, Trojan horses, spyware, etc.), so you can't always install software from the Internet without going through additional steps.

Of course, once you install software, you may want to remove that software later. In this chapter, you'll learn all the different ways to install software on a Mac.

There are three ways that you can install software on your Mac:

- Download a program from the Internet
- Install a program from a DVD
- Install a program from the Mac App Store

Of these three, installing a program from a DVD or from the Mac App Store are the two safest methods. When you install software from the Internet, you need to take extra precautions.

Note One big advantage of installing software from the Mac App Store is that if you ever delete a program by mistake or lose your Mac, you can always reconnect to the Mac App Store to download and reinstall the software without having to find serial codes or installation DVDs.

© Wallace Wang 2016
W. Wang, *Mac OS X for Absolute Beginners*, DOI 10.1007/978-1-4842-1913-3_9

Finding Software on the Mac App Store

The Mac App Store contains a library of software that Apple has examined to make sure it's safe. The disadvantage of the Mac App Store is that it doesn't contain all available OS X software.

To access the Mac App Store, you need an Apple ID, which is linked to a credit card. That allows you to purchase software securely without needing to retype a credit card number each time you want to buy another program from the Mac App Store.

> **Note**   To get a free Apple ID, visit `https://appleid.apple.com`.

The Mac App Store serves two purposes. One, it provides a place for you to search for and purchase programs. Two, it provides a way to update any programs currently installed on your Mac.

To view the Mac App Store, make sure that you have an Internet connection and then follow these steps:

1. Click the Apple icon in the upper-left corner of the menu bar.

2. Click App Store to open the App Store window, as shown in Figure 9-1.

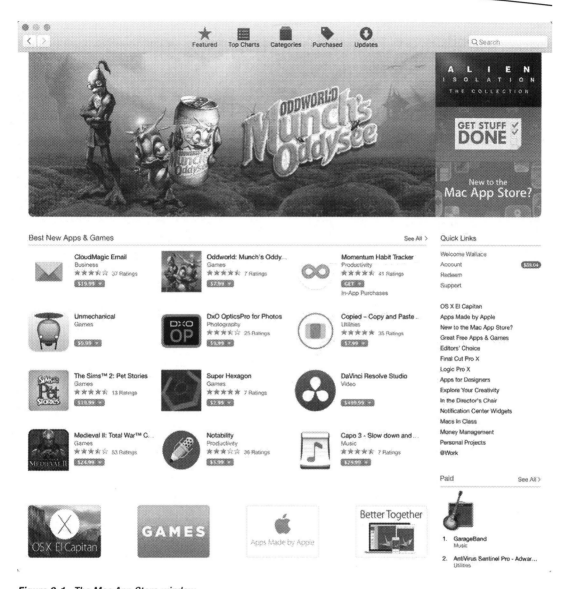

Figure 9-1. The Mac App Store window

There are several ways to search for a program within the Mac App Store. The App Store window organizes software into the following three groups:

- Featured
- Top Charts
- Categories

The Featured group lists the newest or most popular programs that Apple wants to highlight (see Figure 9-1).

The Top Charts category lists the most popular paid programs, the most popular free programs, and the programs earning the most money through the Mac App Store (see Figure 9-2).

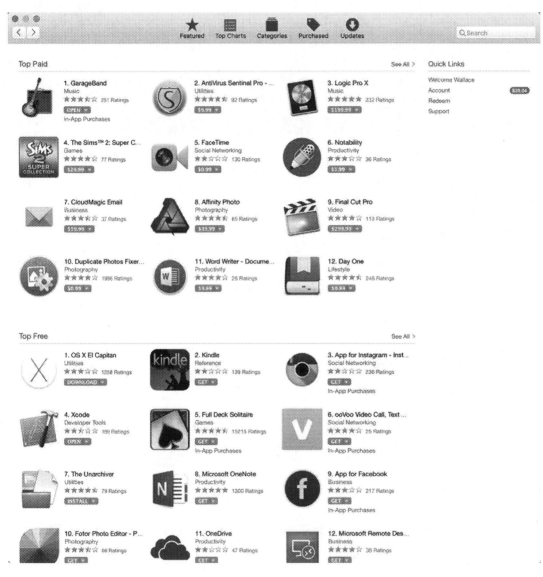

Figure 9-2. *The Top Charts category lists the most popular programs in the Mac App Store*

The Categories group lists software according to their function, such as medical, video, finance, games, or travel, as shown in Figure 9-3.

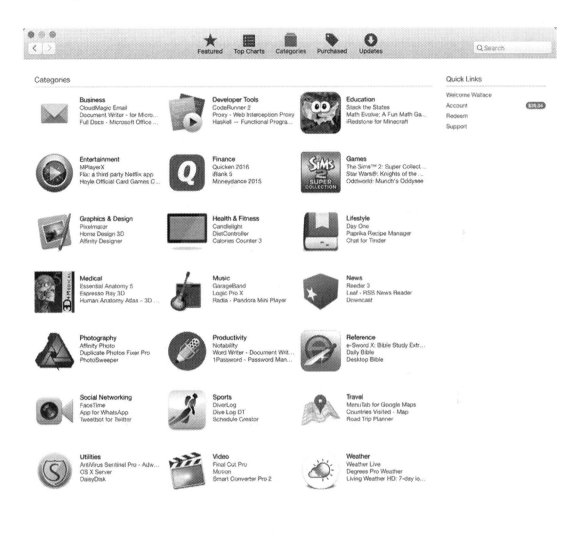

Figure 9-3. The Categories group lists available software by function

By clicking a particular group, you can browse through all available software in that group, such as all games or all sports programs.

Another way to browse through the Mac App Store is to search it. To search for a program by name or by function, follow these steps:

1. Click the Apple icon in the upper-left corner of the menu bar.

2. Click App Store to open the Mac App Store window (see Figure 9-1).

3. Click in the Search field in the upper-right corner of the App Store window.

4. Type all or part of a program name or category type (such as health or finance) and press Return. The App Store window lists all programs that match your search criteria, as shown in Figure 9-4.

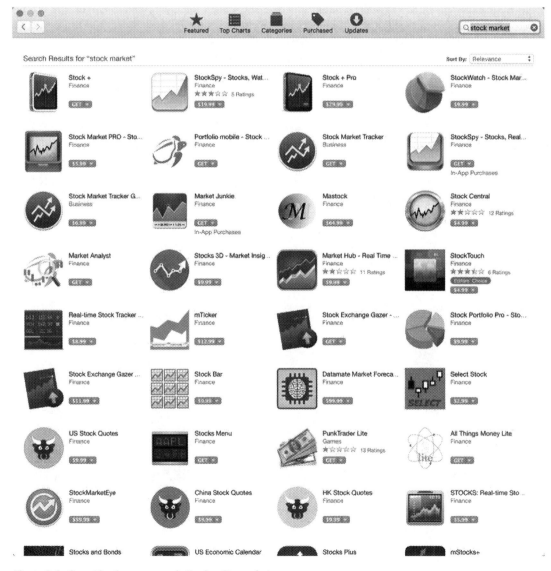

Figure 9-4. Searching for a program in the App Store window

Viewing Software on the Mac App Store

Whether you search for a program or you find a program through the Featured, Top Charts, or Category groups, you can view more details about a particular program by clicking its icon. When you select a program, the App Store window displays more information about that program, such as price, description, and screenshots, as shown in Figure 9-5.

Figure 9-5. *Viewing an individual program in the App Store*

If you scroll down, you see reviews of the program, which can help you decide whether to buy it (see Figure 9-6).

Figure 9-6. Viewing program reviews

Installing Software from the Mac App Store

Once you find a program that you like, you can install it by clicking the price button or the Get button, as shown in Figure 9-7.

Figure 9-7. Paid programs display a price button but free programs display the Get button

If you click a price button, you need to enter your Apple ID password to verify that you want to purchase the program. If you click the Get button to download a free program, the Get button turns into an Install button, which you need to click to install the software on your Mac.

If you have already purchased (whether the program cost money or was free) and downloaded a program from the Mac App Store, you simply see an Open button to show that you have already installed the program on your Mac. Clicking the Open button starts the program on your computer.

Installing Software from the Internet

Not all programs available for the Mac appear in the Mac App Store. Some developers prefer to distribute their software themselves, so you can find plenty of programs available for downloading.

Some of these programs are free but many cost money. The typical way to distribute software over the Internet is to bundle it in a special file called a .dmg, which stands for Disk iMaGe file.

A .dmg file essentially contains all the files of an entire program, so the first step is to download the program's .dmg file to your Mac, which usually stores downloaded files in the Downloads folder, as shown in Figure 9-8.

Figure 9-8. A .dmg file contains all the files of a program condensed in a single file

Once you've saved a .dmg file on your Mac, the next step is to open that .dmg file by double-clicking it. When you open a .dmg file, the following two things happen (also see Figure 9-9):

- The .dmg file creates a virtual disk that appears in the sidebar of the Finder window

- A Finder window opens and displays the program icon and the Applications folder

Figure 9-9. *Opening a .dmg file*

To install the program on your Mac at this point, follow these steps:

1. Move the pointer over the program icon. Hold down the left mouse button (or press a finger on the trackpad) and drag the program icon over the Applications folder.

2. Release the left mouse button or trackpad when the program icon appears directly over the Applications folder. The program is now installed in the Applications folder.

3. Click the eject icon (it looks like a triangle above a horizontal line) that appears to the right of the virtual disk icon in the sidebar of the Finder window. This removes the Finder window of the .dmg file that you just opened.

Note To complete the installation process, you may need to type a serial code when you first start the program. Once done, you won't have to type it again. However, keep the serial code in a safe place in case you need to install the software again at a later date.

Installing Software Blocked from Running

One huge danger of downloading and installing software from the Internet is that you may not know whether the program is legitimate or not. Many malicious hackers create malware (malicious software) designed to delete files or steal important information such as passwords or credit card numbers.

To protect you from downloading and running malware by mistake, your Mac may prevent you from opening a program that you just installed from a .dmg file. This warning message identifies the program that you're trying to run (including the time and web site that you downloaded it from), as shown in Figure 9-10.

"Cura" can't be opened because it is from an unidentified developer.

Your security preferences allow installation of only apps from the Mac App Store and identified developers.

Safari downloaded this file today at 9:31 AM from software.ultimaker.com.

OK

Figure 9-10. OS X may block you from running a program for the first time

To modify your computer's security settings and allow a program to run for the first time, click the OK button to make the warning message go away, and then follow these steps:

1. Click the Apple icon on the menu bar in the upper-left corner of the screen.

2. Choose System Preferences. The System Preferences window appears.

3. Click the Security & Privacy icon. The Security & Privacy window appears.

4. Click the General tab. The bottom of the window explains which program your Mac may have stopped from installing, as shown in Figure 9-11.

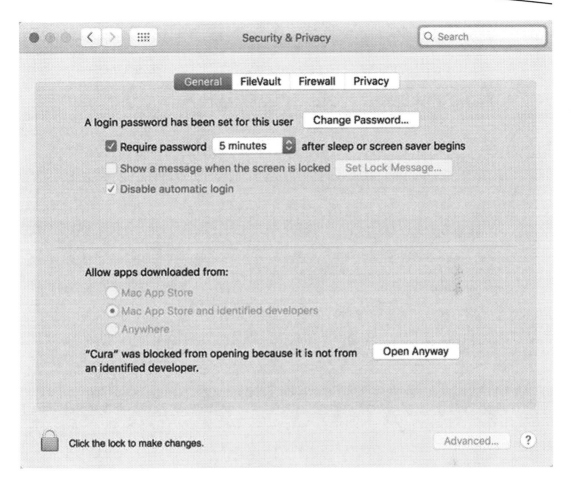

Figure 9-11. *The Security & Privacy window shows you which .dmg file it blocked from installing*

5. Click the Open Anyway button. Another message asks if you're sure that you want to open the .dmg file (see Figure 9-12).

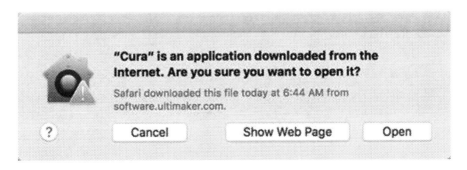

Figure 9-12. *A message asks if you want to open a .dmg file*

6. Click the Open button. A window asks for your password to verify that you want to open and run the blocked program.

7. Type the password that lets you access your Mac and then click the OK button. You can now run your newly installed program. You won't have to go through these steps again for this particular program.

Modifying Security Preferences for Downloaded Software

If you want to modify the security features of OS X for downloaded software, you can change its settings to one of three options:

▓   Mac App Store: Allows installation of software downloaded from the Mac App Store only

▓   Mac App Store and identified developers: Allows installation of software from the Mac App Store and major software publishers, such as Microsoft and Adobe

▓   Anywhere: Turns off security features that block potential malware

Restricting software so that it is only downloadable from the Mac App Store provides the most security, but not all programs are available through the Mac App Store. As a result, this option can keep you from installing legitimate programs downloaded from web sites.

Allowing software to be installed from anywhere is the most dangerous option since it eliminates all possible security features. In general, it's not a good idea to choose this option because it could allow malware to install itself on your Mac without your acknowledgement.

The default option of Mac App Store and identified developers is the safest choice. Unless you otherwise have a good reason, it's best to use this option.

To modify security preferences, follow these steps:

1. Click the Apple icon on the menu bar in the upper-left corner of the screen.

2. Choose System Preferences. A System Preferences window appears.

3. Click the Security & Privacy icon. A Security & Privacy window appears.

4. Click the General tab. The bottom of the window displays a lock icon in the bottom-left corner, as shown in Figure 9-13. Notice that the bottom of the window shows your download security options grayed out.

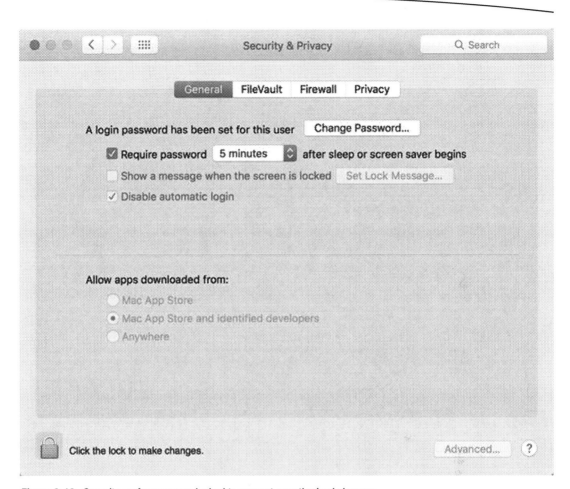

Figure 9-13. Security preferences are locked to prevent unauthorized changes

5. Click the lock icon in the bottom-left corner of the Security & Privacy window. A window appears, asking for your password, as shown in Figure 9-14.

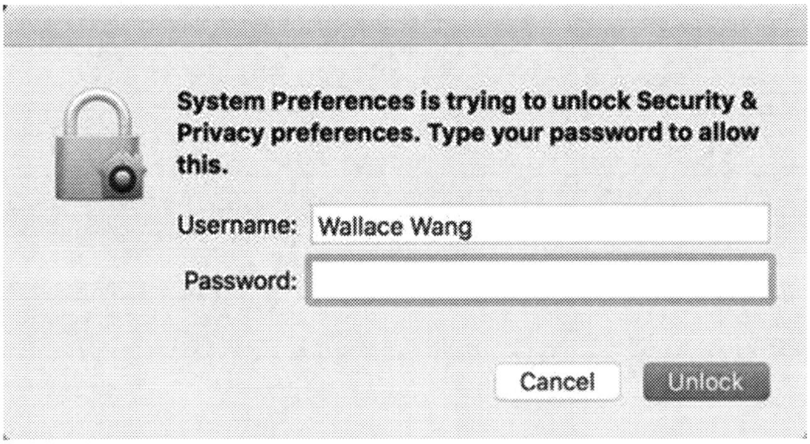

System Preferences is trying to unlock Security & Privacy preferences. Type your password to allow this.

Username: Wallace Wang

Password:

Cancel   Unlock

Figure 9-14. To change security preferences, you must type your password

6. Type your password in the Password field and click the Unlock button. The Security & Privacy window now lets you choose the download security options, as shown in Figure 9-15.

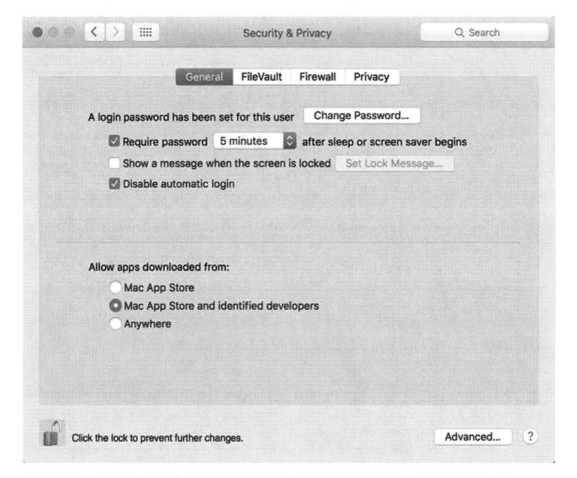

Figure 9-15. *After unlocking, the Security & Privacy window now lets you choose a different security setting*

7. Click a radio button, such as Mac App Store or Anywhere.

8. Click the lock icon to lock your choice.

9. Click the red button in the upper-left corner (the close button) to make the Security & Privacy window disappear.

Installing Programs from a DVD

If you buy software in a store, it will likely be on a DVD. To install software on a DVD, you must have a DVD drive. Older Mac models come with a built-in DVD drive but newer models do not.

To install software on a Mac without a DVD drive, you have to either plug an external DVD drive into your Mac or download the program file (.dmg) from the software publisher's web site.

When you install software from a DVD (or sometimes even from the Internet), the program may appear as a .pkg (package) file. When you double-click a .pkg file to open it, it typically runs its own installation program.

To install software from a DVD, follow these steps:

1. Insert the software DVD into the DVD drive of your Mac. A window appears, displaying an installation program icon, as shown in Figure 9-16.

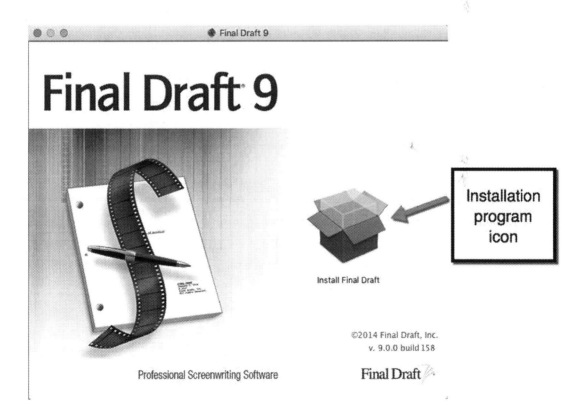

Figure 9-16. Software on a DVD typically contains its own installation programs

2. Double-click the installation program icon and follow the steps to install the program, such as defining the location to store the program.

Note   After you install software from a DVD, store the DVD and any serial codes in a safe place in case you need to reinstall the software later.

Uninstalling Programs

Once you have installed a program, you may want to remove it from your Mac one day. To remove or uninstall a program, follow these steps:

1. Click the Finder icon on the Dock. A Finder window appears.

2. Click the Go menu and choose Applications (Go ➤ Applications). Look for the program that you want to uninstall.

3. Choose one of the following:

    a. Move the pointer over the program icon that you want to uninstall. Hold down the left mouse button (or press one finger on the trackpad). Drag the icon over the Trash icon on the Dock. Release the mouse or trackpad.

    b. Click the program icon that you want to uninstall. Click the File menu and choose Move to Trash (File ➤ Move to Trash).

    c. Right-click the program icon that you want to uninstall, and when a pop-up menu appears, choose Move to Trash.

To permanently delete a program from your Mac, right-click the Trash icon on the Dock. When a pop-up menu appears, choose Empty Trash.

If you change your mind about uninstalling a program after you've moved it to the Trash, follow these steps:

1. Right-click the Trash icon on the Dock. A pop-up menu appears.

2. Choose Open. A Finder window appears, listing the contents of the Trash.

3. Right-click the program icon that you want to keep. A pop-up menu appears.

4. Choose Put Back. The Finder puts the program icon back in the Applications folder (or whichever folder that it was originally stored in).

Summary

Installing software is the most common way to customize your Mac so that it can perform the tasks you need. You can buy software through the Mac App Store, from a retail store, or directly from a software publisher's web site.

The safest way to get software is either from the Mac App Store or from the software publisher's official DVD installation disc.

When downloading and installing software from the Internet, make sure that you trust the source to avoid infecting your computer with malware by mistake. OS X provides three security settings for protecting your Mac:

- Mac App Store
- Mac App Store and identified developers
- Anywhere

If you choose the Anywhere option, OS X will not block any new programs from running. If you choose either the Mac App Store option or the Mac App Store and Identified Developers option, then OS X alerts you when you first try to run a program downloaded from the Internet.

To uninstall a program from a Mac, just drag the program icon out of the Applications folder (or wherever it might be stored) and drop it in the Trash icon on the Dock.

The more you use a Mac, the more likely you'll need to install programs and occasionally uninstall programs that you no longer use. With the right software, you can customize your Mac to perform nearly any task.

Chapter 10

Customizing the Screen

You're going to spend most of your time looking at the screen of your Mac, so why not customize its appearance to make your computer uniquely yours? Customization can be for fun, such as displaying pictures of your family or pets on the screen, or practical, such as creating shortcuts to make your tasks easier and faster.

The following are some of the ways that you customize your screen:

- Change the desktop wallpaper
- Choose screen savers
- Create shortcuts

> **Note** When you customize the way that your Mac looks and behaves, it won't look or behave like any other Mac. If you use multiple Mac computers, you may want to customize all of them identically.

Changing the Desktop Wallpaper

The desktop fills the entire screen, so it is the first image that you see when you turn on your Mac. In the old days, computer screens displayed a solid black or white background. While you could still use a solid color, you also have the option to display pictures, which is called *wallpaper*.

Like real wallpaper, the wallpaper on your desktop simply provides decoration on the screen. You can place any picture you want on the desktop, including photos that you captured on your digital camera or pictures that you downloaded from the Internet.

If you get tired of looking at the same picture all the time, you can even have different pictures appear at random intervals. Wallpaper doesn't do anything useful, but it does make using a Mac a little more fun.

© Wallace Wang 2016
W. Wang, *Mac OS X for Absolute Beginners*, DOI 10.1007/978-1-4842-1913-3_10

When you want to change the desktop wallpaper, you must choose the location of a particular picture. Every Mac lets you choose from three different options to choose a folder that contains a picture:

- Apple: Lets you choose images or solid colors provided by Apple

- Photos: Lets you choose any images stored in the Photos app that you captured with a digital camera

- Folders: Lets you use pictures stored in any folder on your Mac, such as the Pictures folder or any other folder that you have created

To change your desktop wallpaper, follow these steps:

1. Click the Apple icon in the upper-left corner of the menu bar.

2. Click System Preferences to open the System Preferences window.

3. Click the Desktop & Screen Saver icon, as shown in Figure 10-1.

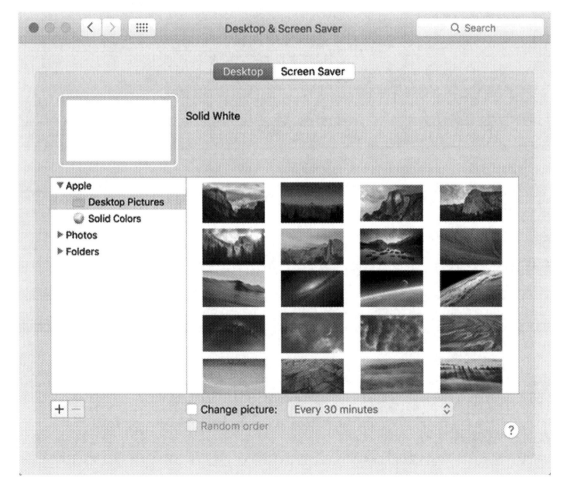

Figure 10-1. The Desktop & Screen Saver window

4. Click the Desktop tab.

5. Click the gray disclosure triangle that appears to the left of Apple. This displays two options: Desktop Pictures and Solid Colors (see Figure 10-1).

6. Click the Desktop Pictures folder to see the variety of wallpaper images provided by Apple.

7. Click any image that you like. The desktop wallpaper changes to your chosen image, as shown in Figure 10-2.

Figure 10-2. Apple provides several images that you can use as your desktop wallpaper

8. Click Solid Colors. The Desktop & Screen Saver window displays different colors that you can choose from to display a solid color on the desktop, as shown in Figure 10-3.

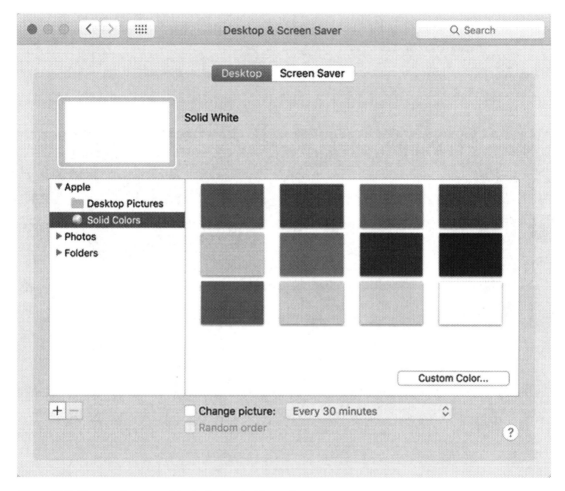

Figure 10-3. You can choose a solid color for the desktop wallpaper

9. Click the disclosure triangle to the left of Photos. A list of different photo categories appears, including Moments, Years, and Albums, as shown in Figure 10-4.

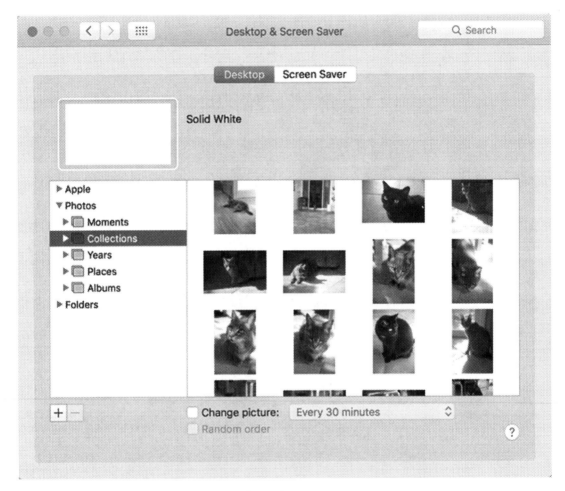

Figure 10-4. You can choose from pictures stored in the Photos app

10. Click the disclosure triangle to the left of a Photos category, such as Places or Collections. A list of photos appears.

11. Click the disclosure triangle to the left of the Folders category.
    A list of folders on your Mac appears, including the Pictures folder.
    Clicking a folder displays all images stored in that folder,
    as shown in Figure 10-5.

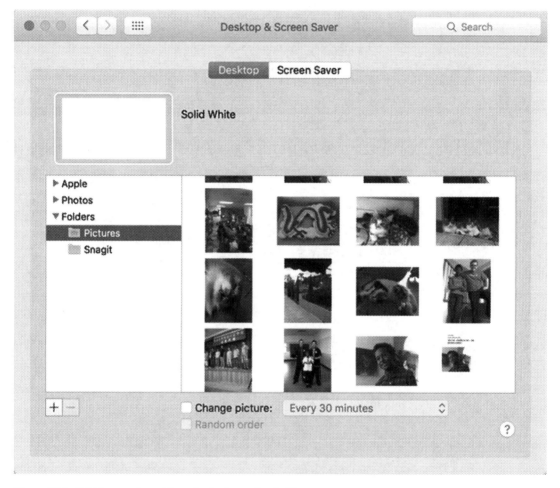

Figure 10-5. *A folder can store pictures to display on the desktop*

12. Click the + button to add a new folder under the Folders category, or
    click an existing folder and click the – button to remove a folder from
    the Folders category.

13. Click the red button (the close button) in the upper-left corner of the
    Desktop & Screen Saver window to make it disappear.

Choosing Pictures Randomly or Sequentially

Normally when you select a desktop wallpaper, your selection is permanent until you select another wallpaper image. However, if you like variety, you can periodically alternate your desktop wallpaper with a different image, such as every 30 minutes.

OS X can pick a new picture in the same folder in two different ways:

- Sequentially choose another picture in the same folder by file name

- Randomly choose another picture in the same folder

If a folder contains ten images, then OS X will only use those ten images. Ideally, you want to choose a folder with plenty of images that you won't mind viewing and displaying to anyone who can look at your Mac screen.

> **Note**   Make sure that you don't choose a folder that contains potentially embarrassing or inappropriate images.

To change desktop wallpaper images, follow these steps:

1. Click the Apple icon in the upper-left corner of the menu bar.

2. Click System Preferences to open the System Preferences window.

3. Click the Desktop & Screen Saver icon (see Figure 10-1).

4. Select the "Change picture" check box. The pop-up menu on the right no longer appears grayed out.

5. Click in the pop-up menu and choose a time interval, as shown in Figure 10-6.

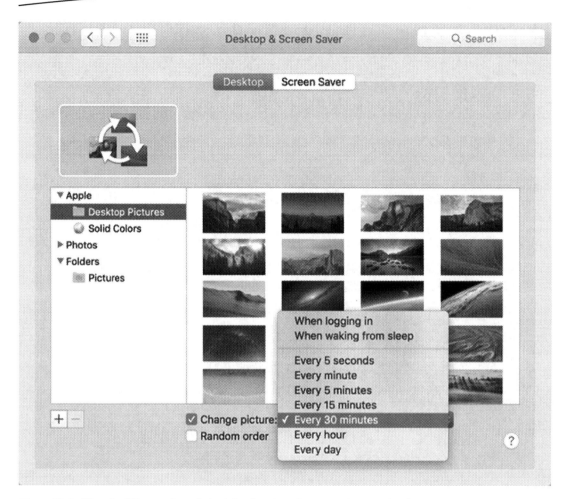

Figure 10-6. When the "Change picture" check box is selected, you can choose a time interval

6. (Optional) Select the "Random order" check box if you want OS X
    to pick a picture at random. If this check box is clear, OS X picks
    pictures sequentially so that you see the pictures in the same order.

7. Click the red button (the close button) in the upper-left corner of the
    Desktop & Screen Saver window to make it disappear.

Defining How to Display a Small Picture

If you choose an Apple wallpaper image or a solid color, it fills the entire screen. However,
other types of pictures, such as those you took with a digital camera, may not be large
enough to fill the entire screen.

OS X provides five different ways to use images that do not fill the entire screen:

* Fill Screen: Expands a picture so that it fills the entire screen, but part of the picture may be cut off to do so

* Fit to Screen: Expands a picture until its width or height fills the screen, which could leave empty space on the sides

* Stretch to Fit Screen: Stretches the height and width of a picture to make it fill the entire screen, but may skewer the appearance of images

* Center: Displays the image in its original size in the center of the screen

* Tile: Displays the image in rows and columns to fill the screen, as shown in Figure 10-7

Figure 10-7. Tiling displays the same image multiple times in rows and columns

To make a small picture the desktop wallpaper, follow these steps:

1. Click the Apple icon in the upper-left corner of the menu bar.

2. Click System Preferences to open the System Preferences window.

3. Click the Desktop & Screen Saver icon (see Figure 10-1).

4. Select a picture in any folder except the Apple Desktop Pictures or Solid Colors folder.

5. Click the pop-up menu and choose an option, as shown in Figure 10-8.

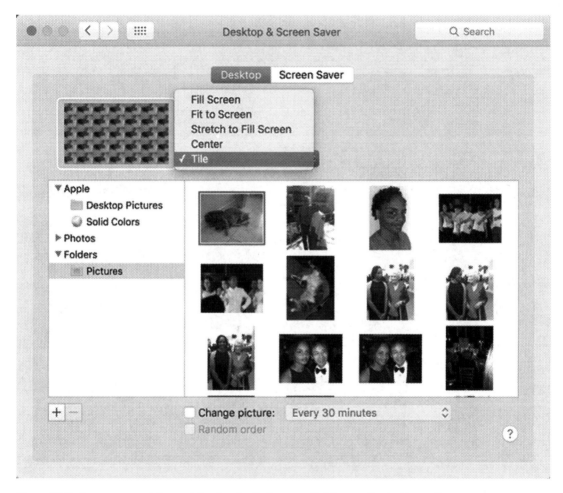

Figure 10-8. A pop-up menu lets you define how to display a small picture as the desktop wallpaper

6. Click an option in the pop-up menu, such as Fit to Screen or Center.

7. Click the red button (the close button) in the upper-left corner of the Desktop & Screen Saver window.

Defining a Screen Saver

Back when computers used cathode-ray tube (CRT) monitors, leaving the same image on the screen for long periods could literally burn that image into the glass screen. If you look at old arcade games or automated-teller machines, you can sometimes see this faint, ghost-like image on the screen, even though the screen may be turned off.

To prevent the screen from burning a static image in the glass, people used special programs called *screen savers*. The idea behind screen savers was that displaying a constantly changing image on the screen reduced the chance of one image appearing on the screen long enough to burn it into the glass.

Nowadays, screen savers are far less important because flat-screen monitors pose far less risk of burning a static image on the screen. Nevertheless, some people still prefer screen savers to make sure burn-in never occurs and to provide a pleasant display if you don't use your Mac for a fixed period, such as five minutes.

Since screen savers are still popular, OS X provides a series of built-in screen savers that you can choose from. When choosing a screen saver, you need to choose a type and a time interval of inactivity to wait before the screen saver starts running.

To choose a screen saver for your Mac, follow these steps:

1. Click the Apple icon on the menu bar in the upper-left corner of the screen.

2. Choose System Preferences. A System Preferences window appears.

3. Click the Desktop & Screen Saver icon. A Desktop & Screen Saver window appears.

4. Click the Screen Saver tab. A list of different screen savers appears on the left of the window, as shown in Figure 10-9.

Figure 10-9. The Screen Saver tab lists different types of screen savers for your Mac

5.   Click a screen saver option, such as Floating or Sliding Panels.

6. Click the "Start after" pop-up menu and choose a time interval to wait before the screen saver starts running, as shown in Figure 10-10. This time interval begins after detecting no activity from the mouse, trackpad, or keyboard.

Figure 10-10. Choosing a time interval from the "Start after" pop-up menu

7. Click the Screen Saver Options button. The options to modify vary by the screen saver type. Figure 10-11 shows one example.

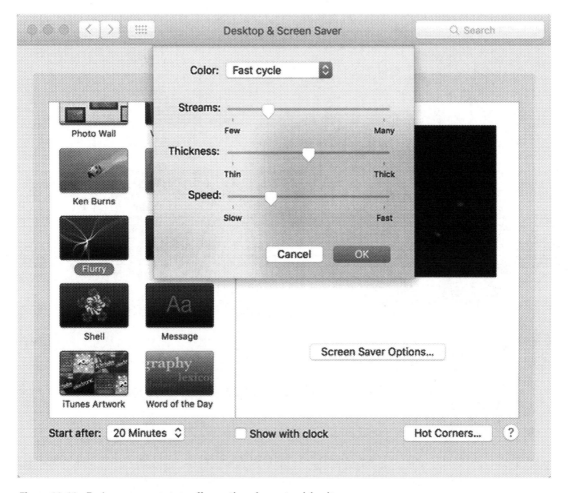

Figure 10-11. *Each screen saver type offers options for customizing its appearance*

8. Modify any options for your particular screen saver and click OK.

9. Click the red button (the close button) in the upper-left corner of the Desktop & Screen Saver window to make it disappear.

Defining Hot Corner Shortcuts

Normally, you have to choose a command from a pull-down menu or type a keystroke shortcut, such as Command+S to save a file or Command+O to open a file on the Mac.

As another way to create shortcuts, you can use *hot corners*. A hot corner is one of four corners on the screen where you can move the pointer. As soon as you shove the pointer in one corner, your hot corner can perform one of the following tasks:

- Start Screen Saver: Starts your screen saver right away, which is handy when you need to step away from your Mac and don't want anyone to see what you're currently working on.

- Disable Screen Saver: Keeps the screen saver from running no matter how long you may be away from your Mac.

- Mission Control: Displays all open windows on the screen at once so that you can pick an open window by clicking it.

- Application Windows: Hides all windows except for the currently active window that you're using right now.

- Desktop: Temporarily hides all open windows and displays the desktop.

- Dashboard: Opens Dashboard, a screen that displays simple utility programs.

- Notification Center: Displays the Notification Center window on the right side of the screen.

- Launchpad: Displays the Launchpad screen.

- Put Display to Sleep: Powers down your monitor to conserve power. Unlike a screen saver, putting your display to sleep simply blacks out your screen.

You can define up to four hot-corner shortcuts, but each hot corner can only represent one shortcut. You can assign the same shortcut to two or more different hot corners if you want, but you cannot assign more than one shortcut to a hot corner.

To define a hot-corner shortcut, follow these steps:

1. Click the Apple icon on the menu bar in the upper-left corner of the screen.

2. Choose System Preferences. A System Preferences window appears.

3. Click the Desktop & Screen Saver icon. A Desktop & Screen Saver window appears.

4. Click the Screen Saver tab. A list of different screen savers appears on the left side of the window (see Figure 10-9).

5. Click the Hot Corners button. An image shows the four corners of the screen.

6. Click the pop-up menu for one of the corners. A menu appears, as shown in Figure 10-12.

Figure 10-12. Defining a hot corner

7. Click a shortcut, such as Application Windows or Launchpad.

8. Click the OK button.

9. Click the red button (the close button) in the upper-left corner of the Desktop & Screen Saver window to make it disappear.

Note   To remove a shortcut from a hot corner, just select the – option for that particular hot corner.

Password Protecting a Mac

When you don't use your Mac for a fixed amount of time, the screen saver starts displaying moving images on the screen. If you put your display to sleep to conserve power, it displays a blank screen.

The moment you touch the mouse, trackpad, or keyboard, your screen saver stops running or your Mac wakes up from sleep and turns the power back on to the monitor. However, this allows anyone to walk up to your Mac, tap the keyboard, mouse, or trackpad, and immediately get access to your computer.

To prevent this, you may want to turn on password protection. That way, if someone turns off your screen saver or wakes up your Mac from sleep by tapping the keyboard, mouse, or trackpad, they won't be able to access your Mac without typing a password first.

If you want to limit access to your Mac, it's a good idea to turn on password protection. To do so, follow these steps:

1. Click the Apple icon on the menu bar in the upper-left corner of the screen.

2. Choose System Preferences. A System Preferences window appears.

3. Click the Security & Privacy icon. A Security & Privacy window appears.

4. Click the General tab.

5. Click the lock icon in the bottom-left corner of the Security & Privacy window. Type your password in the password text field when it appears. The lock icon changes into an unlocked padlock icon and all options under the General tab appear visible so that you can choose them, as shown in Figure 10-13.

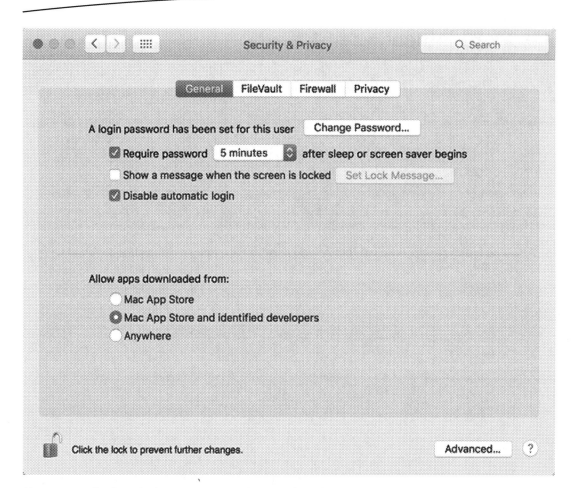

Figure 10-13. The General tab lets you choose various security options for your password

6. Select the "Require password" check box and click the pop-up menu to choose a time interval to wait before requiring a password to access your Mac again.

7. (Optional) Select the "Show a message when the screen is locked" check box and then click the Set Lock Message to show a message on the screen.

8. Make sure that the "Disable automatic login" check box is selected because it keeps someone from turning your Mac off and on again to gain access.

9. (Optional) Click the Advanced button. Another set of security options appears at the top of the Security & Privacy window, as shown in Figure 10-14.

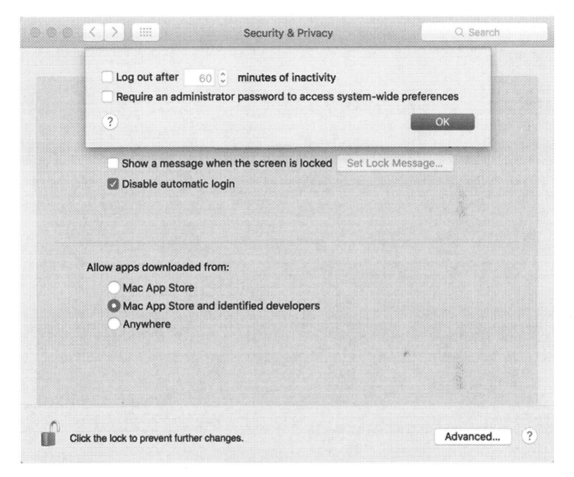

Figure 10-14. The Advanced button displays additional security options

10. Select the "Log out after ___ minutes of inactivity" check box. This completely logs out your account after a fixed time interval and requires a password to get back into your account.

11. Click the OK button.

12. Click the red button (the close button) in the upper-left corner of Security & Privacy window to make it disappear.

Saving Power

If you have a laptop, you'll be especially concerned about saving power since it can prolong your battery. Even if you have a desktop Mac, you may still want to save power to reduce your electricity bill.

With a laptop, there are slightly different power setting options on your laptop for when it is running on batteries or plugged into an electrical outlet, as shown in Figures 10-15 and 10-16.

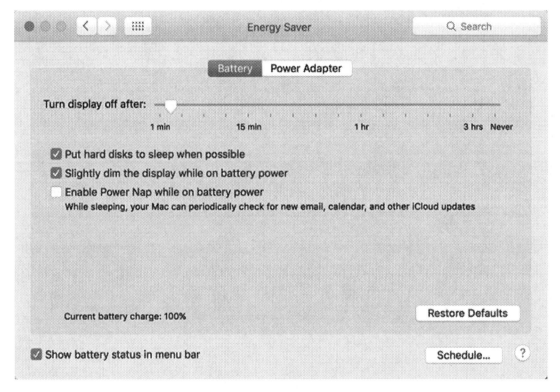

Figure 10-15. The power settings for a laptop running on battery power

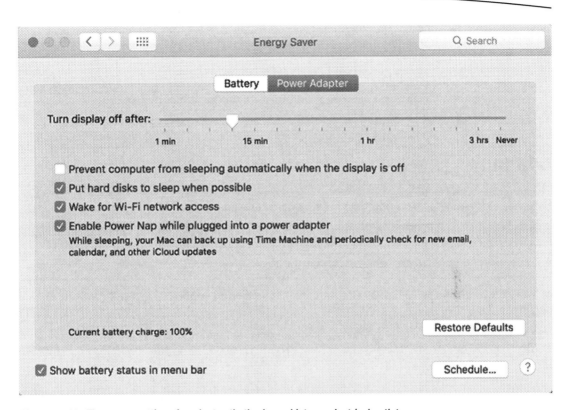

Figure 10-16. The power settings for a laptop that's plugged into an electrical outlet

The following are some of the energy saving options:

- A slider that defines the length of inactive time before turning off the display.

- Prevent computer from sleeping automatically when the display is off: Keeps the computer from conserving power by going to sleep.

- Put hard disks to sleep when possible: Conserves power by reducing electrical use for the hard disk.

- Wake for network access: Wakes a computer if it receives data through the Internet.

- Enable Power Nap: Allows your Mac to conserve power while still performing background tasks, such as backing up your data or checking for new e-mail.

To modify your Mac's energy settings, follow these steps:

1. Click the Apple icon on the menu bar in the upper-left corner of the screen.

2. Choose System Preferences. A System Preferences window appears.

3. Click the Energy Saver icon. An Energy Saver window appears.

4. Select any of the energy saving options. (Click the Restore Defaults button to use the original energy saving settings defined by Apple.)

5. Click the red button (the close button) in the upper-left corner of the Energy Saver window to make it disappear.

Summary

The appearance of your screen doesn't have to be boring. You can customize its look and behavior to make your Mac uniquely your own. The simplest way to change the look of your Mac is to select a desktop wallpaper, which could be an image provided by Apple, a picture from the Internet, or a photo that you captured with your digital camera.

Another way to customize your screen is to choose a screen saver. A screen saver can automatically run after a period of inactivity when you don't touch the keyboard, mouse, or trackpad. When the Mac detects inactivity for a fixed amount of time, it can run a screen saver.

To make using your Mac easier, you can define shortcuts for all four corners of the screen. These hot corners can activate a shortcut the moment that you put the pointer in a corner using the mouse or trackpad.

To restrict access to your Mac, you can password protect it. Not only can a password keep someone from accessing your Mac when they first turn it on, but it can also block someone from using your Mac immediately after your computer wakes up from sleep or when someone turns off the screen saver by tapping the keyboard, mouse, or trackpad.

Don't worry about every possible option available for customizing your Mac. Just choose the features that you need and ignore the rest. By customizing your Mac, you can make it secure, easy, and fun to use every day.

Chapter 11

Customizing the Finder Window

No matter what you need to do, the program you'll likely use most often is the Finder. With the Finder, you can find, open, rename, copy, move, and delete files. By customizing the Finder, you can make it easier to use.

The following are some of the ways that you can customize the Finder:

- Change the sidebar on the left side of the Finder window
- Change the toolbar at the top of the Finder window
- Change the behavior of the Finder window

> **Note** When you customize the way that your Macintosh looks and behaves, it won't look or behave like any other Macintosh. If you use multiple Macintosh computers, you may want to customize them identically.

Changing the Sidebar

The sidebar gives you access to your frequently used folders, such as Documents, Pictures, and Movies. In addition, the sidebar displays a list of external drives connected to your Macintosh, such as an external hard disk or a USB flash drive. If you use tags to identify certain files, you can display tags in the sidebar; one tap of a tag in the sidebar helps you find all files with this tag.

© Wallace Wang 2016
W. Wang, *Mac OS X for Absolute Beginners*, DOI 10.1007/978-1-4842-1913-3_11

Perhaps the simplest way to modify the sidebar in the Finder window is to expand or shrink its width. To change the width of the sidebar, follow these steps:

1. Click the Finder icon on the Dock. A Finder window appears.

2. Move the pointer over the right edge of the sidebar pane until the pointer turns into a double-pointing arrow, as shown in Figure 11-1.

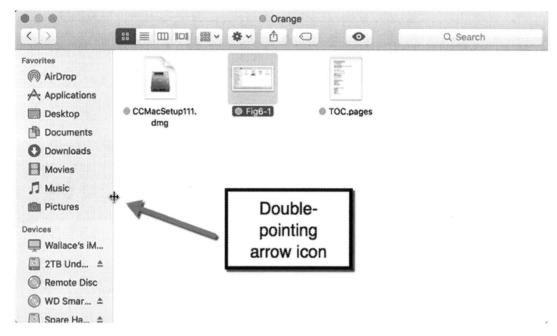

Figure 11-1. Dragging the edge of the sidebar pane can change its width

3. Hold down the left mouse button (or press one finger on the trackpad) and move the mouse (or finger) left and right to change the width of the sidebar pane.

4. Release the mouse (or trackpad) when the sidebar pane is at the width you want.

If you look at the sidebar, you'll see that it already contains different folders under the Favorites category, such as Applications, Downloads, and Pictures.

In general, you'll probably want the Applications folder in the sidebar because that gives you access to all the programs installed on your Macintosh. Likewise, you'll probably want to keep the Documents folder on the sidebar so that you can quickly find any files that you have created.

However, you may not want some of the other folders in the sidebar. For example, if you don't save movies on your computer, you probably won't care to open the Movies folder. Likewise, if you don't use AirDrop, you probably won't want the AirDrop icon cluttering up the sidebar.

Since the sidebar exists to make it easier for you to access a folder, you can choose which folders appear in the sidebar. To modify (add or remove folders) that appear in the sidebar of the Finder window, follow these steps:

1. Click the Finder icon on the far left end of the Dock. A Finder window appears and the Finder menu appears on the menu bar.

2. Click the Finder menu title and choose Preferences (Finder ➤ Preferences). A Finder Preferences window appears.

3. Click the Sidebar icon. A list of different folders appears, as shown in Figure 11-2. Check marks indicate the folders that appear in the Finder sidebar.

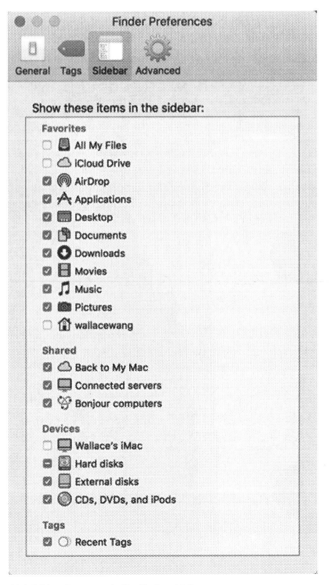

Figure 11-2. Choosing which folders to appear in the Finder sidebar

4. Select the folders that you want to appear in the Finder sidebar by making sure that a check mark appears to its left. Prevent folders from appearing in the Finder sidebar by keeping the check box empty.

5. Click the red close button in the upper-left corner to close the Finder Preferences window.

By taking the time to place the folders that you use most often in the Finder sidebar, you can access your favorite folders quickly and easily.

Adding Custom Folders to the Finder Sidebar

If you customize the Finder sidebar through the Finder Preferences window (see Figure 11-2), you can only choose to display the most common folders, such as Documents, Music, or Movies.

Fortunately, you can add any folder to the Finder sidebar by following these steps:

1. Click the Finder icon on the far left end of the Dock. A Finder window appears and the Finder menu appears on the menu bar.

2. Find the folder that you want to place on the Finder sidebar.

3. Move the pointer over that folder. Hold down the left mouse button (or press one finger on the trackpad) and drag the folder over the sidebar. A horizontal line appears in the sidebar to show you where the folder will appear when you release the mouse button or trackpad, as shown in Figure 11-3.

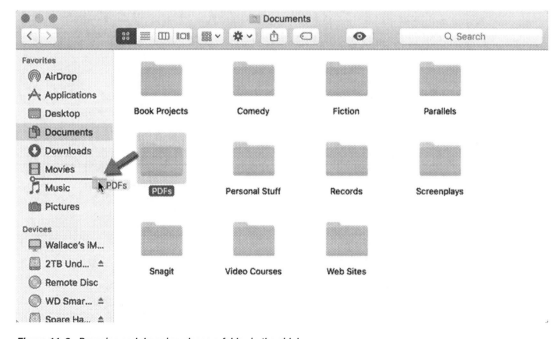

Figure 11-3. Dragging and dropping places a folder in the sidebar

4. Release the mouse or trackpad. Your chosen folder now appears in the Finder sidebar.

> **Note**   When you drag and drop a folder on the sidebar, you do not move the folder from its original location.

If you don't like the drag-and-drop method, follow these steps to choose another way to place a folder on the sidebar:

1. Click the Finder icon on the far left end of the Dock. A Finder window appears. The Finder menu is on the menu bar.

2. Click the folder that you want to place on the sidebar.

3. Click the File menu and choose Add to Sidebar (File ➤ Add to Sidebar) or press Command+Control+T.

> **Note**   Besides adding folders to the sidebar, you can add individual files as well. This lets you find and access important files quickly and easily.

In case you don't like the order that the Finder sidebar displays your folders, you can rearrange them any way that you want. To rearrange folders in the sidebar, follow these steps:

1. Click the Finder icon on the far left end of the Dock. A Finder window appears and the Finder menu appears on the menu bar.

2. Move the pointer over a folder in the sidebar. Hold down the left mouse button (or press one finger on the trackpad) and drag up or down.

3. Release the mouse or trackpad when the folder appears in the position that you like.

If you realize that you don't use a particular folder often enough, you can always remove it from the sidebar. To remove a folder from the sidebar, follow these steps:

1. Click the Finder icon on the far left end of the Dock. A Finder window appears. The Finder menu is on the menu bar.

2. Right-click over the folder in the sidebar that you want to remove. A pop-up menu appears.

3. Choose Remove from Sidebar, as shown in Figure 11-4.

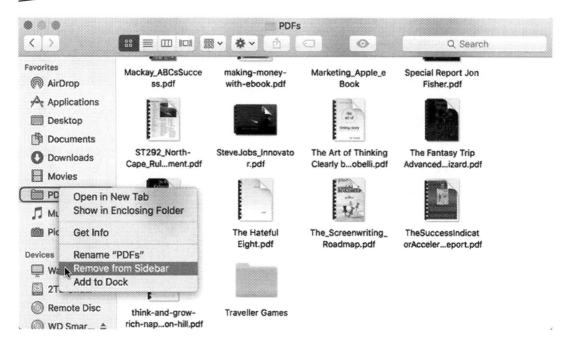

Figure 11-4. Removing a folder from the sidebar

When you remove a folder from the sidebar, you don't physically change that folder's contents or original location.

Customizing the Default Folder to Display

Each time that you start the Finder or choose File ➤ New Folder Window from the Finder menu bar, the Finder window displays the contents of a default folder.

Generally, you might want to open the Documents folder each time you create another Finder window, but if you want to make the Finder window display a different folder, you can choose another folder to open by default.

To define a default folder, follow these steps:

1. Click the Finder icon on the far left end of the Dock. A Finder window appears. The Finder menu is on the menu bar.

2. Click the Finder menu title and choose Preferences (Finder ➤ Preferences). A Finder Preferences window appears.

3. Click the General icon. The "New Finder windows show" pop-up menu displays the current default folder, such as Documents, as shown in Figure 11-5.

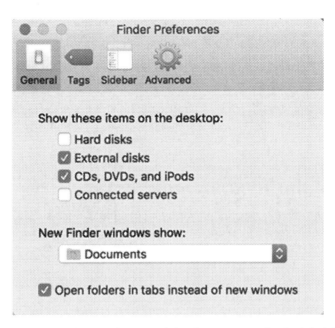

Figure 11-5. The General icon in the Finder Preferences window lets you customize the default folder

4. Click in the "New Finder windows show" pop-up menu to display a menu, as shown in Figure 11-6.

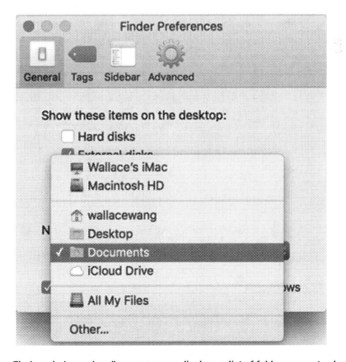

Figure 11-6. The "New Finder windows show" pop-up menu displays a list of folder names to choose

5. Click a folder name, such as Desktop or Documents. Click Other…
    to select any folder on your Macintosh.

6. Click the red close button in the upper-left corner to close the Finder
    Preferences window.

You can only choose one default folder to appear each time that you open a new Finder
window. By defining a default Finder folder, you get quick access to the folder that you need
most often.

Customizing the Toolbar

The top of every Finder window contains various icons that provide a shortcut to common
commands, as shown in Figure 11-7. Some of these icons represent commands for deleting
an item, changing the way a folder's contents look, or sharing an item with others.

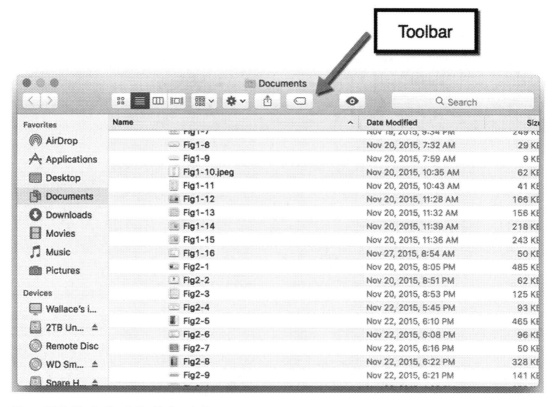

Figure 11-7. The toolbar in the Finder window

The following are some of the ways to customize the toolbar:

- Change the appearance of icons to display text in addition to or instead of icons
- Rearrange the position of icons on the toolbar
- Add or remove icons from the toolbar

Before you customize the Finder toolbar, you need to understand the purpose of the default toolbar icons so that you can better decide whether to keep or remove them (see Figure 11-8).

Figure 11-8. The default toolbar icons

Under the Back category, you see Back and Forward buttons that work much like the back and forward buttons on a browser. To see how these buttons work, follow these steps:

1. Click the Finder icon on the far left end of the Dock. A Finder window displays the contents of its default folder, such as Documents.

2. Click any folder in the sidebar, such as Downloads or Music. The Finder window displays the contents of this new folder but also highlights the Back button.

3. Click the Back button on the Finder toolbar. The Finder window now goes back to the folder displayed in step 1. Notice that the Forward button is now highlighted.

4. Click the Forward button. The Finder window now goes back to the folder that you chose in step 2. By clicking the Back and Forward buttons, you can go back to the last folder that you opened or go forward to the folder that you had open prior to clicking the Back button.

Under the View category, there are four options to display items in the Finder window: as icons, in a list, in columns, or in Cover Flow.

Icons make it easier to find an item but they take up more space (see Figure 11-9).

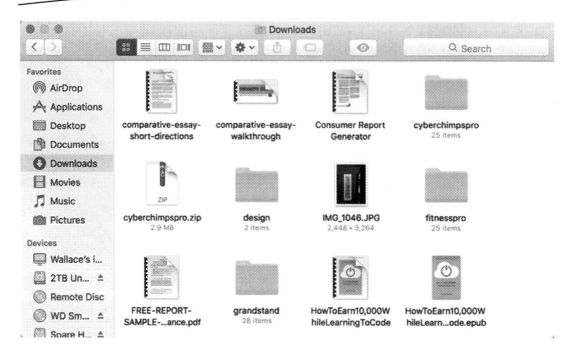

Figure 11-9. Icon view

Lists take up less space and show more information, but they are harder to read (see Figure 11-10).

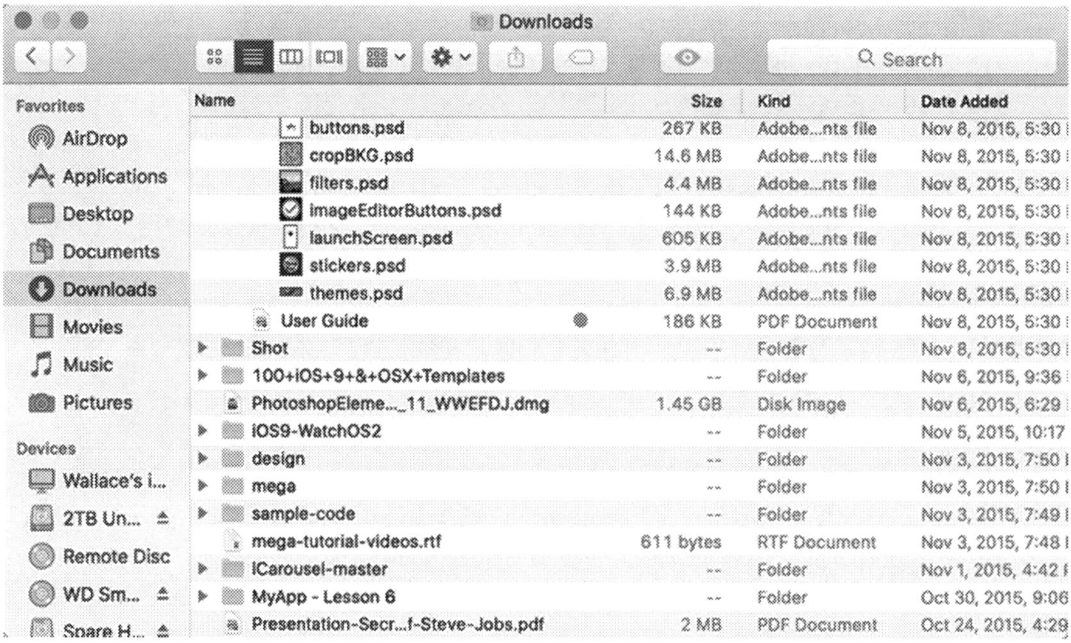

Figure 11-10. List view

Columns show the hierarchy of folders but are as hard to read as lists (see Figure 11-11).

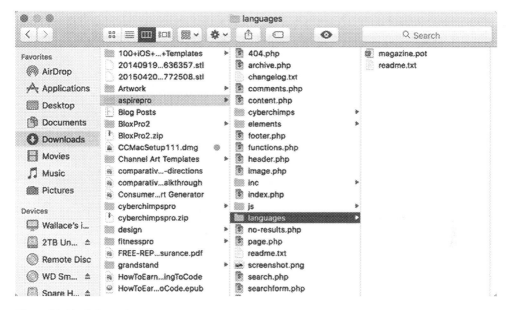

Figure 11-11. Column view

Cover Flow lets you view the contents of files but takes up more space (see Figure 11-12). By clicking an icon in the View category, you can change the way that the Finder window displays its contents.

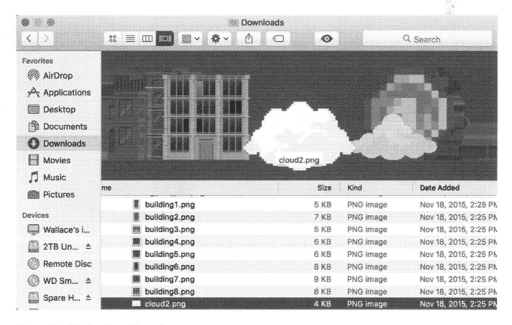

Figure 11-12. The Cover Flow view

The Arrange icon lets you rearrange how the Finder displays items, such as alphabetically by name, chronologically by date created or modified, or by file size. By choosing a different way to arrange items in the Folder window, you can quickly find items, such as the most recent file that you created or modified (see Figure 11-13).

Figure 11-13. Using the Arrange icon to change the way the Finder window displays items

The Action icon (it looks like a gear icon) lets you perform common tasks on a file or folder, such as creating a new folder, showing a preview of the file's contents, or opening the Info window of a file or folder.

When you click the Actions icon, you get a pull-down menu. This pull-down menu displays slightly different commands, depending on whether you selected a file, a folder, or nothing at all.

To see how the Actions icon displays different commands in its pull-down menus, follow these steps:

1. Click the Finder icon on the far left end of the Dock. A Finder window appears and displays the contents of its default folder, such as Documents.

2. Click the Action icon. A pull-down menu appears, as shown in Figure 11-14.

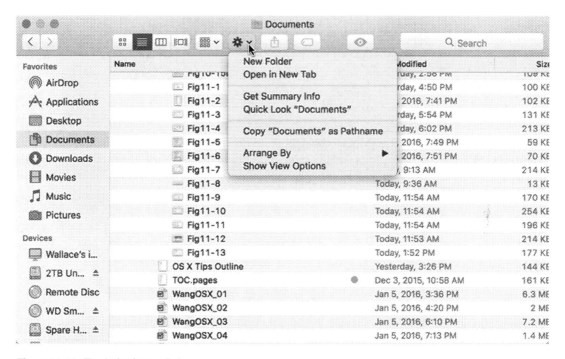

Figure 11-14. *The Action icon pull-down menu*

3. Click any file.

4. Click the Action icon again. Notice that this time, the pull-down menu displays slightly different commands, as shown in Figure 11-15.

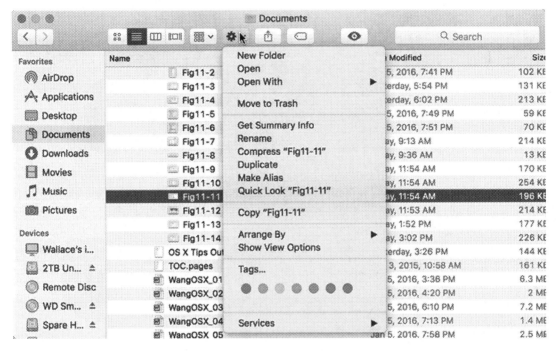

Figure 11-15. The Action icon pull-down menu with a file selected

Basically, the Action icon duplicates most of the commands on the File menu.

The Share icon lets you select one or more files or folders and send them to someone by e-mail. If you select a graphic file, you can also share a file through popular social networks, such as Twitter, Facebook, or Flickr, as shown in Figure 11-16.

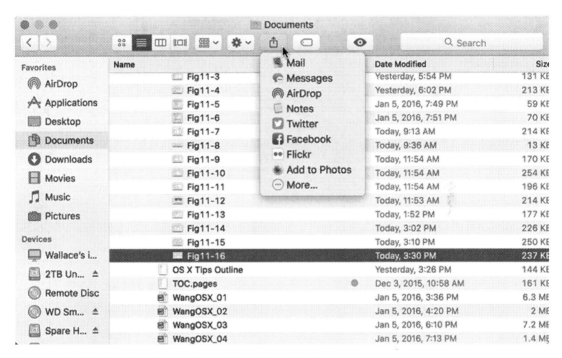

Figure 11-16. *The Share icon lets you share a file or folder with others*

The Tags icon lets you place a tag on a file to help you find it later, as shown in Figure 11-17.

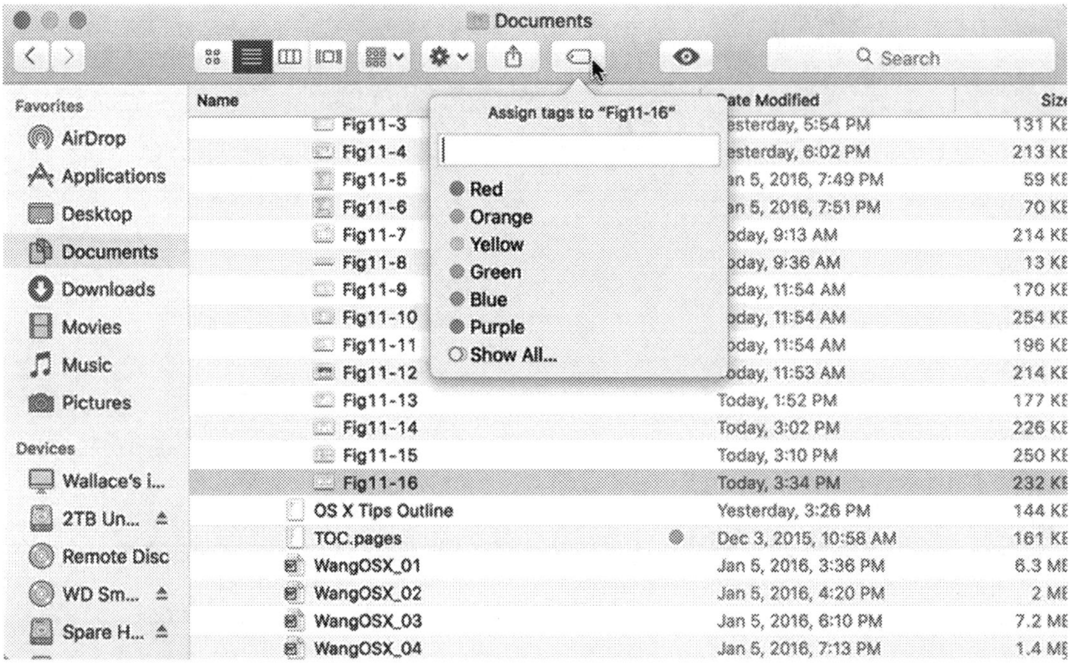

Figure 11-17. *The Tags icon lets you place a tag on a file*

The Quick Look icon lets you preview the contents of a file without opening it in a program. If you click a word processor document, the Quick Look icon lets you browse the contents of that file. If you click a graphic image, you'll see that image in a separate window, as shown in Figure 11-18. If you click a movie or audio file, you'll see that movie or hear that audio file.

Figure 11-18. The Quick Look icon lets you view the contents of a file, such as a picture stored in a graphic file

Changing the Appearance of the Toolbar Icons

The toolbar on the Finder usually displays icons, but you can change its appearance in several ways:

- Icon and Text: Displays the icon and provides a descriptive label
- Icon Only: Displays icons
- Text Only: Displays only descriptive text
- Hide Toolbar: Hides the toolbar

To change the appearance of the Finder's toolbar, follow these steps:

1. Click the Finder icon on the far left end of the Dock. A Finder window appears.

2. Right-click the toolbar (but not on any icons) to make a pop-up menu appear, as shown in Figure 11-19.

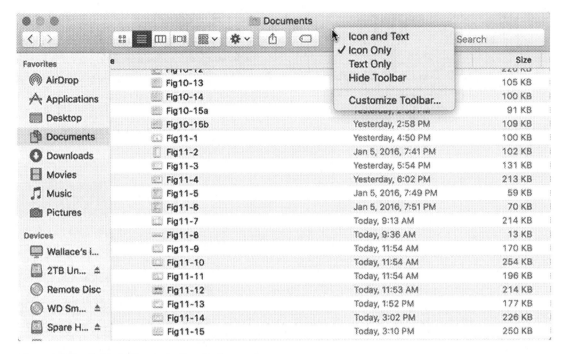

Figure 11-19. Right-clicking the toolbar displays a pop-up menu

3.   Choose an option, such as Icon and Text, Icon Only, or Text Only.
      The Finder toolbar changes appearance based on your choice.

The appearance of the toolbar icons is solely for your own personal preference. Toolbar icons work identically whether they're displayed as text, icons, or a combination of icons and text.

Customizing the Toolbar

Rather than modify the appearance of the toolbar icons, you can add or remove icons on the toolbar. This lets you remove those icons you don't need and replace them with icons you use most often.

To customize the toolbar, follow these steps:

1.   Click the Finder icon on the far left end of the Dock. A Finder window appears.

2.   Click the View menu and choose Customize Toolbar (View ➤ Customize Toolbar). You can also right-click the toolbar (but not on any icons) to bring up a pop-up menu to choose Customize Toolbar. A list of icons shows what you can add to the toolbar (see Figure 11-20).

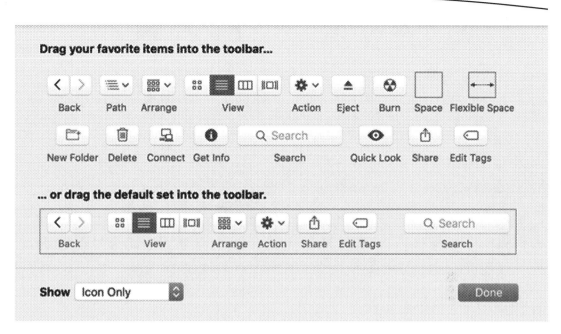

Figure 11-20. You can add a variety of different icons on the toolbar

3.   Move the pointer over an icon. Hold down the left mouse button (or press one finger on the trackpad) and drag the icon over the toolbar, as shown in Figure 11-21.

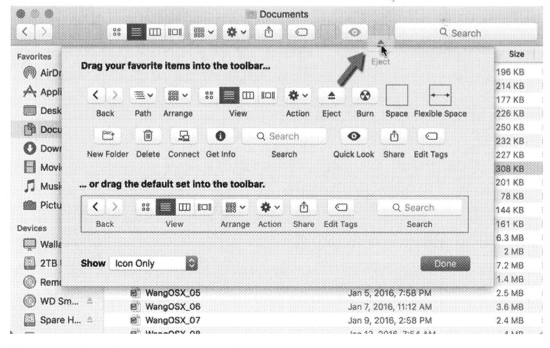

Figure 11-21. Drag and drop an icon onto the toolbar

4. Release the mouse (or trackpad) when the icon appears where you want it on the toolbar.

5. Click the Done button.

To remove an icon from the toolbar, repeat these steps—except rather than dragging and dropping an icon onto the toolbar, drag and drop the icon anywhere off the toolbar.

Using Tabs

The simplest way to copy a file from one folder to another is to open two Finder windows and then drag a file from one Finder window into the second Finder window. If you'd rather not clutter your screen with multiple Finder windows, you can use tabs instead.

Tabs let you view the contents of two or more folders within a single Finder window. You can view the contents of different folders just by clicking a different tab.

Creating a Finder Tab

The following describes the two ways to create a tab in the Finder window (also see Figure 11-22):

* Click the File menu and choose New Tab (File ➤ New Tab)

* Press Command+T

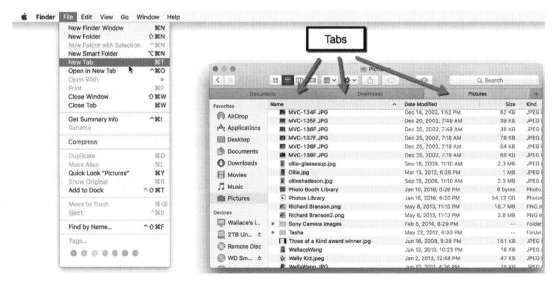

Figure 11-22. Creating tabs in the Finder window

You can create as many tabs as you want but the more tabs that you create, the more crowded the Finder window will look.

Once you've created a tab, you can click that tab and select a folder. The name of the currently displayed folder appears in the tab, such as Downloads or Documents.

To copy a file from one folder to another, you can drag a file directly over a tab. So if you have a tab that displays the Documents folder, you could drag a file and drop it directly on the Documents tab.

If you don't like the order of your tabs, you can rearrange their position by dragging a tab left or right with the mouse or trackpad.

Merging (and Separating) Finder Tabs

If you have multiple Finder windows open, you can merge all open Finder windows into tabs within a single Finder window. To do this, click the Window menu and choose Merge All Windows (Window ➤ Merge All Windows).

If you have two or more tabs already displayed within a Finder window, you can separate tabs so that they appear in their own Finder window. To do this, click the Window menu and choose Move Tab to New Window (Window ➤ Move Tab to New Window).

It's possible to have multiple Finder windows open and tabs within one or more Finder windows.

Closing Finder Tabs

Once you've opened tabs within a Finder window, you can always close them. To close a tab, follow these steps:

1. Click the Finder icon on the far left end of the Dock. A Finder window appears.

2. Move the pointer over the tab in the Finder window that you want to close. A close icon (an X) appears on the left side of the tab, as shown in Figure 11-23.

Figure 11-23. The close icon appears on a tab when the pointer appears over that tab

3. Click the close icon of the tab that you want to remove. The tab disappears.

Summary

You'll likely use the Finder every time that you use a Macintosh, so take some time to understand how you can customize its features. Place your favorite folders in the sidebar for easy access. Modify the toolbar so that your most frequently used commands are available at all times.

The Finder toolbar contains a set of default icons, but you'll probably want to remove icons that you don't use and replace them with the icons you use most often. The less cluttered the toolbar, the less complicated the Finder window will look.

Remember, you can always modify the Finder toolbar at any time by adding new icons or removing old ones. You might also experiment with modifying the way the toolbar looks so that you can make the toolbar easier to read.

To avoid cluttering your screen with multiple Finder windows, you can create tabs. You can merge multiple Finder windows in tabs or separate tabs into their own Finder window. Tabs help keep your screen organized.

The Finder is one of the most crucial programs that you'll use to manage files on your Macintosh. A little time spent modifying the Finder today will make your Macintosh much easier to use from now on.

Chapter 12

Organizing Windows

No matter how big your screen may be (even if you have multiple screens), there never seems to be enough room to show everything. You can minimize windows or temporarily hide them, but a more elegant solution might be to use multiple desktops.

When you first start your Mac, you'll see the desktop displaying its wallpaper background image. Any program windows you open all appear on this desktop. If you open too many windows, your desktop becomes cluttered.

To solve this problem, you have several options:

- Minimize one or more windows to tuck them out of sight on the Dock
- Hide windows
- Use Mission Control to view all open windows
- Use Mission Control to create multiple desktops

Minimizing a Window

Any window can be temporarily tucked out of sight by minimizing it so that it appears as a thumbnail image on the Dock next to the Trash icon. When you want to use a minimized window again, just click its thumbnail image on the Dock.

To minimize a window, you have the following three options (also see Figure 12-1):

- Click the yellow (middle) minimize button that appears in the upper-left corner of every window
- Press Command+M
- Click the Window menu and choose Minimize (Window ➤ Minimize)

© Wallace Wang 2016
W. Wang, *Mac OS X for Absolute Beginners*, DOI 10.1007/978-1-4842-1913-3_12

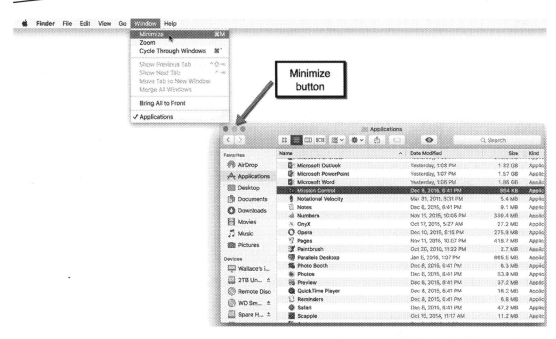

Figure 12-1. The minimize button on a window

When you minimize a window, it appears as a thumbnail image on the Dock next to the Trash icon, as shown in Figure 12-2. To help you identify the program that the window belongs to, the program icon appears in the bottom-right corner of the thumbnail image.

Figure 12-2. Minimized window appears on the Dock

To open a minimized window, click its thumbnail image on the Dock.

Although minimizing windows helps you keep your desktop organized, it can be troublesome to minimize windows individually. The more minimized windows that you create, the more crowded those minimized windows appear on the Dock. For that reason, OS X offers another way that hides windows completely from view.

Hiding Windows

Because minimizing multiple windows can clutter the Dock, OS X can hide them completely. To hide windows, you have two choices:

■ Hide all windows belonging to one program

■ Hide all windows except those belonging to one program

Hiding all windows except those belonging to one program can be useful when you only want to work in one program but don't want to close or minimize windows belonging to other programs.

> **Note**   Unlike minimizing windows, hiding windows gives you no clue as to the number of hidden windows.

To hide windows, follow these steps:

1. Click the Application menu on the menu bar. The Application menu is whatever program you're currently using, such as Pages, Safari, or Excel.

2. Do one of the following, as shown in Figure 12-3:

   a. Hide (Application name), such as Hide Finder or Hide Pages: Hides only the windows belonging to the currently active program

   b. Hide Others: Hides all windows except those of the currently active window

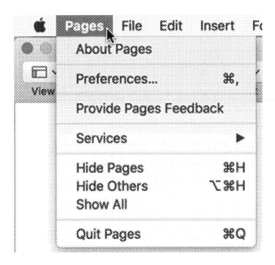

Figure 12-3. A typical Application menu

You can hide windows from any Application menu. When you want to display any hidden windows on the screen again, click any Application menu and choose Show All.

Using Mission Control

If you have multiple open windows all over your screen, they may overlap and hide other open windows. When an open window is hidden behind another open window, one quick way to see all open windows on the screen at once is to use Mission Control.

Mission Control displays all open windows (but not hidden or minimized windows) as thumbnail images on the screen. This lets you see all your open windows so that you can click the one you want, as shown in Figure 12-4.

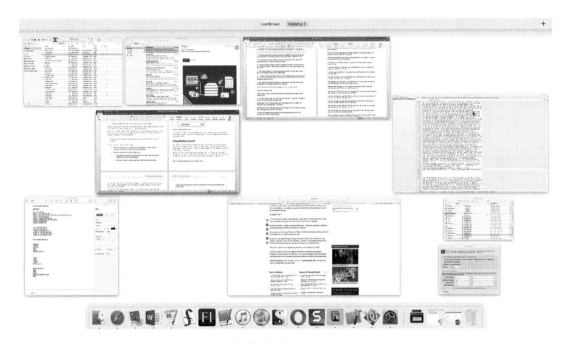

Figure 12-4. Displaying multiple open windows in Mission Control

The moment you click a thumbnail image of a window in Mission Control, your chosen window appears on the screen in normal size so that you can start working in that window.

To see how Mission Control works, follow these steps:

1. Open two or more windows on your Mac, preferably using different programs, such as the Finder, Safari, and Keynote.

2. Click the Finder icon on the Dock. A Finder window appears.

3. Click Applications in the sidebar of the Finder window.

4. Double-click the Mission Control icon. Mission Control displays all of your open windows as thumbnail images on the screen.

5. Click any thumbnail image of an open window. That window becomes the currently active window on the screen and appears in normal size.

Note   If you don't want to click any open window in Mission Control, you can exit out of Mission Control by pressing the Esc key on the keyboard or by clicking in a blank space between any thumbnail images of windows.

Opening the Applications folder and double-clicking the Mission Control icon can be cumbersome, so one option is to drag the Mission Control icon onto the Dock. Now you can open Mission Control with one click.

A second shortcut to opening Mission Control is to use a keystroke shortcut. The default keystroke shortcut is Control+Up arrow (try it on your Mac now), but you can define any keystroke shortcut you wish.

A third shortcut to opening Mission Control with a trackpad is to swipe three fingers up on the trackpad. To exit out of Mission Control, you can swipe three fingers down on the trackpad.

To define a keystroke shortcut for opening Mission Control, follow these steps:

1. Click the Apple icon on the menu bar to display a pull-down menu.

2. Click System Preferences. A System Preferences window appears.

3. Click the Mission Control icon. The Mission Control window appears, as shown in Figure 12-5.

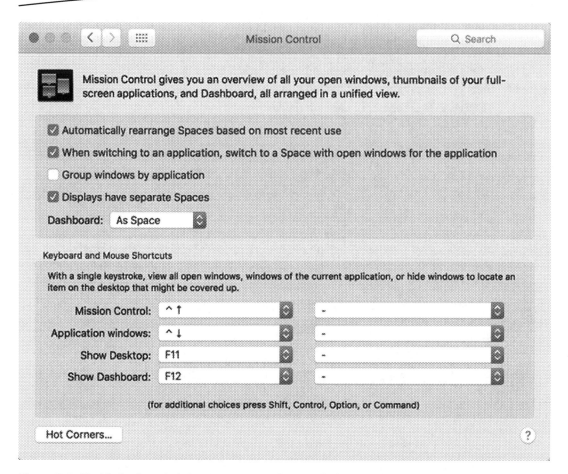

Figure 12-5. The Mission Control window lets you customize how Mission Control works

4.   Click the Mission Control pop-up menu and choose a different keystroke shortcut to run Mission Control.

5.   Click the red button (the close button) in the upper-left corner of the Mission Control window to make it disappear.

If you look at the Mission Control window, you can see three additional options for defining keystroke shortcuts:

- Application windows (Control+Down arrow)
- Show Desktop (F11)
- Show Dashboard (F12)

Note   If you're using a laptop, you'll need to press the Fn key at the same time you press a function key, such as F11 or F12. That's because laptops assign hardware controls to the function keys, such as adjusting screen brightness or audio volume.

The Application windows shortcut (Control+Down arrow) displays the thumbnail images of all the windows in the currently active program. You can see which program is currently active by looking at the Application menu next to the Apple icon on the menu bar.

So if Microsoft Word is the currently active program, you see Word next to the Apple icon on the menu bar. Then if you press Control+Down arrow, you'll only see thumbnail images of all currently open (not minimized or hidden) Word documents, as shown in Figure 12-6.

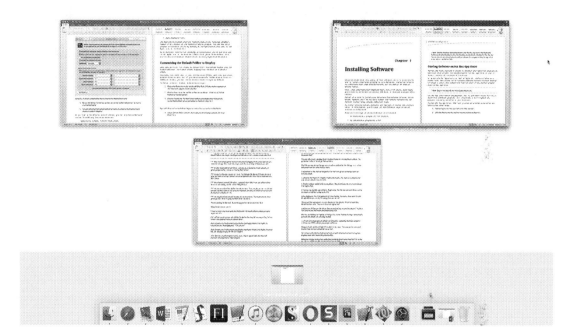

Figure 12-6. The Application windows keystroke shortcut lets you view only open windows in the currently active program

The Show Desktop shortcut (F11) temporarily hides all open windows so that you can see the desktop. To display all open windows once more, press the Show Desktop shortcut keystroke again (such as F11).

The Show Dashboard shortcut (F12) displays simple utility programs that appear on the screen, such as the clock and the calendar, as shown in Figure 12-7.

Figure 12-7. The Dashboard displays simple utility programs

Using Multiple Desktops

Perhaps the most useful feature of Mission Control is the ability to display multiple desktops. Normally, you only use one desktop. Any windows that you open appear on the one desktop, so the more programs you use, the more open windows clutter it.

The idea behind multiple desktops is to help you organize related programs. For example, you might open your word processor documents in one desktop, your browser and e-mail program in a second desktop, and a game in a third desktop.

Now, instead of having all open windows cluttering a single desktop, you can organize programs in different desktops and switch between desktops.

> **Note** OS X initially has two desktops. One desktop is what you see on your Mac. The second desktop is used to display the utility programs of Dashboard (see Figure 12-7).

Creating Additional Desktops

Each time you turn on your Mac for the first time, it displays a single desktop. To create additional desktops, follow these steps:

1.   Open Mission Control using any method you like (such as pressing Control+Up arrow). Mission Control displays all open windows as thumbnail images. A + icon appears in the upper-right corner of the screen, as shown in Figure 12-8.

Figure 12-8. *The plus (+) icon lets you add a new desktop to Mission Control*

2. Click the + icon. Mission Control adds a new desktop thumbnail and gives it a number, such as Desktop 2, as shown in Figure 12-9.

Figure 12-9. *Clicking the + icon creates a new desktop*

3. Click the newly created desktop thumbnail image, such as Desktop 2. Your desktop appears with no open windows.

4. Open Mission Control again and then click your first desktop, such as Desktop 1. Notice that if you have any open windows on Desktop 1, they appear again.

Rather than constantly manage multiple open windows on a single desktop, Mission Control lets you create multiple desktops. Now you can isolate related windows in separate desktops and each desktop won't appear cluttered with so many open windows.

Switching Between Desktops

Once you've created two or more desktops, you can switch between them. The following are three different ways to switch between desktops:

■ Open Mission Control and click the desktop thumbnail image that you want to use

■ With a trackpad, swipe three fingers left or right to view each additional desktop

■ Press Control+Left arrow or Control+Right arrow to view each additional desktop

Moving Windows Between Desktops

On each desktop, you can open programs and arrange windows any way that you like. One limitation is that if you open a program in one desktop, you cannot open that program in another desktop. This helps keep windows from the same program isolated in the same desktop.

If you open a program in one desktop and later want to move it to a different desktop, you can.

If you have an open program window on one desktop and you would like to move it to another desktop, follow these steps:

1. Open Mission Control using any method you like (such as pressing Control+Up arrow). Mission Control displays all open windows as thumbnail images.

2. Move the pointer over the window that you want to move to another desktop.

3. Hold down the left mouse button (or press one finger on the trackpad) and move the pointer over the desktop where you want it to appear, as shown in Figure 12-10.

Figure 12-10. Dragging a window to another desktop

4. Release the mouse (or trackpad).

5. Click a desktop image at the top of the screen to open that desktop.

By dragging and dropping windows from one desktop to another, you can have different windows from the same program in separate desktops. For example, you might to open two documents in Microsoft Word and place one document window in one desktop and a second document window in another desktop.

Rearranging Desktops

The order that you create desktops is the order that they'll appear. If you need to switch back and forth between two desktops, you might want to place them next to each other so that you don't have to view other desktops when pressing Control+Left arrow or Control+Right arrow.

To rearrange desktops, follow these steps:

1. Open Mission Control using any method that you like (such as pressing Control+Up arrow). Mission Control displays all open windows as thumbnail images.

2. Move the pointer over a desktop thumbnail image at the top of the screen.

3. Hold down the left mouse button (or press one finger on the trackpad). Move the pointer left or right to rearrange the position of all your desktops.

4. Release the mouse (or trackpad) when the desktop is in the order that you want it.

Deleting a Desktop

Once you've created two or more desktops, you may eventually want to delete one. If you delete a desktop that has open windows in it, they'll automatically appear in another desktop, but you may want to move all windows to a specific desktop yourself.

To delete a desktop, follow these steps:

1. Open Mission Control using any method that you like (such as pressing Control+Up arrow). Mission Control displays all open windows as thumbnail images.

2. Hold down the Option key and move the pointer to the top of the screen. Thumbnail images of all your desktops appear. Move the pointer over the desktop thumbnail that you want to delete. A close button (an X in a circle) appears in the upper-left corner of each desktop thumbnail, as shown in Figure 12-11.

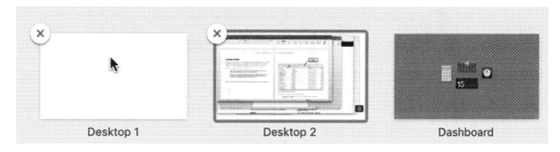

Desktop 1   Desktop 2   Dashboard

Figure 12-11. When holding the Option key down, a close button appears in the upper-left corner of each desktop image

3. Click the close button of the desktop that you want to delete. Your chosen desktop disappears and any open windows on that desktop move to another desktop.

Using Split View

Some (but not all) OS X programs support a feature called *split view*. The idea behind split view is to allow you to place two windows side by side, as shown in Figure 12-12.

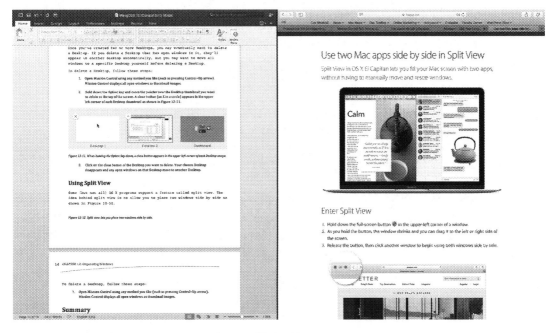

Figure 12-12. Split view lets you place two windows side by side

To identify which program's windows support split view, hover the pointer over the green button in the upper-left corner of the window. If a window does not support split view, you'll see a zoom button (+). If a window does support split view, you'll see a full-screen button (two triangle icons pointing in opposite directions), as shown in Figure 12-13.

**Zoom button
(Split view not supported)**

**Full screen button
(Split view supported)**

Figure 12-13. Identifying windows that support split view

To open split view, follow these steps:

1. Move the pointer over the green, full-screen button of a program window. (If a zoom button appears, you won't be able to make that window appear in split view.)

2. Hold down the left mouse button (or press a finger on the trackpad) until the window shrinks slightly.

3. Release the mouse or trackpad. The window shifts to one side of the screen (see Figure 12-12).

To exit out of split view, press the Esc key on the keyboard.

Using Full-Screen Mode

To allow you to focus on a single window without distractions, some (but not all) programs support full-screen mode. To identify which program windows support full-screen mode, look at the green button in the upper-left corner of each program window. If you see a full-screen button (see Figure 12-13), then that program window supports full-screen mode.

Full-screen mode expands a single window to fill the entire screen and even temporarily hides the menu bar.

To exit out of full-screen mode, move the pointer to the top of the screen until the menu bar and window title bar reappear. Then click the green button in the upper-left corner of the window again to display the window normally.

Summary

The ability to open multiple windows lets you multitask and refer to the contents of one window while working in another. However, too many windows can clutter the screen and prove more confusing than helpful.

That's why OS X offers several ways to help organize and reduce the clutter. You can minimize individual windows to temporarily tuck them out of sight on the Dock. You can also completely hide windows and make them appear again when you want them.

If you have multiple open windows on the screen, you might want to use Mission Control, which displays open windows as thumbnail images. By letting you see all open windows at once, you can click the one that you want to use.

Mission Control also lets you create multiple desktops. By using desktops, you can organize each desktop with different windows and switch between desktops. This lets you keep each desktop organized for a specific task.

Some, but not all, program windows support full-screen mode and split view. Full screen mode expands a window to fill the entire screen to block out distractions and let you focus on the contents of one window. Split screen lets you view two windows side by side so that you can easily refer to both of them at the same time.

With so many different ways to organize windows, you can use the methods that you like best to keep yourself from getting distracted and getting overwhelmed by so much information displayed on the screen at once. By taking the time to learn different ways to organize your program windows, you can find a way that makes you more efficient and productive.

Part III

Having Fun

The real reason that people buy a computer isn't simply to do more work, but to have fun. Even if you don't play video games, you can still find ways to have fun with your Macintosh, such as viewing and organizing pictures captured with a digital camera. In addition to letting you view and modify still images, your Macintosh also lets you watch and edit video.

Perhaps the most common trait that people enjoy is listening to music. Whether you listen to classical, jazz, country, hip-hop, rock, or rap, you can store, organize, and listen to your favorite songs and recording artists by turning your Macintosh into a sophisticated jukebox or radio.

Or, you may want to read e-books on your Macintosh. Instead of lugging around stacks of heavy and cumbersome printed books, you can literally store thousands of e-books on your Macintosh. Whenever you want to read a novel or a non-fiction e-book, you can turn your Macintosh into an e-book reader.

Computers are supposed to be fun to use, so find what you enjoy most—the chances are good that you'll find a way to have fun playing with it on your Macintosh.

Chapter 13

Playing with Photos

Taking pictures can be fun. With digital cameras in every smartphone and tablet, it's easy to capture pictures wherever you go without worrying about taking a camera with you.

One of the biggest problems with taking pictures is finding a place to store them. If you take too many pictures, you'll eventually run out of room to store any more, so you need to know how to get photos off a smartphone, tablet, or camera and on to a Mac for safekeeping.

There are three ways to transfer pictures from an external device (such as a smartphone or tablet) to a Mac:

- Use the Photos program
- Use the Image Capture program
- Use the Finder to copy individual pictures

Using the Photos Program

Included with every Mac is a program called Photos, which can store pictures, organize them, and edit them. Best of all, Photos can automatically import pictures off a smartphone or tablet to make transferring photos fast, simple, and easy.

When you add pictures to the Photos program, it stores them in a special file called the Photos Library. No matter how many pictures that you add to Photos, they all get stored in this single file.

Once you've stored pictures in Photos, you can view them in chronological order, or you can group related pictures together in albums, as shown in Figure 13-1. You can also do light editing on pictures, such as adjusting the brightness.

© Wallace Wang 2016
W. Wang, *Mac OS X for Absolute Beginners*, DOI 10.1007/978-1-4842-1913-3_13

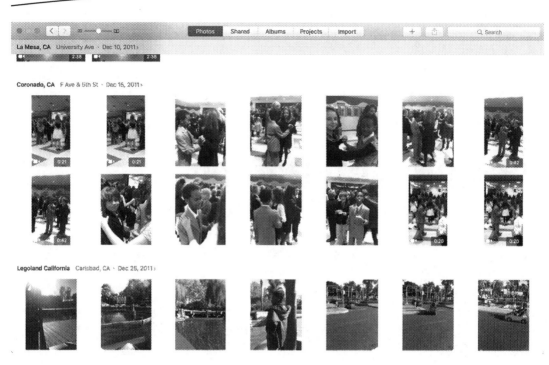

Figure 13-1. *The Photos program can organize pictures in chronological order*

Finally, you can share pictures with others through e-mail or social networks like Flickr or Facebook, or even create projects from your pictures, such as printing a book, greeting cards, or a calendar. For many people, Photos is the only program that they need to save, modify, and view their pictures.

Adding Pictures to Photos

To add pictures to the Photos library file, you can either connect a cable to an external camera (such as a smartphone or tablet) or retrieve pictures stored in a separate folder, such as the Pictures folder or a USB flash drive.

The Photos program automatically loads every time that you connect a camera to your Mac through a cable. When the Photo program loads and connects to your camera, it displays a list of photos that are stored on your camera but not copied to Photos, as shown in Figure 13-2.

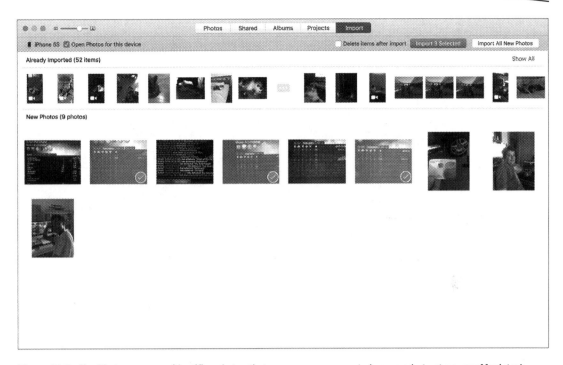

Figure 13-2. *The Photos program identifies photos that appear on a connected camera but not on your Macintosh*

To add all new pictures, click the Import All New Photos button in the upper-right corner.

To selectively add pictures, click the picture (or pictures) that you want to add and then click the Import Selected button. Each time that you click a picture, a check mark appears to show that it's selected. If you click a selected picture a second time, the check mark disappears.

If you want to delete pictures off your smartphone, tablet, or camera after copying them into the Photos program, click the "Delete items after import" check box.

> **Note**   When the "Open Photos for this device" check box is selected, the Photos program opens automatically every time that you connect your camera to your Mac. If you clear this check box, then the Photos program will not open automatically when you plug your camera into your Mac.

Viewing Pictures in Photos

Once you've saved pictures in the Photos program, you can view them in chronological order or by albums. Since most cameras place a date and time stamp on each photo, the Photos program can determine the order that you captured your pictures.

To view pictures in chronological order, open the Photos program and click the Photos tab (see Figure 13-1). Then double-click any picture that you want to view, as shown in Figure 13-3.

Figure 13-3. Double-clicking a picture expands it so that you can see more detail

Once you've selected a picture, you can edit or share it.

Editing Pictures in Photos

Editing a picture lets you fix slightly flawed pictures, such as changing brightness, cropping out unwanted parts, or rotating. The following are some of the ways to edit a picture:

- Enhance: Brightens an image to correct pictures that are too dark

- Rotate: Flips a picture on its side

- Crop: Lets you select a rectangular portion of the image to keep; the rest of it is removed

- Filters: Lets you change the appearance of a picture as seen through different visual filters

- Adjust: Lets you change the color of an image

- Retouch: Lets you drag the pointer over parts of an image you want to remove, such as eliminating blemishes on a person's face

- Red-Eye: Lets you remove the red glow in a person's eyes that occur when a picture is captured using flash

Note The Red-Eye tool only appears when the Photos program detects red eye in a picture. To make the Red-eye tool appear all the time, click the View menu and choose Always Show Red-Eye Control (View ➤ Always Show Red-Eye Control).

Each type of editing tool displays different options for modifying an image in different ways. To edit a picture stored in Photos, follow these steps:

1. Double-click the picture that you want to edit. Your chosen picture appears (see Figure 13-3).

2. Click the Edit button in the upper-right corner. The Edit menu appears on the right edge of the screen, as shown in Figure 13-4.

Figure 13-4. The Edit menu displays common editing tools

3. Click an editing tool on the right edge of the screen, such as Enhance or Retouch and modify the image, as shown in Figure 13-5.

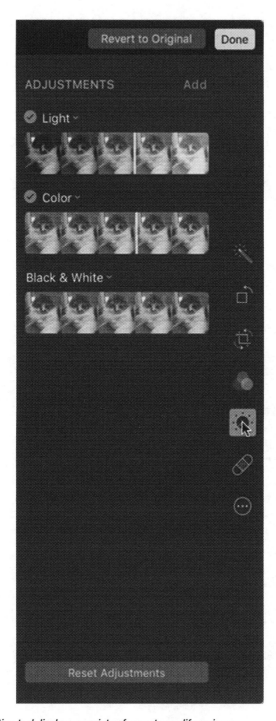

Figure 13-5. *The Adjust editing tool displays a variety of ways to modify an image*

4. Click the Done button in the upper-right corner when you're done.

Organizing Pictures in Albums

Just as you can organize physical pictures in albums, you can also organize digital pictures in albums. The big difference is that physical photos can only appear in one album at a time. With digital albums, you can place the same photo in multiple albums.

For example, you might have one album containing pictures only of your pet dog and a second album containing pictures only of your son. Yet the same dog picture could appear in both albums if there's a picture of your dog with your son.

Albums simply give you a way to group related photos together so that you can easily find them again, as shown in Figure 13-6. Photos provides several different types of albums:

- Standard albums: These albums contain any pictures that you want, based on your own criteria.

- Smart albums: These albums contain pictures based on criteria that you specify, such as pictures taken on a certain date or place.

- Faces: This album uses facial recognition to store pictures of faces, both human and animal.

- Last Import: This album contains the last images that you imported into Photos.

- Favorites: This album contains any pictures that you marked as a favorite.

- Panoramas: This album contains panoramic pictures captured with an iOS device, such as an iPhone or iPad.

- Videos: This album contains videos.

- Slo-mo: This album contains slow motion video captured with an iOS device, such as an iPhone or iPad.

- Time-lapse: This album contains time-lapse video captured with an iOS device, such as an iPhone or iPad.

- Bursts: This album contains photo bursts captured with an iOS device, such as an iPhone or iPad.

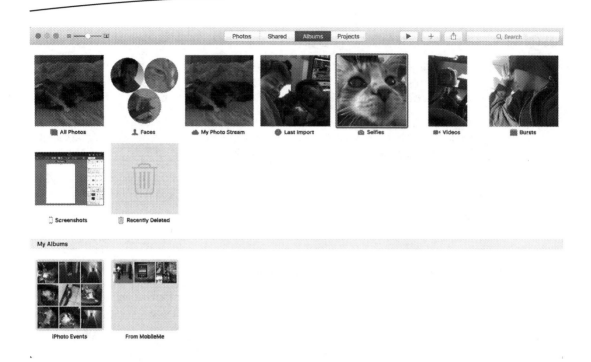

Figure 13-6. Photos can organize your pictures in different types of albums

Your Photos program may not display all of these different album types. For example, if you haven't captured any slow motion or panoramic images, you won't see a Slow-mo or Panoramas album in the Photos program.

Out of all these album types, standard albums are the ones that you can create. The other album types occur automatically.

Creating Standard Albums

You can create as many standard albums as you want and fill them with pictures based on your own criteria, such as pictures from a certain location or pictures that evoke a certain emotion.

Once you create a standard album, you'll need to fill that album with pictures that you manually place (or remove) in that album.

To create a standard album, follow these steps:

1. Click the File menu and choose New Album (File ➤ New Album) or press Command+N. A Create New Album dialog box appears, as shown in Figure 13-7.

Note If you select one or more pictures before choosing to create a new album, those selected pictures automatically appear in your new album.

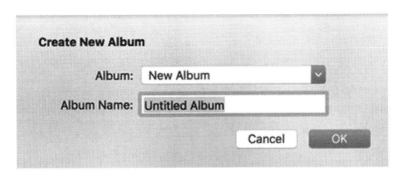

Figure 13-7. Creating a new album

2. Click in the Album Name text field and type a descriptive name for your album, such as Vacation Photos or Birthday Party April 2018.

3. Click the OK button. Photos creates an empty album.

Adding Pictures to a Standard Album

Once you've created an album, you can add pictures to it. Adding pictures essentially means making a copy of that picture and storing it in an album, so if you ever delete that album (or that picture in that album), you'll still have a copy of that picture stored in the Photos library.

To add pictures to a standard album, follow these steps:

1. Click the Albums tab. A list of available albums appears (see Figure 13-6).

2. Double-click the album that you want to use.

3. Click the View menu and choose Show Sidebar (View ➤ Show Sidebar). The sidebar appears on the left side of the Photos window, listing your current album, as shown in Figure 13-8.

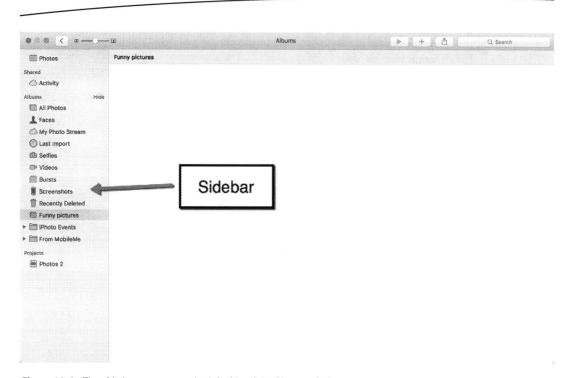

Figure 13-8. *The side bar appears on the left side of the Photos window*

4. Click the View menu and choose Photos (View ➤ Photos) or press Command+1 to display all the pictures stored in the Photos library.

5. Move the pointer over a picture that you want to add to the album. Hold down the left mouse button (or press a finger on the trackpad) and drag the picture over the album name that appears in the sidebar, as shown in Figure 13-9.

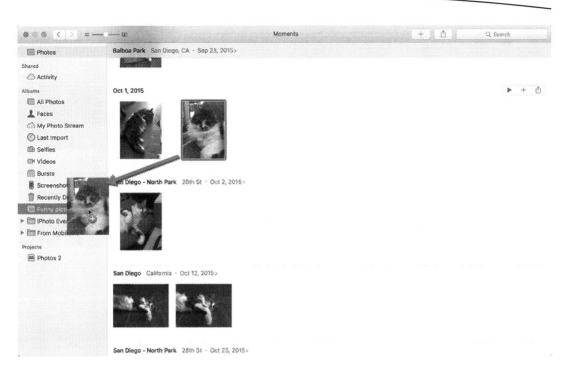

Figure 13-9. Dragging a picture over the album name in the sidebar

6. Release the mouse button (or trackpad) when a white plus sign appears inside a green circle. Your chosen picture now appears in your album.

Removing Pictures from a Standard Album

If you added a picture to an album and later decide you don't want it there any more, you can always remove it. To remove a picture from a standard album, follow these steps:

1. Click the Albums tab. A list of available albums appears (see Figure 13-6).

2. Double-click the album that you want to modify. All the pictures stored in that album appear.

3. Right-click the picture that you want to remove. A pop-up menu appears.

4. Choose Remove from Album, as shown in Figure 13-10.

Figure 13-10. Removing a picture from an album

> **Note**   Removing a picture from an album does not physically delete that picture from your Photos library.

Tagging Pictures

Each time that you capture a photo with a digital camera, it may tag that file with a generic file name along with the date when and the location where it was captured, as shown in Figure 13-11.

Figure 13-11. Captured images often store information about the location and device that captured it

To help you find a particular file, you might want to add additional tags, such as marking some pictures as your favorite, typing in a description of that image, or adding identifying keywords about the pictures, such as the name of the person in the picture. Tags give you a way to find a particular picture quickly without endlessly scrolling through your entire library of pictures.

To tag a picture, follow these steps:

1. Right-click a picture that you want to tag. A pop-up menu appears, as shown in Figure 13-12.

Figure 13-12. Right-clicking a picture displays a pop-up menu

2. Click Get Info. An Info window appears (see Figure 13-11).

3. Add a tag, such as one or more of the following:

    a. Click the Heart icon in the upper-right corner to mark a picture as
        a Favorite.

    b. Click in the Add a Title text field to add a title for your picture.

    c. Click in the Add a Description text field to add a description.

    d. Click in the Add a Keyword text field to add a keyword, such as
        the name of a person in the picture.

When typing descriptions or keywords, be consistent. For example, you probably wouldn't
want to label one picture as "Hawaii" and a similar picture as "Honolulu" since searching for
one tag (Hawaii) wouldn't help you find the other picture.

Since you can make up your own descriptions, titles, and keywords, use words that you'll
remember. That way you'll be able to search for all pictures tagged with the same keywords,
titles, or descriptions.

Searching with Tags

Once you've tagged your pictures, you can use those tags later to help you find a particular image. For example, if you captured a dozen pictures in Paris over the years, then you might tag it with the Paris keyword. Now you can easily find all pictures tagged with the Paris keyword.

To search for a picture using a tag, follow these steps:

1. Click in the Search field in the upper-right corner of the Photos window.

2. Type part or all of the tag that you want to find. As you type, a list of matching pictures appears, as shown in Figure 13-13.

Figure 13-13. *Searching lets you find all pictures matching a particular title, description, or keyword*

3. Click the picture that you want to view.

Creating Smart Albums

When you create a standard album, you must add (or remove) pictures to that album yourself. A much easier way is to create smart albums.

A smart album automatically adds pictures based on certain criteria, such as all pictures that were captured on a certain date, or contained specific people or tags.

Smart albums work best if all the pictures stored in your Photos library are tagged. That way you won't risk missing a picture just because it wasn't tagged.

> **Note**   The main difference between a standard album and a smart album is that a smart album adds pictures automatically, whereas a standard album forces you to manually add pictures to it.

To create a smart album, follow these steps:

1. Click the File menu and choose New Smart Album (File ➤ New Smart Album). A window asks you to set criteria for the pictures to add to the smart album, as shown in Figure 13-14.

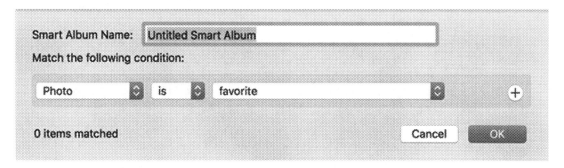

Figure 13-14. Defining which types of files should automatically appear in the smart album

2. Click in the Smart Album Name text field and type a descriptive name for your smart album.

3. Click the far left pop-up menu. A list of different options appears, as shown in Figure 13-15.

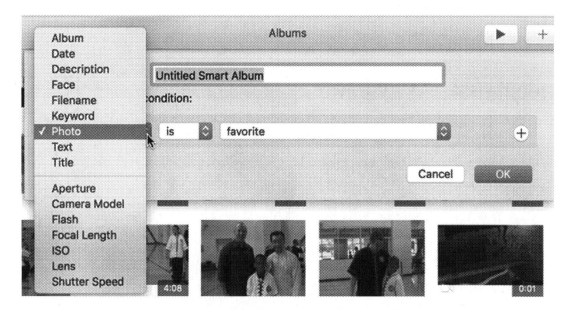

Figure 13-15. Defining criteria for the type of pictures to include in a smart album

4. Click in the far right pop-up menu to define different options for the choice that you made in step 3, as shown in Figure 13-16. Depending on which option you chose in step 3, these options offer different choices.

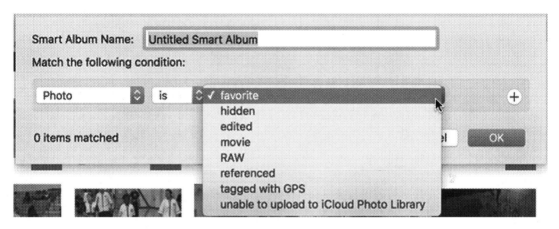

Figure 13-16. Defining additional criteria for adding pictures to a smart album

5. (Optional) If you want to add more criteria, click the plus sign in a circle that appears to the far right, as shown in Figure 13-17. You can add multiple criteria to ensure that the smart album only includes pictures that you want.

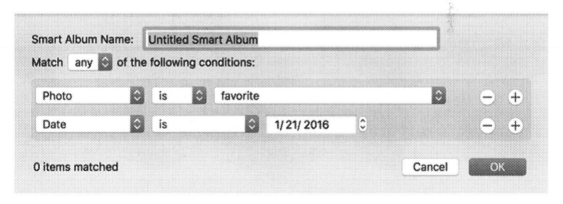

Figure 13-17. Defining additional criteria for adding pictures to a smart album

6. Click the OK button when you're done defining enough criteria to choose which type of pictures automatically appear in your smart album.

Once you've defined the criteria for a smart album, it continues to use it to add new pictures automatically. Just make sure that you remember the criteria you defined for each smart album so that you'll know how to tag new pictures so that they'll automatically appear in the right smart albums.

Exporting a Picture

Photos is handy for storing pictures but you'll likely want to share them with others. Photos can send a picture directly to e-mail, or as a text message, or to a common social network like Facebook or Twitter.

Since Photos stores all pictures in its own Photos Library file, you may want to export a picture out of Photos to save it as a separate file. That way you can use it in another program.

To share a picture, follow these steps:

1.   Click the picture that you want to share. (Hold down the Shift key and click multiple pictures to select more than one to share at a time.)

2.   Click the Share icon in the upper-right corner of the Photos program to display a pop-up menu, as shown in Figure 13-18.

Figure 13-18. Clicking the Share icon displays a menu offering different ways to share a picture

3.   Click one of the following choices:

   a.   iCloud Photo Sharing: Lets you share photos with others through an online album

   b.   Mail: Lets you send a picture as a file attachment in an e-mail message

   c.   Messages: Lets you send a picture as a text message

d. AirDrop: Lets you wirelessly send a picture to a Mac or iOS device

e. Notes: Lets you store a copy of a picture in the Notes program

f. Facebook: Lets you post a picture on Facebook

g. Flickr: Lets you post a picture on Flickr

If you want to save a picture as a separate file, you need to export that picture. When you export a picture out of Photos, you can define the following:

▤ A file format (JPEG, TIFF, or PNG)

▤ A file name

▤ Additional information about the file, such as the keywords or descriptions used to tag that picture

To export a picture out of Photos, follow these steps:

1. Click the picture that you want to save as a separate file. (Hold down the Shift key and click multiple pictures to select more than one to share at a time.)

2. Click the File menu, choose Export, and choose Export again (File ➤ Export ➤ Export), as shown in Figure 13-19. A dialog asks for a file format and file name, as shown in Figure 13-20.

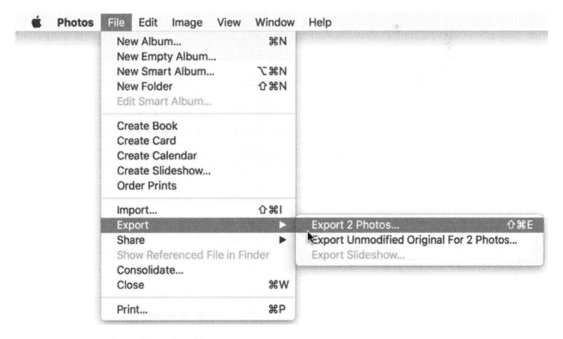

Figure 13-19. Exporting a picture from Photos

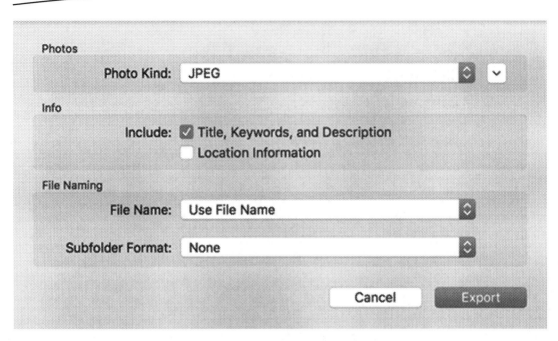

Figure 13-20. Defining a file format and file name for an exported picture

3. Click in the Photo Kind pop-up menu and choose a file format (JPEG, TIFF, or PNG).

4. Select (or clear) the Include check boxes, such as Location Information.

5. Click the File Name pop-up menu and choose how you want to name your pictures.

6. Click the Export button. A window lets you choose a folder to store your exported pictures.

7. Click a folder to store your pictures and click the Export button. Your chosen pictures now appear as separate files that you can use in other programs, such as a desktop publishing program or a website editor.

Using the Image Capture Program

Photos is handy for storing and managing your pictures because it automatically asks to import pictures every time that you plug an external camera into your Mac. However, if you don't want to use the Photos program or if you want to store pictures as separate files in a folder, you can use the Image Capture program instead.

Unlike the Photos program, the Image Capture program won't run automatically when you connect a camera to your Mac. You also can't edit pictures with the Image Capture program or share pictures with others by e-mail or social networks like Facebook.

To use the Image Capture program to store pictures as files on your Mac, follow these steps:

1. Connect your camera to your Mac.

2. Click the Finder icon on the Dock. A Finder window appears.

3. Click Applications in the sidebar of the Finder window.

4. Double-click the Image Capture program icon. The Image Capture window appears.

5. Click the camera under the Devices category in the left pane. All available pictures on your chosen camera appear, as shown in Figure 13-21.

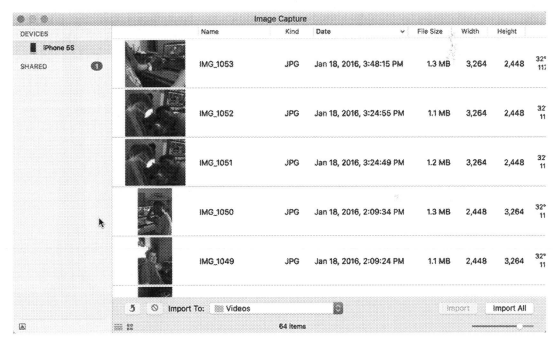

Figure 13-21. The Image Capture window displays a camera name and all pictures on that camera

6. Click the picture that you want to copy from your camera. (Hold down the Command key and click multiple pictures to select more than one picture.)

7. Click the Import To pop-up menu and choose a folder to store your pictures, as shown in Figure 13-22. (If you choose Other, you'll be able to choose a folder not listed on the Import To pop-up menu.)

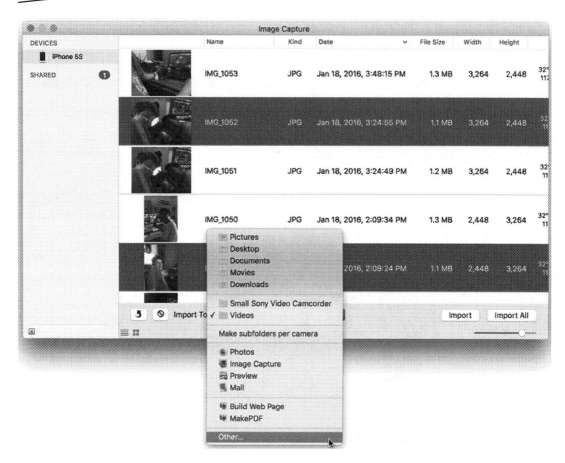

Figure 13-22. The Import To pop-up menu lets you define where to save copies of your pictures

8.   Click the Import button.

Summary

Almost every smartphone and tablet comes with a built-in camera, which means you can easily capture pictures at any time. The trick is getting those pictures off your camera and on to your Mac for safekeeping.

The two main programs for copying pictures off a camera are the Photos program and the Image Capture program. The Image Capture program treats pictures as separate files and simply copies them off a camera on to a folder on your Mac.

The Photos programs can copy pictures off a camera, and organize, share, and edit them as well. Unlike the Image Capture program, the Photos program stores all pictures in a single file called the Photos Library.

You can use the Photos program and the Image Capture program to copy still pictures and video off any camera connected to your Mac. Whenever you have pictures, use either Photos or Image Capture to save your pictures on your computer.

Chapter 14

Watching and Editing Video

Cameras can capture both still images and video. Once you have video on your Mac, you can view, edit, or save it to a DVD if your Mac has a DVD drive (either internal or external).

Video files may be stored in different types of file formats, such as:

- .mpg, .m4v: MPEG-4 format
- .mpg, .mpeg: MPEG-1 format
- .mov, .qt: QuickTime format
- .avi: Audio Video Interleave format (commonly associated with Windows)
- .wmv: Windows Media Video (commonly associated with Windows)

The best video file formats for OS X are the MPEG and QuickTime formats. Your Mac may be able to recognize other video file formats, but if you are unable to play a video file on your Mac, you may need to convert it to the .mpg, .m4v, or .mov formats.

> **Note** The Photos program (see Chapter 13) can also store and organize video files as well as still images.

Once you get a video in a format that your Mac can recognize, you can then manipulate the video in different ways.

© Wallace Wang 2016

W. Wang, *Mac OS X for Absolute Beginners*, DOI 10.1007/978-1-4842-1913-3_14

Watching a Video with Quick Look

The most common use for any video file is to watch it. The simplest and fastest way to watch a video is to use the Quick Look feature that lets you view the contents of a file without running a program to open that file first.

To use the Quick Look feature to watch a video, follow these steps:

1. Click the Finder icon on the Dock. A Finder window appears.

2. Click the video file that you want to view.

3. Do one of the following:

    a. Press the spacebar

    b. Press Command+Y

    c. Click the File menu and choose Quick Look (File ➤ Quick Look)

    d. Right-click the video file, and when a pop-up menu appears, choose Quick Look

4. Click the close button (the X) in the upper-left corner of the Quick Look window when you're done watching the video.

When you open a video file using Quick Look, the video appears in a window, as shown in Figure 14-1.

Figure 14-1. *Quick Look displays a video file in a separate window*

The Quick Look window displays several controls for viewing a video:

- Pause/Play: Toggles between playing the video and pausing it
- Mute/Volume: Toggles between muting the volume and increasing it
- Scrubber Bar: Rewinds or forwards the video

If you click the Open with QuickTime Player button in the upper-right corner, you can open the video file in the QuickTime Player program. This gives you the option of saving the video in a different file format or doing basic editing to trim the length of the video.

Watching a Video with the QuickTime Player

You can open the QuickTime Player within the Quick Look window or by double-clicking the QuickTime Player program icon in a Finder window. The QuickTime Player gives you more control over watching a video than the Quick Look window; you can adjust the volume, export the video in different resolutions, or even strip out the video and retain only the audio.

In addition, the QuickTime Player lets you do basic video editing, such as trimming the beginning or end of a video.

To open and watch a video in the QuickTime Player like the one shown in Figure 14-2, you can use one of the following methods:

- Load the QuickTime Player and then choose File ➤ Open to select the video you want to view

- Right-click the video file that you want to open, and when a pop-up menu appears, choose Open With ➤ QuickTime Player

- Click a video file and open it in the Quick Look window. Then click the Open with QuickTime Player button

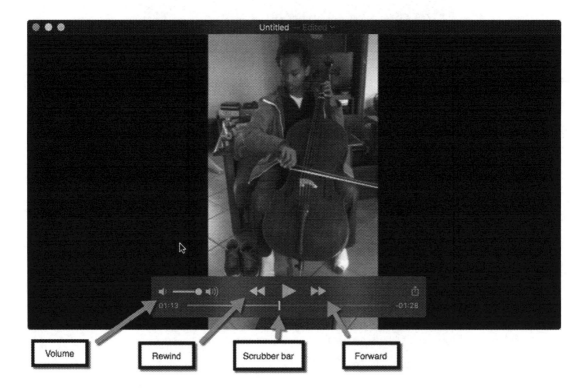

Figure 14-2. The Photos program can organize pictures in chronological order

Exporting a Video in Different Resolutions

If the QuickTime Player program can load and play a video, then you can export that video as a QuickTime video (.mov) in several different resolutions, as follows (also see Figure 14-3):

- 1080p: Up to 1920 × 1080 resolution

- 720p: Up to 1280 × 720 resolution

- 480p: Up to 640 × 480 resolution

- iPad, iPhone, iPod touch & Apple TV: Lets you optimize your file for a specific Apple device

- Audio Only: Strips away the video and only saves the audio portion

- iTunes: Lets you share a movie on iTunes

Figure 14-3. Exporting a video in different resolutions

If you choose the "iPad, iPhone, iPod touch & Apple TV" option in the Export submenu, you'll see an additional dialog for choosing a size for your file, as shown in Figure 14-4.

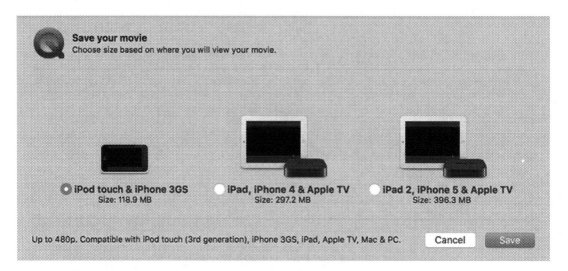

Figure 14-4. Defining an optimum file size for different Apple devices

The smaller the device that you choose (such as an iPod touch), the smaller the file size. Small file sizes can be viewed on larger devices but the resolution won't be optimized for that larger screen. So if you save a video for an iPod touch, it won't look as good when viewed on an Apple TV or iPad.

After you choose a resolution and file size, you can then specify a folder and a file name to save your exported video.

Trimming Video in the QuickTime Player

Trimming a video shortens that video clip to get rid of unwanted images at the beginning or end of a video. To trim a video, follow these steps:

1.   Open a video with the QuickTime Player program.

2.   Click the Edit menu and choose Trim (Edit ➤ Trim) or press Command+T. The QuickTime Player displays clips of your video with a handle at the beginning and end of the video, as shown in Figure 14-5.

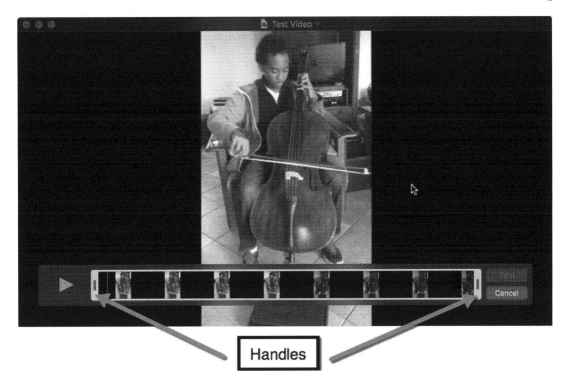

Figure 14-5. Trimming a video

3. Move the pointer over the handle at the beginning or end of the video clip. Notice that the Trim button appears dimmed.

4. Hold down the left mouse button (or press a finger on the trackpad). Drag the mouse (or slide your finger on the trackpad) left or right to exclude a portion of the video at the beginning or end.

5. Release the left mouse button (or lift your finger off the trackpad). The Trim button appears so that you can select it.

6. Click the Trim button. The QuickTime Player trims your video.

Note   If you make a mistake trimming a video, choose Edit ➤ Undo or press Command+Z to undo any changes you made.

Splitting Video into Clips

Trimming shortens a video. Another way to edit a video is to split a video into clips. Once you've split a video into clips, you can rearrange the clips so that images that appeared earlier can appear later and vice versa.

To split a video into clips, follow these steps:

1. Open a video with the QuickTime Player program.

2. Click the View menu and choose Show Clips (View ➤ Show Clips).
   The QuickTime Player displays multiple clips of your video, as shown
   in Figure 14-6. A red vertical line (called the *playhead*) appears on the
   far left.

Figure 14-6. Displaying a video as multiple clips

3. Move the pointer over the playhead.

4. Hold down the left mouse button (or press a finger on the trackpad)
   and drag the mouse (or slide a finger on the trackpad) to move the
   playhead between any two clips.

5. Click the Edit menu and choose Split Clip (Edit ➤ Split Clip) or press
   Command+Y. QuickTime Player splits the video into separate clips,
   as shown in Figure 14-7. You can repeat steps 3 to 5 as often as
   necessary to keep splitting a video into multiple clips.

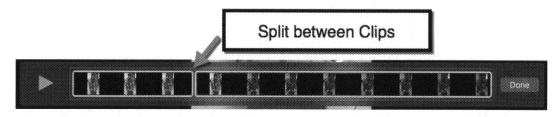

Figure 14-7. Splitting a video into two separate clips

6. Click the Done button when you're finished splitting your video into
   separate clips.

Rearranging Clips

Once you've split your video into at least two separate clips, you can rearrange them in any
order. To rearrange clips, follow these steps:

1. Split your video into at least two separate clips.

2. Click the clip that you want to move to a new location. QuickTime
   Player highlights your chosen clip.

3. Hold down the left mouse button (or press a finger on the trackpad).

4. Move the mouse (or slide your finger on the trackpad) left or right to rearrange the clip. The existing clips move out of the way to make room for the new location of the moved clip.

5. (Optional) Click the Edit menu and choose one of the following to change the visual orientation of your chosen clip:

    a. Rotate Left

    b. Rotate Right

    c. Flip Horizontal

    d. Flip Vertical

6. Click the Done button when you're finished rearranging clips.

Note   If you open video in another QuickTime Player window, you can copy/cut clips from one video and paste them into another video.

Capturing a Video of the Screen

If you've ever tried to explain to someone how to use a Mac, you know how frustrating and limited words can be. Since it's not always possible to peek over someone's shoulder and show them how to use a Mac, you can do the next best thing and record a video of your screen instead.

When you record a video of your screen, others can see exactly what you click and choose. Even better, you can record audio so that you can narrate what you're doing.

Note   QuickTime Player can only record audio from your Mac's built-in microphone. QuickTime Player cannot record any audio playing out of your Mac.

To record the actions on your screen, follow these steps:

1. Open the QuickTime Player program.

2. Click the File menu and choose New Screen Recording (File ➤ New Screen Recording). A Screen Recording window appears.

3. Click the Options icon to display a pull-down menu, as shown in Figure 14-8.

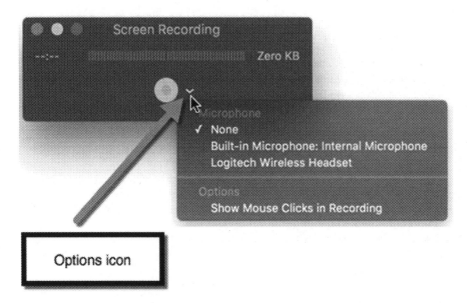

Figure 14-8. The Screen Recording window

4. Choose how you want to record audio, such as None or Built-in Microphone.

5. Click the red Record button. A message appears letting you know to click to record the full screen or part of the screen.

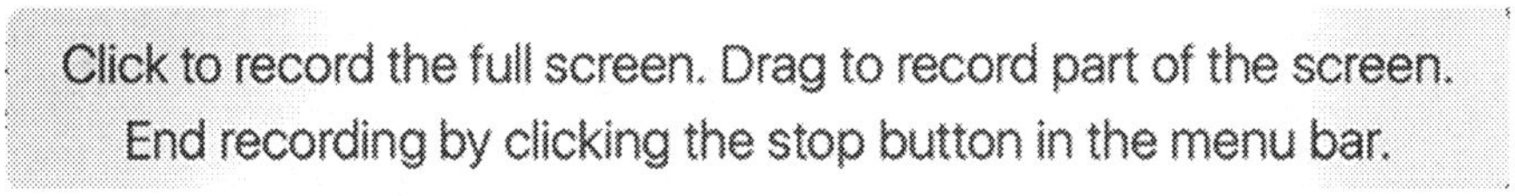

Click to record the full screen. Drag to record part of the screen.
End recording by clicking the stop button in the menu bar.

Figure 14-9. You can record the entire screen or just part of it

6. Click to record the full screen or drag the mouse (or press and slide a finger on the trackpad) to define the part of the screen that you want to record. A Start Recording button appears on the screen.

7. Click the Start Recording button. Anything you say and do on the screen is recorded.

8. Click the Stop button on the menu bar to stop recording, as shown in Figure 14-10. Your recorded video now appears in a separate QuickTime Player window.

Figure 14-10. The Stop button appears on the menu bar in the upper-right corner of the screen

Burning a Video to a DVD

Most Macs no longer have a built-in DVD drive, but you can always connect an external DVD drive to any Mac. If you have a DVD drive, you can burn a video to a DVD.

Burning a video to a DVD creates a playable DVD. If you copy a video *file* to a DVD, then that video won't play in ordinary DVD players; it can only be read by other computers.

To burn a video file to a DVD, follow these steps:

1. Make sure that you have a DVD drive connected to your Mac with a blank DVD inside it.

2. Click the Finder icon on the Dock. A Finder window appears.

3. Right-click the video file that you want to burn to a DVD. A pop-up menu appears, as shown in Figure 14-11.

Figure 14-11. Right-clicking displays a pop-up menu with the Burn command

4.   Click Burn to burn your video on to the DVD in the DVD drive.

> **Note**   If your Mac has a DVD drive, you can also play DVDs, such as movies, using the DVD Player program, which mimics the controls and features of a DVD player.

Summary

OS X provides basic features for playing, capturing, and editing video. If you need video-editing features that are more advanced, you can use the iMovie program that comes with every Mac. With iMovie, you can add titles, transition, and audio in more ways than the QuickTime Player can offer.

For simple screen capturing and recording, you can use the QuickTime Player. However, if you want to record audio from a microphone and audio playing out of your Mac, you'll need a dedicated video recording program.

Likewise, if you have a DVD drive connected to your Mac and you want to burn videos to DVDs in different ways, you need to get a dedicated CD/DVD burning program.

If you regularly work with video captured from different cameras, you may want to get a special video file converter. That way, no matter what file format a video might be stored in, you'll be able to view and edit it.

With so many smartphones and tablets available, capturing video is getting even easier than before. Capture your memories in video and then store them on your Mac for safekeeping. Once stored on your Mac, your video files are always available for viewing, editing, or sharing whenever you like.

Chapter 15

Playing Music

Listening to music is yet another way that you can enjoy using your Mac. You can listen to music stored on a CD (if you have a CD/DVD drive connected to your Mac), music streamed over the Internet, or music stored as audio files on your computer. You can listen to music while working on your computer, or you can turn your Mac into a stereo and let it play music while you do something else.

Besides playing music, you can also purchase music online. You can buy your favorite songs or albums and play them right away on your Mac.

There are three ways to play audio files such as music on a Mac:

- Use Quick Look
- Use the QuickTime Player
- Use iTunes

Playing Audio with Quick Look

Quick Look is meant to let you peek at the contents of any file without the hassle of opening a program to do it. With Quick Look, you can play a portion of an audio file or the entire file if you wish.

Quick Look can open and play a variety of audio file formats, including .mp3, .wav, .aac, .mov, and .qt. If you have an audio file stored in a different file format, Quick Look may not be able to play it.

To listen to an audio file with Quick Look, follow these steps:

1. Click the Finder icon on the dock. A Finder window appears.

2. Click the audio file that you want to hear.

© Wallace Wang 2016
W. Wang, *Mac OS X for Absolute Beginners*, DOI 10.1007/978-1-4842-1913-3_15

3. Do one of the following to open the Quick Look window (also see Figure 15-1):

a. Press the spacebar.

b. Press Command+Y.

c. Click the File menu and choose Quick Look (File ➤ Quick Look).

d. Right-click the video file, and when a pop-up menu appears, choose Quick Look.

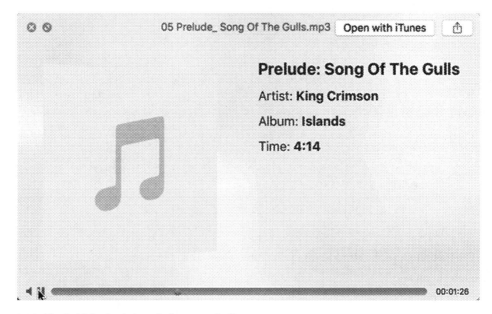

Figure 15-1. *The Quick Look window playing an audio file*

4. Click the close button (the X) in the upper-left corner of the Quick Look window when you're done listening to the audio file.

Playing Audio with the QuickTime Player

One drawback of using Quick Look to play an audio file is that you can't play an audio file in Quick Look and use the Finder at the same time. If you want to listen to an audio file while using the Finder, you have to use the QuickTime Player.

To play an audio file with the QuickTime Player, follow these steps:

1. Start the QuickTime Player.

2. Click the File menu and choose Open File (File ➤ Open File). Select the audio file that you want to play. A QuickTime Player window appears, as shown in Figure 15-2.

Figure 15-2. Playing an audio file in the QuickTime Player

3. Click the close button (the X) in the upper-left corner of the QuickTime
    Player window when you're done listening to the audio file.

Note   Unlike Quick Look, which can only play one audio file at a time, you can open as many audio
files as you wish in the QuickTime Player.

Playing an Audio File in iTunes

The biggest limitation of playing audio files in Quick Look or the QuickTime Player is that
you can only play one audio file at a time. If you want to hear multiple audio files one after
another, you can play audio files in iTunes instead.

With iTunes, you can import audio files either by buying them online or by importing them
off your hard disk or flash drive. You can also create playlists to play related audio files one
after another.

Of course, before you can play any audio files in iTunes, you must import them into iTunes first.

Importing Audio Files into iTunes

Although there are many varieties of audio file formats, iTunes can only play the more
popular audio file formats, such as:

  ▦ .aac: The file format used when you purchase music within iTunes

  ▦ .aiff and .wav: Two file formats that provide the best audio quality but at
     the expense of larger file sizes

  ▦ Apple Lossless Encoder: Apple's format that is similar to AIFF but takes
     up much less space

  ▦ .mp3: The most popular file format for storing audio files

Note   If you have an audio file stored in a different format, you may have to convert it to another
file format before importing it into iTunes.

To import a compatible audio file into iTunes, follow these steps:

1. Open the iTunes program.

2. Click the File menu and choose Add to Library (File ➤ Add to Library). A dialog appears.

3. Click the audio file that you want to add to your iTunes library. (You can hold down the Command key to select more than one file.) If you select a folder, you will add all audio files stored in that folder.

4. Click the Open button. iTunes adds your selected audio file in the Music library and the Recently Added playlist.

Importing Audio CDs into iTunes

If your Mac has a DVD drive, you can have iTunes automatically ask you to import audio tracks off a CD every time that you insert it into your DVD drive. This makes it convenient to save audio CD tracks as digital files in iTunes so that you can play them again without inserting the CD back into your Mac again.

To make iTunes automatically ask if you want to import audio files every time you insert an audio CD into a DVD drive, follow these steps (if your Mac has a DVD drive connected to it):

1. Click the Apple menu in the upper-left corner of the screen to display a pull-down menu.

2. Choose System Preferences. A System Preferences window appears.

3. Click the CDs & DVDs icon. The CDs & DVDs window appears, as shown in Figure 15-3.

Figure 15-3. *You can make iTunes load automatically every time you insert an audio CD into your DVD drive*

4. Click the "When you insert a music CD" pop-up menu and choose Open iTunes. From now on, iTunes automatically loads each time that you insert a music CD into your DVD drive. To make iTunes automatically import audio tracks, you need to define how iTunes behaves when you insert an audio CD into your DVD drive.

5. Open iTunes, click the iTunes menu, and choose Preferences (iTunes ➤ Preferences). A General Preferences window appears.

6. Click the General tab and click the "When a CD is inserted" pop-up menu. Choose Ask to Import CD, as shown in Figure 15-4.

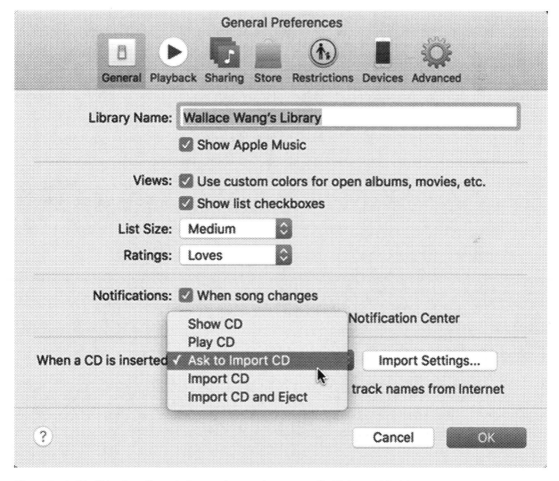

Figure 15-4. Modifying how iTunes behaves when you insert an audio CD into a DVD drive

7. Click the OK button.

8. Insert an audio CD into the DVD drive of your Mac. iTunes asks if you want to import the audio tracks into iTunes, as shown in Figure 15-5.

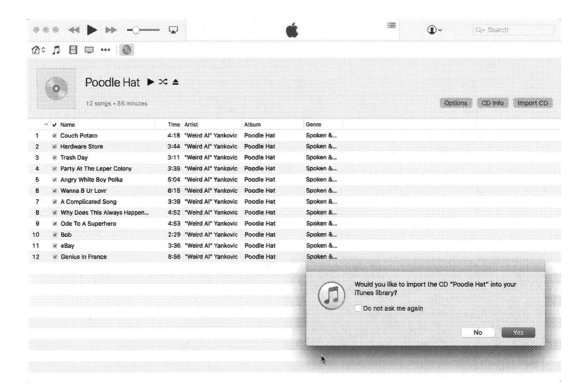

Figure 15-5. Inserting a music CD can automatically import audio tracks into iTunes

9. Click the Yes button to import all audio tracks from the CD. Click the No button if you don't want to import any audio tracks from the CD.

Playing Audio in iTunes

Once you have audio files stored in iTunes, you can play them individually or in groups, such as all songs from a single album. In addition, you can play an audio file once or have it loop multiple times. This is particularly handy for a long audio track, such as a relaxing meditation audio file, that you want to keep playing until you finally turn it off.

Playing a Single Audio Track

If you just want to play a single audio track stored in your iTunes library, follow these steps:

1. Open iTunes.

2. Click the View menu and choose Music. Click Music in the left pane under the Library category, or press Command+1. A list of all audio tracks stored in iTunes appears, as shown in Figure 15-6.

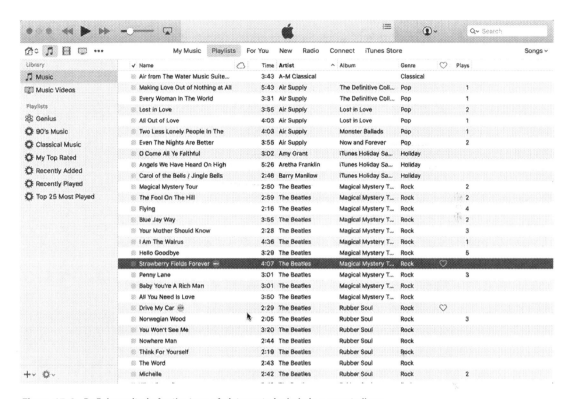

Figure 15-6. Defining criteria for the type of pictures to include in a smart album

3. Click an audio track that you want to play.

4. Click the Controls menu and choose Play (Controls ➤ Play). Press the spacebar or click the Play button in the upper-left corner of the iTunes window. Your chosen audio track starts playing.

While an audio track is playing, you'll see controls at the top of the iTunes window, as shown in Figure 15-7. The following includes ways to control an audio track:

▓ Previous: Plays the previous audio track (if any).

▓ Play/Pause: Toggles between playing and pausing an audio track.

▓ Next: Plays the next audio track (if any).

▓ Scrubber: Shows the current position of the audio track and lets you drag a slider to move the audio track to a specific position.

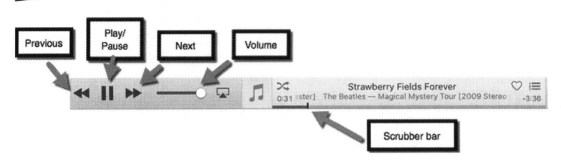

Figure 15-7. Controls for playing an audio track in iTunes

If you're just playing a single audio track, the Previous button starts playing the audio track from the beginning and the Next button stops playing the audio track.

Playing Multiple Audio Tracks

Most likely, you won't want to load iTunes just to play a single audio track. Instead, you're more likely to play multiple audio tracks. To play multiple audio tracks, follow these steps:

1. Open iTunes.

2. Click the check box to the left of each audio track that you want to play, as shown in Figure 15-8.

☑ Starless	12:19	King Crimson	Red	Rock
The Night Watch	4:41	King Crimson	Starless And Bible...	Rock
☑ Trio	5:41	King Crimson	Starless And Bible...	Rock
☑ Fracture	11:13	King Crimson	Starless And Bible...	Rock
People	5:54	King Crimson	Thrak	Other
☑ VROOOM	7:20	King Crimson	Thrak	Rock

Figure 15-8. Selecting multiple audio tracks

3. Click the Controls menu and choose Play (Controls ➤ Play). Press the spacebar or click the Play button in the upper-left corner of the iTunes window. Your chosen audio tracks start playing.

> **Note** If you click the Controls menu and choose Shuffle and On (Controls ➤ Shuffle ➤ On), you can play your selected audio tracks in random order.

Making Playlists

Many people have favorite songs that they want to hear together, such as all songs from a particular album or similar types of songs, such as love songs or songs you just like the best. When you want to play groups of related songs, you can create a playlist.

A playlist defines a group of songs that you can play sequentially or randomly. Instead of taking time to select the audio tracks you want to hear, you can just select the playlist that you want to hear.

The following are three ways to create a playlist:

- Create a playlist and then choose audio tracks to store in that playlist.

- Select multiple audio tracks and create a playlist from those selected audio tracks.

- Create a smart playlist where iTunes automatically adds new audio tracks based on different criteria.

Creating a Playlist

If you want to create a playlist and then choose audio tracks to store in that playlist afterward, follow these steps:

1. Open iTunes.

2. Click the File menu, choose New, and then choose Playlist (File ➤ New ➤ Playlist), or press Command+N. iTunes displays an empty playlist window with a generic name (Playlist) selected so that you can type a more descriptive name for your playlist, as shown in Figure 15-9.

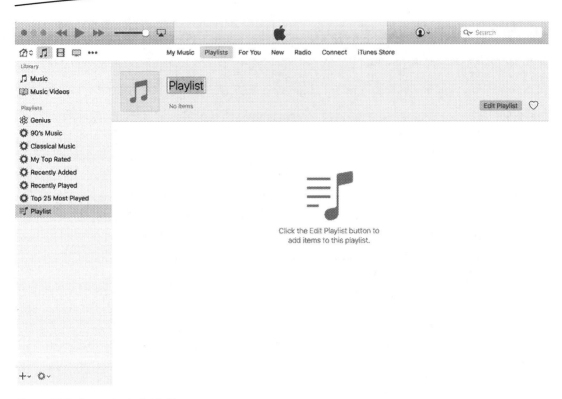

Figure 15-9. *An empty playlist in iTunes*

3. Type a descriptive name for your playlist and press Return.

4. Click the Edit Playlist button. iTunes displays a list of audio tracks currently stored in iTunes that you can drag into the playlist pane on the right side of the iTunes window, as shown in Figure 15-10.

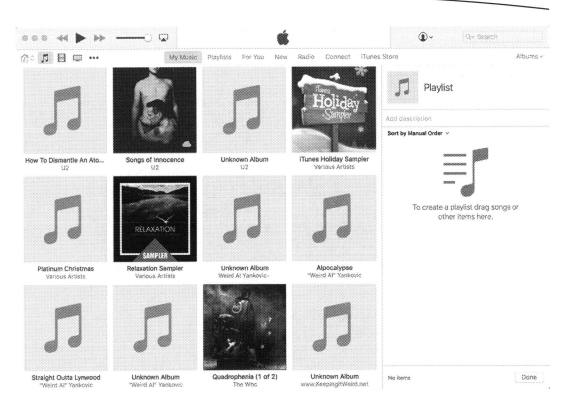

Figure 15-10. *Adding audio tracks to a playlist*

5. Click an album that contains the audio tracks you want to add to your playlist. A list of audio tracks in that album appears.

6. Move the pointer over an audio track that you want to add to your playlist, hold down the left mouse button (or press a finger on the trackpad), and drag the mouse (or slide your finger on the trackpad) so drag the audio track over the playlist box, as shown in Figure 15-11.

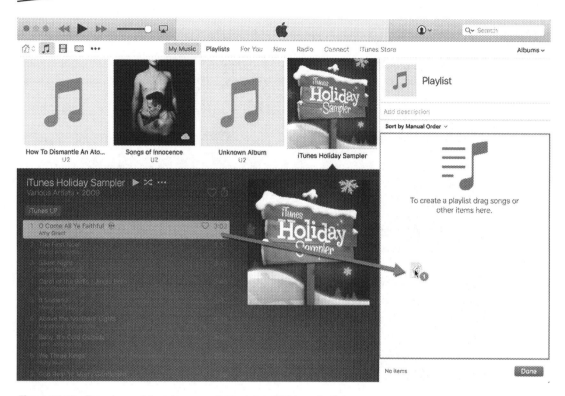

Figure 15-11. Dragging and dropping an audio track to add it to a playlist

7. Release the left mouse button (or lift your finger off the trackpad) when the audio track appears over the playlist box. iTunes adds your audio track to the playlist. Repeat steps 5 to 7 for each additional audio track that you want to add to the playlist.

8. (Optional) You can drag and drop audio tracks up or down to rearrange their order.

9. Click the Done button when you're finished adding audio tracks to your playlist.

Creating a Playlist from a Selection of Audio Tracks

Creating an empty playlist and then filling it with audio tracks is fine, but it's often faster to select multiple audio tracks and then add those selected audio tracks to a playlist right away.

Then you can add new audio tracks later if you wish. Selecting audio tracks first is especially useful when grouping audio tracks from the same album together. To select audio tracks and then create a playlist, follow these steps:

1. Open iTunes.

2. Click the View menu and choose Music (View ➤ Music), or press Command+1 to view all audio tracks stored in your iTunes library.

3. Hold down the Command key and click each audio track that you want to add to your playlist.

4. Click the File menu, choose New, and then choose Playlist from Selection (File ➤ New ➤ Playlist from Selection). iTunes creates a playlist with your chosen audio tracks.

Creating a Smart Playlist

The biggest problem with creating a playlist is that it only contains the audio tracks that you specifically add. If you add new audio tracks to your iTunes library, none of those new audio tracks will appear in your playlists until you specifically add them.

To overcome this limitation, iTunes offers *smart playlists*. A smart playlist lets you define criteria for which audio tracks to include, such as certain recording artist names, year released, or length.

Each time you add new audio tracks to your iTunes library, iTunes checks to see if any of these new audio tracks match the criteria defined by your smart playlist. If so, then it adds those audio tracks to your playlist automatically.

iTunes already has several smart playlists, such as Recently Added and Recently Played. Because smart playlists can add (or remove) audio tracks automatically, they can help you group related audio tracks with no extra effort on your part.

For smart playlists to work, your audio tracks must contain certain information, such as the genre, album, recording artist name, or song name. When you import audio tracks off a music CD, this information will already be recorded with each file. If you import audio files from another source, you need to tag that audio file with descriptive information, such as the recording artist name and other details that can help identify that audio file for your smart playlists.

If you want to add (or edit) an audio track to give it more descriptive information, follow these steps:

1. Open iTunes.

2. Click the audio track that you want to tag with additional information.

3. Click the File menu and choose Get Info (File ➤ Get Info), or press Command+I to view all audio tracks stored in your iTunes library. A window displays tags for your chosen audio track, as shown in Figure 15-12.

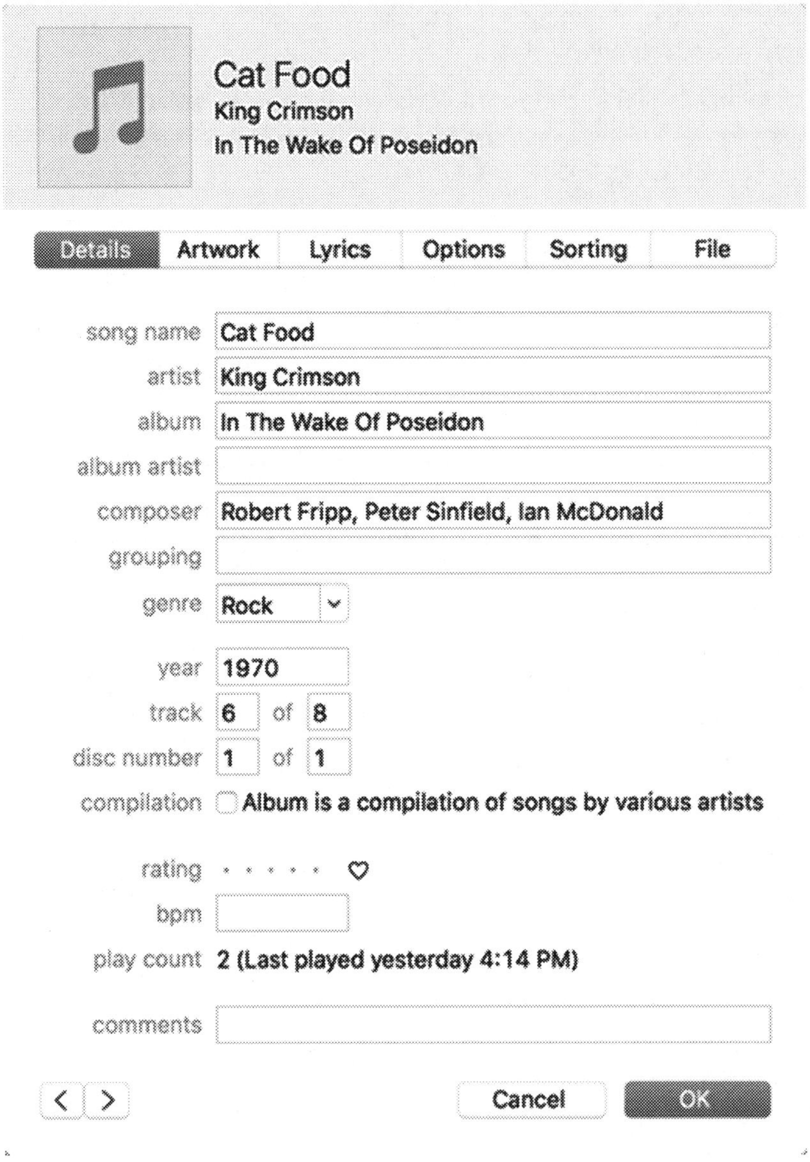

Cat Food
King Crimson
In The Wake Of Poseidon

| Details | Artwork | Lyrics | Options | Sorting | File |

song name Cat Food

artist King Crimson

album In The Wake Of Poseidon

album artist

composer Robert Fripp, Peter Sinfield, Ian McDonald

grouping

genre Rock

year 1970

track 6 of 8

disc number 1 of 1

compilation ◯ Album is a compilation of songs by various artists

rating · · · · · ♡

bpm

play count 2 (Last played yesterday 4:14 PM)

comments

‹ ›   Cancel   OK

Figure 15-12. Displaying information about an audio track

4.   Edit any information about your chosen audio track and click the OK
     button when you're done.

Once you've made sure that all of your audio tracks have descriptive information, you can
then use that information to create a smart playlist. When creating a smart playlist, you can
choose several options:

▪   Limit to: Lets you set a maximum limit to your smart playlist, such as the
     number of audio tracks it can contain, the time length of all audio tracks,
     or the file size of all audio tracks.

■ Match only checked items: Only selects audio tracks that are checked (in check box) in your Music library.

■ Live updating: Constantly adds or removes audio tracks from your smart playlist as you add new audio tracks to your iTunes library.

To create a smart playlist, follow these steps:

1. Open iTunes.

2. Click the File menu, choose New, and then choose Smart Playlist (File ➤ New ➤ Smart Playlist). A Smart Playlist window appears, as shown in Figure 15-13.

Figure 15-13. Creating a smart playlist

3. Make sure that the "Match the following rule" check box is selected, and then click the pop-up menu on the far left. A list of different options appears, as shown in Figure 15-14.

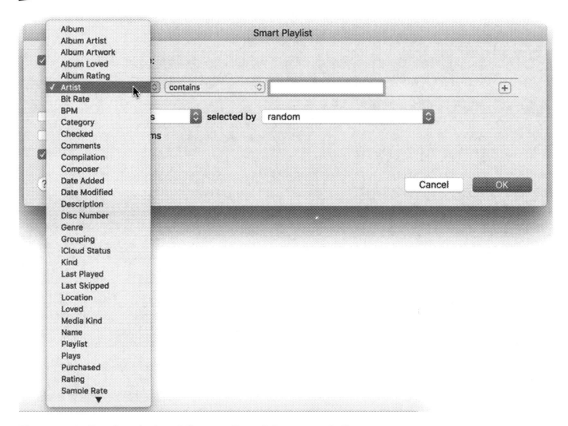

Figure 15-14. Choosing criteria to define an audio track for a smart playlist

4. Click the second pop-up menu to the right. Choose from varying options, such as "contains" or "is greater than".

5. Click in the text field and type a number or name, depending on the criteria that you chose in step 3.

6. (Optional) Click the plus sign (+) if you want to create additional rules and then repeat steps 3 to 5.

7. Select any additional options, such as "Live updating" or "Match only checked items".

8. Click the OK button. Your smart playlist appears in the left pane of the iTunes window.

Note iTunes comes with several smart playlists already defined, such as Recently Added, Recently Played, and Genius. The Genius smart playlist tries to include similar songs in your iTunes library along with suggesting new songs that you might enjoy.

Editing a Playlist

After you've created a playlist, you can always edit it at any time. For example, you might want to edit a smart playlist if it's choosing audio tracks you don't want. To edit a playlist, follow these steps:

1. Open iTunes.

2. In the left pane of the iTunes window, click the playlist that you want to edit.

3. Click the Edit Playlist button in the upper-right corner of the iTunes window. If you're editing a smart playlist, you can define or delete rules for choosing which audio tracks to add automatically. If you're editing a regular playlist, you can add or remove audio tracks manually.

Listening to a Playlist

Playlists are handy when you want to play certain types of audio tracks for long periods of time without any additional effort on your part. To listen to a playlist, follow these steps:

1. Open iTunes.

2. In the left pane of the iTunes window, click the playlist that you want to hear. Your chosen playlist appears in the right pane of the iTunes window.

3. Click the first audio track in the playlist that you want to hear. (It doesn't necessarily have to be the first audio track at the top of your playlist.)

4. (Optional) Click the Controls menu, choose Shuffle, and then choose On (Controls ➤ Shuffle ➤ On). Or, click the Shuffle icon (it looks like two crisscrossing arrows, as shown in Figure 15-15).

Figure 15-15. The Shuffle and Play icons

5. Click the Play button or press the spacebar to start listening to the audio tracks in your playlist.

When listening to a playlist, you have the following options listed under the Controls menu (see also Figure 15-16):

- Pause/Play: Press the spacebar to toggle between pausing and playing an audio track.
- Stop: Press Command+. (period) to stop playing the playlist.
- Next: Press Command+Right arrow to play the next song in the playlist.
- Previous: Press Command+Left arrow to play the previous song in the playlist.
- Shuffle: Toggles between playing your playlist in sequential order and choosing an audio track at random.
- Repeat: Repetitively plays a single audio track or all audio tracks in a playlist.

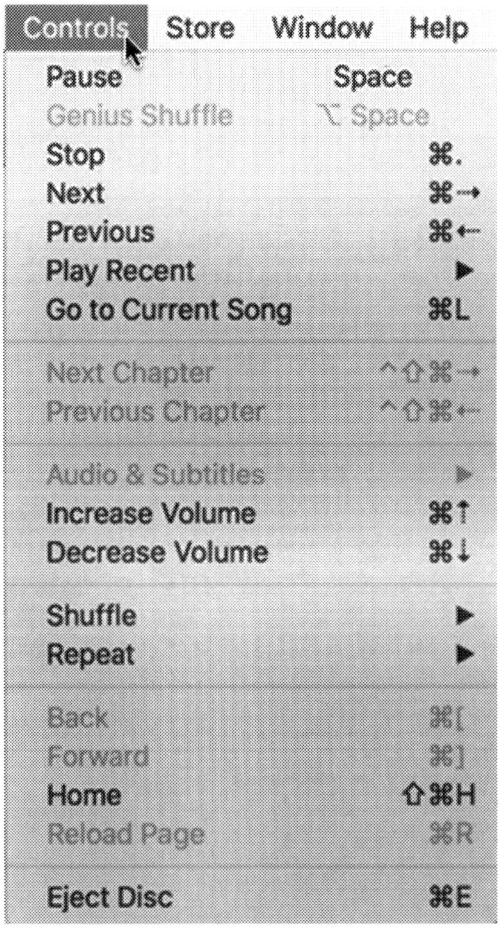

Figure 15-16. The Controls menu lists several options for playing audio tracks in a playlist

Deleting a Playlist

You can delete a playlist at any time. When you delete a playlist, you simply remove the list of audio tracks but you do not delete any of the audio tracks listed in the playlist.

To delete a playlist, follow these steps:

1. Open iTunes.

2. In the left pane of the iTunes window, click the playlist that you want to delete.

3. Click the Edit menu and choose Delete (Edit ➤ Delete). A dialog asks if you want to delete your chosen playlist.

4. Click the Delete button.

Listening to the Radio

Besides using iTunes to listen to your own music, you can also use iTunes to listen to the radio. Many radio stations around the world offer music, news, and information in multiple languages so that you can choose what you like.

There are two ways to listen to the radio in iTunes: Internet radio or Apple Music.

If you choose to listen to Internet radio, it will be free but finding a station can be difficult and the reliability of the broadcast may be uneven.

If you choose to listen to Apple Music, you can only listen to a handful of free stations. To hear other radio stations, you'll need to subscribe to Apple Music.

Listening to Internet Radio

Internet radio gives you the widest selection of available stations, but finding a station to listen to can be challenging. To listen to an Internet radio station, follow these steps:

1. Open iTunes.

2. Click the View menu, choose More, and then choose Internet Radio (or press Command+9). A list of Internet radio station categories appears, as shown in Figure 15-17.

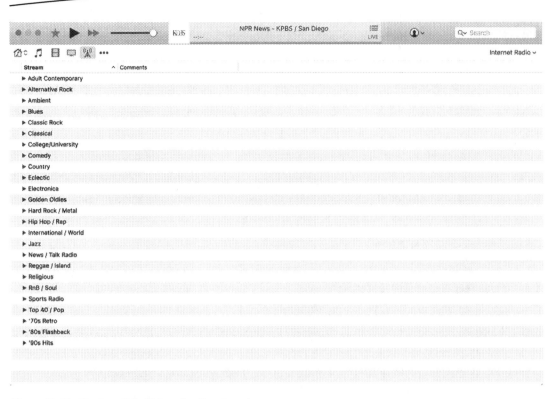

Figure 15-17. Viewing a list of Internet radio categories

3. Click the gray disclosure triangle that appears to the left of a category, such as Classic Rock or Jazz. A list of Internet stations appears, as shown in Figure 15-18.

4. Double-click a radio station to start listening to it.

Figure 15-18. Choosing from a list of Internet radio stations within a category

Listening to Apple Music Radio

Apple Music is a subscription that lets you stream audio. If you want to listen to all possible stations on Apple Music, you'll need to buy a subscription. However, there are a handful of free radio stations available on Apple Music.

To listen to the radio through Apple Music, follow these steps:

1. Open iTunes.

2. Click the View menu and choose Music (or press Command+1).

3. Click Radio in the top middle part of the iTunes window. A list of different types of radio stations appears, as shown in Figure 15-19.

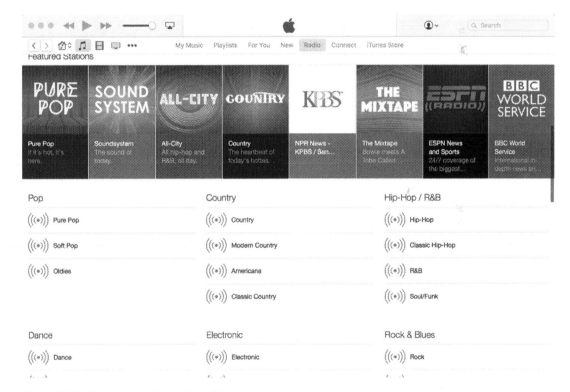

Figure 15-19. Choosing a radio station in iTunes

4. Double-click a radio station or category. Your chosen station starts to play.

Summary

You can play audio files in Quick Look, in the QuickTime Player, or in iTunes. For listening to a single audio file, Quick Look is the fastest and easiest method. For converting an audio file to make the file smaller, use the QuickTime Player.

For playing multiple audio files, use iTunes. With iTunes, you can create a playlist of multiple audio tracks, such as all songs from the same album, or all songs from a specific genre, such as country or jazz.

iTunes can create smart playlists that can automatically organize audio tracks based on criteria that you define, such as artist or genre. A playlist can play audio tracks sequentially or in random order. In addition, you can choose to repetitively play one or more audio tracks so you'll always have something to listen to.

Think of iTunes as your digital jukebox. You can listen to music or radio stations, so you'll never need to use a separate radio ever again.

Chapter 16

Reading e-Books

If you wanted to read a book in the old days, you had to buy a paper copy and lug it around with you wherever you went. If you wanted to read two or more books, you had to carry two or more books. That meant carrying around a lot of bulk and weight just on the off chance you would actually have time to do any reading.

Nowadays, you can load and carry thousands of books of all kinds as e-books. An e-book takes up a minimal amount of space and you can read it on your Mac whenever you want. If you have a laptop, you can read e-books while traveling.

The following are the most common e-book file formats:

- PDF
- ePub
- iBook

PDF (Portable Document Format) files essentially display static text and graphics that others can read but cannot modify.

ePub files are considered the standard for e-books and can be read by most e-book readers, such as the Kindle, Nook, and Kobo.

iBook is Apple's e-book file format that can only be read using the iBooks app on a Mac, iPhone, or iPad. You can download e-books, stored in the iBook format, by opening the iBooks program, clicking the Store menu, and choosing Store Home (Store ➤ Store Home). Although some e-books on the iBookstore are free, most cost money.

Reading an e-Book in a PDF

There are three ways to read a PDF file:

- Quick Look
- Preview
- iBook

© Wallace Wang 2016
W. Wang, *Mac OS X for Absolute Beginners*, DOI 10.1007/978-1-4842-1913-3_16

To use Quick Look to open a PDF file, follow these steps:

1. Click the Finder icon on the dock. A Finder window appears.

2. Click the PDF file that you want to read.

3. Do one of the following to open the Quick Look window (also see Figure 16-1):

   a. Press the spacebar.

   b. Press Command+Y.

   c. Click the File menu and choose Quick Look (File ➤ Quick Look).

   d. Right-click the PDF file, and when a pop-up menu appears, choose Quick Look.

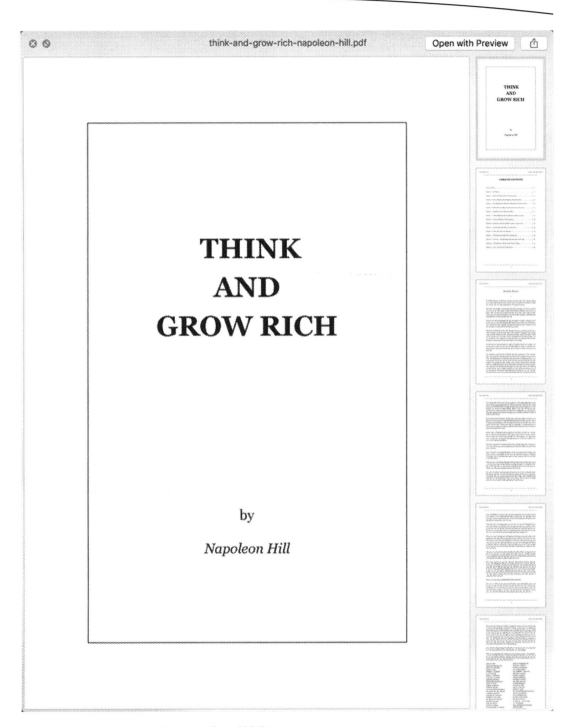

Figure 16-1. The Quick Look window reading a PDF file

4. (Optional) Click the thumbnails on the right to quickly jump to a specific page.

5. Click the close button (the X) in the upper-left corner of the Quick Look window when you're done reading the PDF file.

Reading a PDF File with the Preview Program

Every Mac comes with the Preview program, which opens and displays graphic files (such as JPG or PNG) along with PDF files. The Preview program is more convenient than Quick Look when you want to read, copy, or even mark up a PDF file.

To read a PDF file with the Preview program, follow these steps:

1. Click the Finder icon on the dock. A Finder window opens.

2. Right-click the PDF file that you want to read. A pop-up menu appears.

3. Choose Open With and then choose Preview, as shown in Figure 16-2. The Preview program loads your chosen PDF file.

> **Note**   You can also start the Preview program and then choose File ➤ Open to open the PDF file that you want to read in the Preview program.

Figure 16-2. Opening a PDF file in the Preview program

Once you open a PDF file in the Preview program, you can modify how the pages look, how to navigate around, and even how to modify the file to add comments or your own signature, which is handy for filling out legal documents.

Note   Adobe gives away a free PDF reader program called Adobe Reader, which is the main program for opening PDF files on Windows and Linux PCs. You can download and install Adobe Reader on your Mac if you wish, but it's usually easier just to use the Preview program to open PDF files on a Mac.

Viewing PDF Files

The Preview program gives you several ways to view PDF files, depending on your personal preference.

- Zoom: Magnifies or shrinks text on the screen
- Scroll: Defines how the Preview program displays pages on the screen
- Navigation: Provides different ways to jump to different parts of a PDF file
- Markup: Provides tools for adding comments or notes to a PDF file

To shrink or enlarge text in a PDF file within the Preview program, follow these steps:

1. Open a PDF file within the Preview program.

2. Click the View menu and choose Zoom In/Zoom Out (Command+ to zoom in, Command– to zoom out). If you have a trackpad, you can also pinch two fingers to zoom in and out.

> **Note**   If you click the View menu and choose Actual Size (View ➤ Actual Size), you can quickly return a page to its original magnification.

Changing How to Scroll Pages

There are three options for scrolling through a PDF file:

- Continuous Scroll: Smoothly and continuously scrolls through the pages of the file
- Single Page: Discretely scrolls through the pages so that you can easily see where each page begins and ends
- Two Pages: Displays two pages side by side like an open book

To change how the Preview program scrolls through a PDF file, follow these steps:

1. Open a PDF file within the Preview program.

2. Click the View menu and choose one of the following:
   a. Continuous Scroll (or press Command+1)
   b. Single Page (or press Command+2)
   c. Two Pages (or press Command+3)

You can also view a PDF file as a slideshow or in full screen. Both options display the pages to fill the entire screen. As a slideshow, Back, Forward, Play/Pause, and Close buttons appear at the bottom of the screen, as shown in Figure 16-3.

Figure 16-3. *The Back, Forward, and Play/Pause buttons appear in Slideshow view*

The Play/Pause button toggles between automatically going to the next page and pausing. The Back button returns to the previous page. The Forward button jumps to the next page. The Close button exits out of the Slideshow view.

Full Screen mode fills the contents of the PDF file on the screen but lets you manually advance or reverse the pages by pressing the left or right arrow keys.

To switch to Slideshow or Full Screen mode, follow these steps:

1. Open a PDF file within the Preview program.

2. Click the View menu and choose one of the following:

   a. Slideshow

   b. Enter Full Screen

3. To exit out of Slideshow mode, click the Close button (see Figure 16-3). To exit out of Full Screen mode, press the Esc key on the keyboard.

Slideshow mode is best for turning a PDF file into a presentation. Full Screen mode is best for viewing the pages of a PDF file without the distraction of other windows on the screen.

Navigating Through a PDF File

If a PDF file contains multiple pages, you may find it difficult to continuously scroll up or down through the entire PDF file. To make navigation easier through a large PDF file, the Preview program offers two features:

▧ Thumbnails: Displays shrunken images of each page in the left pane of the Preview window

▧ Contact Sheet: Displays miniature images of each page across the entire screen

With thumbnails, you can scroll up or down the thumbnail list. When you find the page that you want to read, click it to view that page, as shown in Figure 16-4.

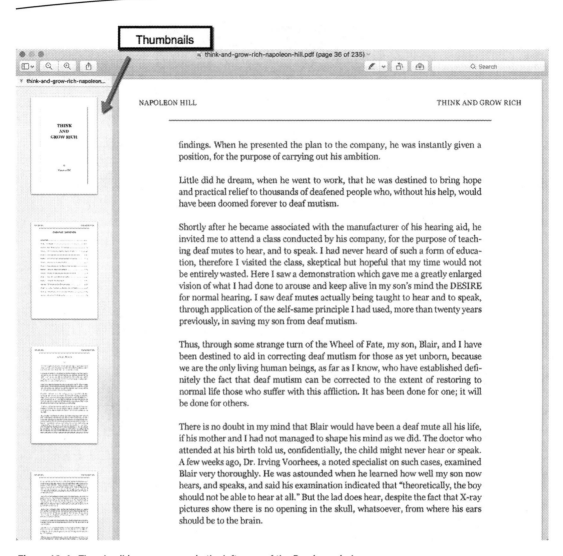

Figure 16-4. *Thumbnail images appear in the left pane of the Preview window*

A contact sheet lets you view several PDF pages as tiny thumbnail images that fill the screen. Click the page that you want to view, as shown in Figure 16-5.

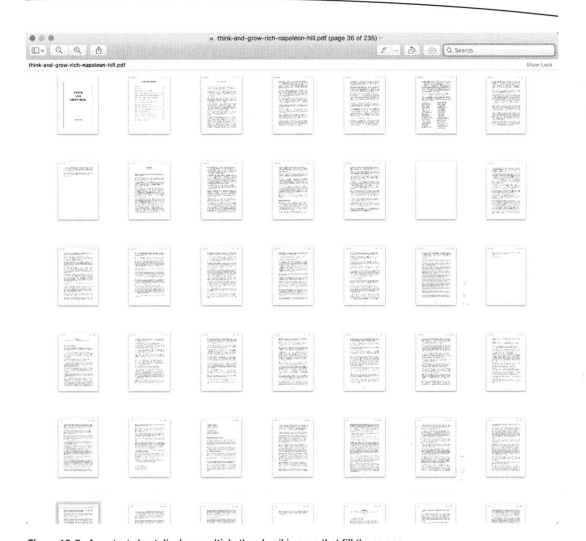

Figure 16-5. A contact sheet displays multiple thumbnail images that fill the screen

To display either thumbnails or a contact sheet, follow these steps:

1. Open a PDF file within the Preview program.

2. Click the View menu and choose one of the following:

   a. Thumbnails

   b. Contact Sheet

3. Click the thumbnail image of the page that you want to go to.

Using Bookmarks

You mark your place in a printed book by inserting a bookmark between two pages. If you're reading a PDF file, you can place a bookmark a page to quickly jump to it later. More than one page can be bookmarked.

You can do three things with bookmarks:

* Place a bookmark

* Jump to a bookmarked page

* Delete a bookmark when it's no longer needed

To place a bookmark, follow these steps:

1. Open a PDF file within the Preview program.

2. Navigate to the page that you want to place a bookmark.

3. Click the Tools menu and choose Add Bookmark (Tools ➤ Add Bookmark) or press Command+D. A red bookmark appears in the upper-right corner of the page.

4. Repeat steps 2 and 3 as often as you wish to place multiple bookmarks throughout a PDF file.

Once you've placed one or more bookmarks in a PDF file, you can jump to a specific page that you have bookmarked by following these steps:

1. Using the Preview program, open a PDF file that contains bookmarks.

2. Click the View menu and choose Bookmarks (View ➤ Bookmarks). The list of bookmarks appears in the left pane, as shown in Figure 16-6.

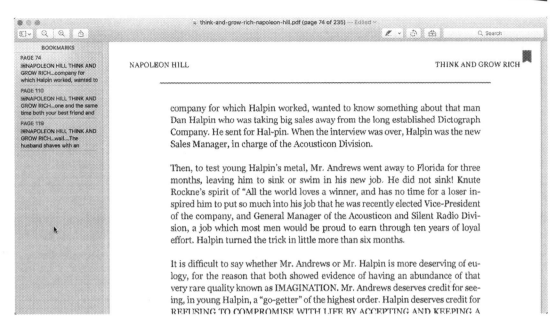

Figure 16-6. The bookmark pane appears in the left side of the Preview window

3. Click any bookmark in the left pane to jump to that specific page in the PDF file.

To delete a bookmark, follow these steps:

1. Using the Preview program, open a PDF file that contains bookmarks.

2. Click the View menu and choose Bookmarks (View ➤ Bookmarks). The list of bookmarks appears in the left pane (see Figure 16-6).

3. In the Bookmarks pane, right-click over the bookmark that you want to delete. A pop-up menu displays the Delete command.

4. Click Delete.

> **Note** When you delete a bookmark, you don't physically delete any pages in the PDF file.

Reading PDF, ePub, and iBook Files

The Preview program can only let you read PDF files. If you want to read ePub or iBook files, you'll have to use the iBooks program. iBooks can also let you read PDF files too so that you can use iBooks for all of your e-book reading needs.

To read PDF, ePub, or iBook files, you must first load them into the iBooks program. To store an e-book file in iBooks, follow these steps:

1.   Open the iBooks program.

2.   Click the File menu and choose Add to Library (File ➤ Add to Library). A dialog appears.

3.   Click the e-book file that you want to add to iBooks and click the Add button.

Finding e-Books in iBooks

Once you've loaded e-book files into iBooks, the next problem is finding them again. When you have a regular bookshelf holding printed books, you must browse through all of your books until you find the one you want. With iBooks, you can browse through your book collection or search by author, category, or title.

iBooks offers several categories to help sort and organize your e-books:

▓   All Books: Displays the cover art of all e-books in iBooks

▓   Collections: Organizes e-books into groups, such as PDF files or science fiction e-books

▓   Authors: Displays a list of author names in the left pane of the iBooks window

▓   Categories: Displays a list of book genre categories in the left pane of the iBooks window

▓   List: Lists the titles of all e-books in iBooks

To view the different categories in iBooks, follow these steps:

1.   Open the iBooks program.

2.   Click a category near the top of the iBooks window, such as Authors or List, as shown in Figure 16-7.

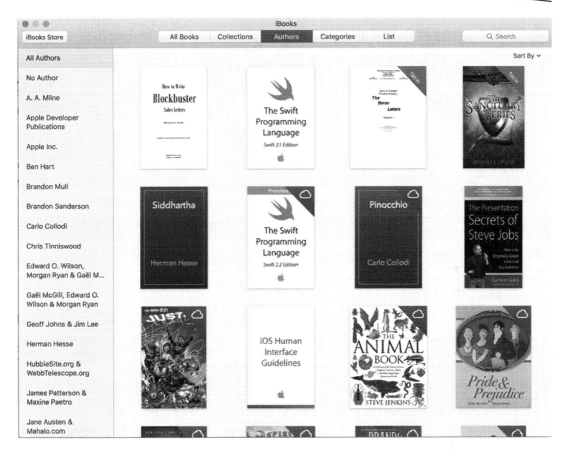

Figure 16-7. *Categories for organizing iBooks*

3. Click the e-book that you want to read.

Making e-Book Collections

iBooks provides a collection for PDF files and another for ePub and iBook files. However, you might want to create collections to organize your e-books in any way that you wish, such as your favorites.

To create your own e-book collection in iBook, follow these steps:

1. Open the iBooks program.

2. Click the File menu and choose New Collection (File ➤ New Collection), or press Command+N. iBooks creates a new collection in the left pane, as shown in Figure 16-8.

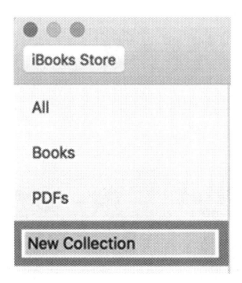

Figure 16-8. Creating a new e-book collection in iBooks

3. Type a descriptive name for your new collection and press Return.

Once you've created a collection, you can store e-books in it. To add e-books to a collection in iBook, follow these steps:

1. Open the iBooks program.

2. Click the All Books category near the top of the iBooks window.

3. Click the e-book that you want to store in your collection.

4. Click the File menu and choose Add to Collection (File ➤ Add to Collection). A submenu pops up, listing all the collections that you've created.

5. Choose the name of the collection in which you want to store the e-book.

You may eventually want to delete a collection. When you delete a collection, you have the option of just deleting the collection (and preserving all e-books inside that collection) or deleting the collection and all the e-books inside it.

To delete a collection, follow these steps:

1. Open the iBooks program.

2. Click the Collections category near the top of the iBooks window. A list of collections appears in the left pane.

3. Click the collection that you want to delete.

4. Click the Edit menu and choose Delete (Edit ➤ Delete). A dialog asks if you want to delete just the collection or the collection along with all e-books stored in it, as shown in Figure 16-9.

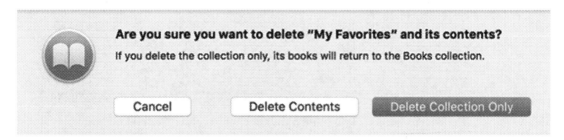

Are you sure you want to delete "My Favorites" and its contents?

If you delete the collection only, its books will return to the Books collection.

Cancel   Delete Contents   Delete Collection Only

Figure 16-9. Deleting a collection in iBooks

5. Click the Delete Collection Only button (or click the Delete Contents button if you also want to delete all the e-books inside it).

Reading e-Books in iBooks

Once you've saved an e-book inside the iBooks program, you can read them. Depending on the type of e-book you want to read (PDF, ePub, or iBooks file), you have different options for reading the e-book.

When you choose to read a PDF file in iBooks, the iBooks program opens the PDF file using the Preview program, which was explained earlier in this chapter.

When you open an ePub or iBook file in iBooks, you can scroll through the pages by pressing the left/right arrow keys or swiping left/right across your mouse or trackpad. To make it easy to read an e-book, you can navigate to particular pages by using the table of contents or bookmarks.

Viewing a Table of Contents

Almost all ePub and iBooks files offer a table of contents. By opening it, you not only see the number of sections that the e-book contains, but you can also click a chapter name or number to immediately jump to it.

To use the table of contents in an ePub or iBooks file, follow these steps:

1. Open the iBooks program.

2. Open the ePub or iBooks file that you want to read.

3. Click the Table of Contents icon (three horizontal lines that appear in the upper-left corner of the iBooks window), as shown in Figure 16-10.

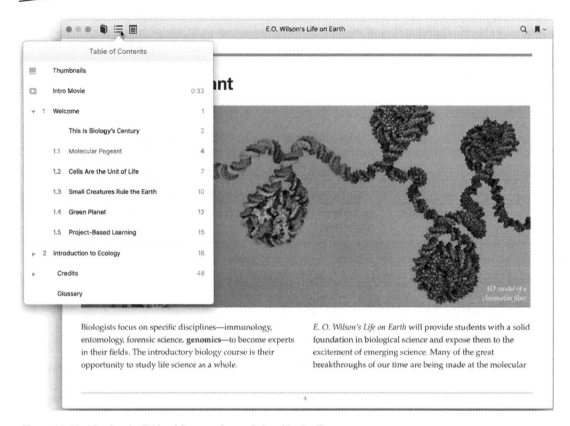

Figure 16-10. Viewing the Table of Contents in an ePub or iBooks file

4.   Click a chapter name or number to jump to it in the e-book.

Using Bookmarks

Bookmarks also aid you in reading ePub and iBook files. You can place as many bookmarks as you wish and remove them at any time. To place a bookmark, follow these steps:

1.   Open the iBooks program.

2.   Open the ePub or iBooks file that you want to read.

3.   Open the page that you want to place a bookmark.

4.   Click the Edit menu and choose Add Bookmark (Edit ➤ Add Bookmark) or press Command+D. iBooks places a red bookmark in the upper-right corner of the page.

Once you've placed one or more bookmarks in an ePub or iBooks file, you can jump to a bookmarked page by following these steps:

1. Open the iBooks program.

2. Open the ePub or iBooks file that you want to read.

3. Click the View Bookmarks icon that appears in the upper-right corner of the iBooks window, as shown in Figure 16-11. A list of bookmarks appears.

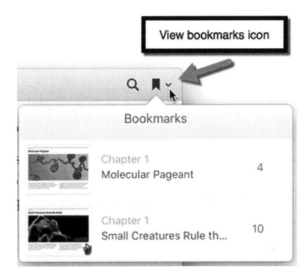

Figure 16-11. The View Bookmarks icon lists all bookmarks in an e-book

4. Click the bookmark that you want to view. iBooks jumps to that bookmarked page.

You can remove a bookmark when you no longer need it in one three ways. The first step is to go to the page with the bookmark, and then do one of the following:

▪ Click the Edit menu and choose Remove Bookmark (Edit ➤ Remove Bookmark)

▪ Press Command+D

▪ Click the red bookmark icon in the upper-right corner of the iBooks window

Deleting e-Books

Each time that you add another e-book to iBooks, it takes up space. Eventually, you may want to remove an e-book from your iBooks library. When you delete an e-book, you're physically removing it from your Mac but retaining a copy in iCloud. You can always reinstall it back into iBooks later.

To delete an e-book from iBooks, follow these steps:

1. Open the iBooks program.

2. Click the e-book you want to remove from iBooks.

3. Click the Edit menu and choose Delete (Edit ➤ Delete), or right-click an e-book and choose Delete. A message asks if you want to delete the e-book and retain a copy on iCloud, as shown in Figure 16-12.

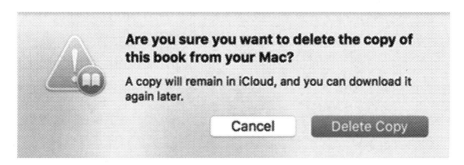

Are you sure you want to delete the copy of this book from your Mac?

A copy will remain in iCloud, and you can download it again later.

Cancel   Delete Copy

Figure 16-12. Deleting an e-book

4. Click the Delete Copy button.

Summary

Since a single e-book takes up so little space, you can store many e-books on your Mac so that you'll always have something to read. An e-book may be stored in a PDF, ePub, or iBook file. If you have a PDF file, you can read it using the Preview program. If you have an ePub or iBook file, you can read it in the iBooks program.

> **Note**   As an alternative to using the iBooks program to read ePub files, you can also download Amazon's free Kindle program or Barnes & Noble's free Nook program. Both programs can open and read ePub files while also letting you shop for more e-books through the Kindle or Nook bookstore.

Two common ways to navigate through any e-book is through the table of contents and bookmarks. Not all e-book files (especially PDF files) contain a table of contents but by viewing a table of contents, you can click a chapter name or number to jump to it.

Another way to navigate through an e-book is through bookmarks. By placing a bookmark, you can save your place or mark a page that you want to reference later. You can view a list of your bookmarks and jump to that page later.

Quick Look is handy for viewing PDF files, but if you want to read long PDF files, you should use the Preview program. For reading ePub or iBooks files, you'll need to use the iBooks program.

Part IV

Getting on the Internet

Back in the old days, every computer was isolated from everyone else. Fortunately, those primitive dark ages of computing are over because now almost everyone's computer can connect with anyone else in the world through the magic of the Internet.

In this part of the book, you'll learn how to connect your Macintosh to the Internet. Once you're connected to the Internet, you can send and receive e-mail to and from people all over the world, explore the world by visiting web sites, chat with your friends and family members through text messages, and see and talk to others using video and audio.

Perhaps the most important advantage of the Internet isn't communicating with other people, but in protecting your data through the magic of iCloud. With iCloud, you can back up your data to the Internet and retrieve it from any device, such as an iPhone or iPad.

The Internet can be the gateway to making your Macintosh even more fun and productive than ever before.

Chapter 17

Browsing the Internet

Back in the old days, you had to read a newspaper or a magazine, listen to the radio, or watch TV to get the latest news. Today, you can get the latest news, often within minutes of it happening, right on your Mac.

The secret to accessing information all over the world lies with the Internet. By connecting to the Internet, you can access a wealth of information that rivals anything your library could offer.

To access the Internet, you need to use a special program called a *browser*. OS X comes with a browser called Safari, which lets you browse web sites on the Internet.

> **Note** Safari is the default browser for OS X but you can always install and use another browser, such as Chrome or Firefox, since all browsers work in similar ways.

Connecting to the Internet

In addition to a browser such as Safari, you also need an Internet connection. Two ways to connect to the Internet are through an Ethernet cable that physically plugs into your Mac (MacBook models require a special adapter because they don't have an Ethernet port) or through Wi-Fi, which doesn't require any wires at all.

An Ethernet connection is the most secure and reliable way to connect to the Internet, but is mostly useful only for desktop computers that don't need to be moved.

Wi-Fi connections are less secure and reliable than Ethernet, but far simpler to use, especially for laptops that may not have an Ethernet port. Wi-Fi is often available at public places such libraries, coffee shops, or airport terminals.

To make sure that you have an Internet connection, follow these steps:

1.   Click the Apple icon on the menu bar. A pull-down menu appears.

2.   Choose System Preferences. A System Preferences window appears.

3.   Click the Network icon. The Network window appears, as shown in Figure 17-1. If a green dot appears to the left of Ethernet or Wi-Fi, you're connected to the Internet.

Figure 17-1. The Network window identifies if you have an Internet connection

4. (Optional) Click Ethernet and click the "Assist me" button to get help connecting to the Internet through an Ethernet cable.

5. Click Wi-Fi. The Network window displays Wi-Fi options, as shown in Figure 17-2.

Figure 17-2. *Connecting to a Wi-Fi network*

6. Click the Network Name pop-up menu and choose a Wi-Fi network to join. A dialog asks for the Wi-Fi password, as shown in Figure 17-3.

Figure 17-3. You must enter a password to access most Wi-Fi networks

7. Type a password and click the Join button. (If you select the "Show password" check box, you'll be able to see the password you typed. Otherwise, the password appears as dots to prevent anyone from peeking over your shoulder to spot the password. If you select the "Remember this network" check box, you won't have to type the password again to access this Wi-Fi network.)

8. Click the close button (the red dot) in the upper-left corner of the System Preferences window to make it go away.

Defining a Default Browser

Safari is the default browser for OS X. However, if you have installed other browsers such as Chrome or Firefox, you may want to use those browsers instead. To define a default browser for your Mac, follow these steps:

1. Click the Apple menu on the menu bar. A pull-down menu appears.

2. Click System Preferences. A System Preferences window appears.

3. Click the General icon. The General window appears, as shown in Figure 17-4.

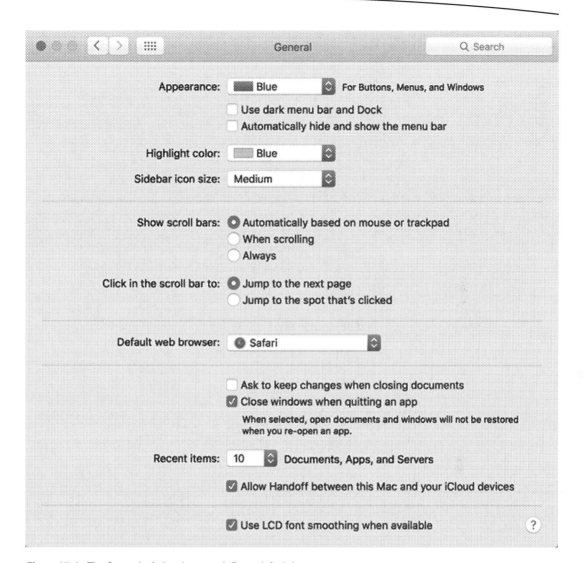

Figure 17-4. The General window lets you define a default browser

4. Click the Default web browser pop-up menu and choose a browser such as Safari. If you have installed other browsers on your Mac such as Chrome or Firefox, you can choose one of those browsers instead.

5. Click the red dot (the close button) in the upper-left corner of the General window to make it go away.

Visiting Web Sites

The main purpose of a browser, such as Safari, is to let you view web sites anywhere on the Internet. Two common ways to find a web site is to enter the web site address (such as www.apple.com) or type a search query such as looking for all web sites that contain information about "Apple computers".

In general, searching for a web site is easier because you just type one or more keywords that you want to find such as "Apple" and "Mac".

Typing a web site address means knowing the exact web site address you want to find and spelling it correctly. If you misspell a web site address, you won't find the web site that you want. The advantage of typing a web site address is that it gets you directly to the web site that you want to view.

> **Note**   Be especially careful when typing a web site address. Malicious hackers often create web sites with domain addresses that match commonly misspelled web site addresses. If you visit a malicious web site, it could lock up your browser and try to install malware on your computer.

To visit a web site by typing its address, follow these steps:

1.   Open the Safari program.

2.   Click in the Search text field at the top center of the Safari window, as shown in Figure 17-5.

Figure 17-5.   The Search text field appears at the top center of the Safari window

3.   Type a web site address (such as www.apress.com) or type a search query (such as "books on OS X") and press Return. Safari displays the web site at the address that you specified or a list of web sites that match your search query ("books on OS X").

> **Note**   When typing a search query, use as many words as possible to avoid finding web sites containing irrelevant information. So rather than just search for "Apple", search for "Apple Mac" or "Apple Mac refurbished" to find more web sites that exactly match your search criteria.

Defining a Default Search Engine

When you type a search query, Safari sends your query to its default search engine, which is Google. If you want, you can choose a different search engine.

Since Google tracks your search queries (so they know which Google ads to show you), some people prefer DuckDuckGo as their search engine since they don't track your search queries like Google does.

Baidu is the most popular search engine in Asia so if you search Asian web sites frequently, you may want to switch to Baidu instead. If for some reason you simply don't like the results Google consistently provides, you can try switching to Yahoo! or Bing.

> **Note** If you define a default search engine for Safari, this won't change the default search engine for any other browsers you may have installed on your Mac, such as Chrome or Firefox.

To define a default search engine for Safari, follow these steps:

1. Open the Safari program.

2. Click the Safari menu and choose Preferences. A Preferences window appears.

3. Click the Search icon. The Search window appears.

4. Click the Search engine pop-up menu and choose a search engine, such as Yahoo! or DuckDuckGo, as shown in Figure 17-6.

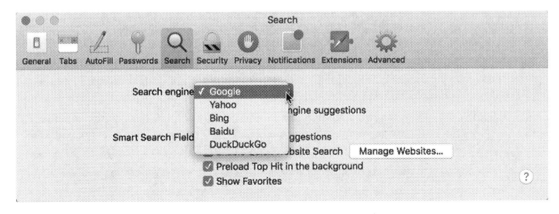

Figure 17-6. The Search text field appears at the top center of the Safari window

5. Click the red dot (the close button) in the upper-left corner of the Search window to make it go away.

Opening Multiple Web Sites

When you first start Safari, you can open and view a single web site. If you want to view another web site, the new web site appears and your previously viewed web site disappears.

In some cases, this might be what you want, but if you want to keep a web site visible while looking at more web sites at the same time, you may need to open additional web sites inside of multiple windows or tabs.

When you open multiple windows, you can arrange the windows on the screen so that you can view them side by side. However, multiple windows can clutter your screen so another alternative is to open multiple web sites as separate tabs inside a single window, as shown in Figure 17-7.

Figure 17-7. Multiple tabs let you view several web sites within a single window

Opening a Web Site in Another Window

To open another web site in a separate window, follow these steps:

1. Open the Safari program.

2. Click the File menu and choose New Window (or press Command+N). Safari displays another window.

3. Click in the Search text field in the new Safari window. Type a web site address or a search query and then press Return.

4. Click the red dot (the close button) in the upper-left corner of the Safari window when you're done using it.

Opening a Web Site in a Tab

Multiple windows make it easy to view two or more web sites side by side. However, if you don't need to view two or more web sites at the same time, you can open multiple web sites in tabs.

Tabs appear in a single window so they take up less space and make it easy to quickly switch from one web site to another. If you want, you can even open multiple windows where each window has two or more tabs.

To open a web site in a tab, follow these steps:

1. Open the Safari program.

2. Create a new tab by choosing one of the following:

    a. Click the "Add new tab" button (it looks like a +) (see Figure 17-7).

    b. Click the File menu and choose New Tab (File ➤ New Tab).

    c. Press Command+T.

3. Click in the Search text field in the new Safari tab. Type a web site address or search query and press Return.

4. When you're done with a tab, move the pointer over the tab so a close button (an X) appears to the left of that tab, as shown in Figure 17-8.

Figure 17-8. A close button appears to the left of a tab when you move the pointer over that tab

5. Click the close button on a tab that you want to close. The tab disappears.

Defining Default Web Sites for New Windows and Tabs

Each time you open another web site in a separate window or tab, Safari displays a default web page. Initially this default web page is your list of Favorite web sites, but you can define a new default web page for both new windows and tabs by following these steps:

1. Open the Safari program.

2. Click the Safari menu and choose Preferences (Safari ➤ Preferences). A Preferences window appears.

3. Click the General tab. The General window appears, as shown in Figure 17-9.

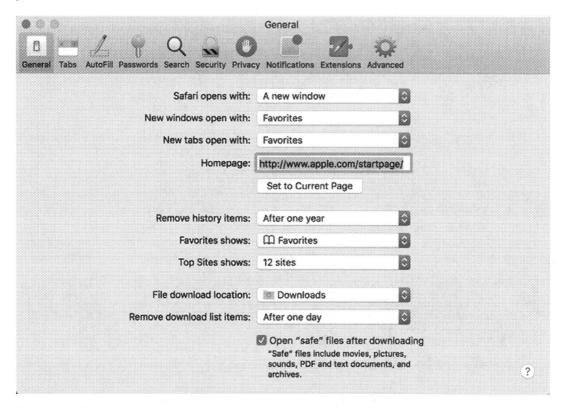

Figure 17-9. The General window lets you define default web pages for new windows and tabs

4. Click in the New windows open with: pop-up menu and choose an option.

5. Click in the New tabs open with: pop-up menu and choose an option.

6. Click the red dot (the close button) in the upper-left corner of the General window to make it go away.

Turning Tabs into Multiple Windows (and vice versa)

If you open another web site in a separate window, you can always merge all open Safari windows into one and display those web sites as tabs within a single Safari window.

Likewise, if you open multiple web sites in separate tabs, you can always display those tabs as different windows instead. By switching between multiple windows and tabs, you can view your web sites the way you like best.

To merge multiple Safari windows into tabs, follow these steps:

1. Open two or more separate windows in Safari.

2. Click the Window menu and choose Merge All Windows, as shown in Figure 17-10. Safari closes all open Safari windows and displays them as tabs in a single window.

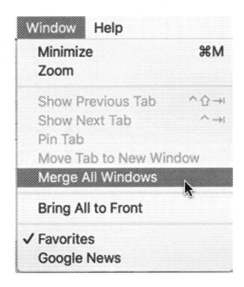

Figure 17-10. *The Merge All Windows command turns multiple windows into tabs*

To display a Safari tab as a separate window, follow these steps:

1. Open a window in Safari that displays two or more tabs.

2. Click the tab that you want to display as a separate window.

3. Click the Window menu and choose Move Tab to New Window (Windows ➤ Move Tab to New Window) (see Figure 17-10). Safari displays your chosen tab in a separate window.

For each tab that you want to display in a separate window, you'll have to repeat steps 2 and 3.

Going Back to Previously Viewed Web Sites

Browsing the Internet encourages you to explore by clicking various links to see something new. The problem is that as you explore the Internet, you may want to return to a previous web site that you recently looked at.

Fortunately, Safari offers two ways to go back to previous viewed web sites:

▓   Use the Show the previous page and "Show the next page" buttons

▓   Use the History menu

The "Show the previous page" and "Show the next page" buttons appear in the upper-left corner of the Safari window, as shown in Figure 17-11.

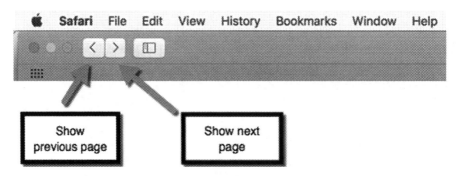

Figure 17-11. The "Show the previous" page and "Show the next page" buttons

Each time that you click a web page link that displays a new web page, you can go back to the previous web page by clicking the "Show previous page" button.

Suppose you visit a financial web page and then visit an animal web page. With the animal web page displayed, clicking the "Show previous page" button returns you to the financial web page. Clicking the "Show next page" button displays the animal web page again.

Essentially, the "Show previous page" and "Show next page" buttons let you go back one web page at a time to what you previously viewed. Until you go back at least one web page, the "Show next page" button remains dimmed and unavailable.

As an alternative to clicking the "Show previous page" and "Show next page" buttons, you can also do one of the following:

▓   Click the History menu and choose Back or Forward

▓   Press Command+[to choose the Back command, or press Command+]
     to choose the Forward command

Going back and forth one web page at a time is slow. If you want to go back to a web site that you viewed earlier in the day but browsed through dozens of other web sites since then, going back one web page at a time is clumsy. A faster alternative is to view your browsing history.

Each time you visit a web site, Safari keeps track of the site in its history list. By viewing this history list, you can see a list of previously visited web sites and just click the one that you want to return to.

To use Safari's history list, follow these steps:

1.   Start Safari and browse different web sites.

2.   Click the History menu. A list of previously viewed web sites appears,
      as shown in Figure 17-12.

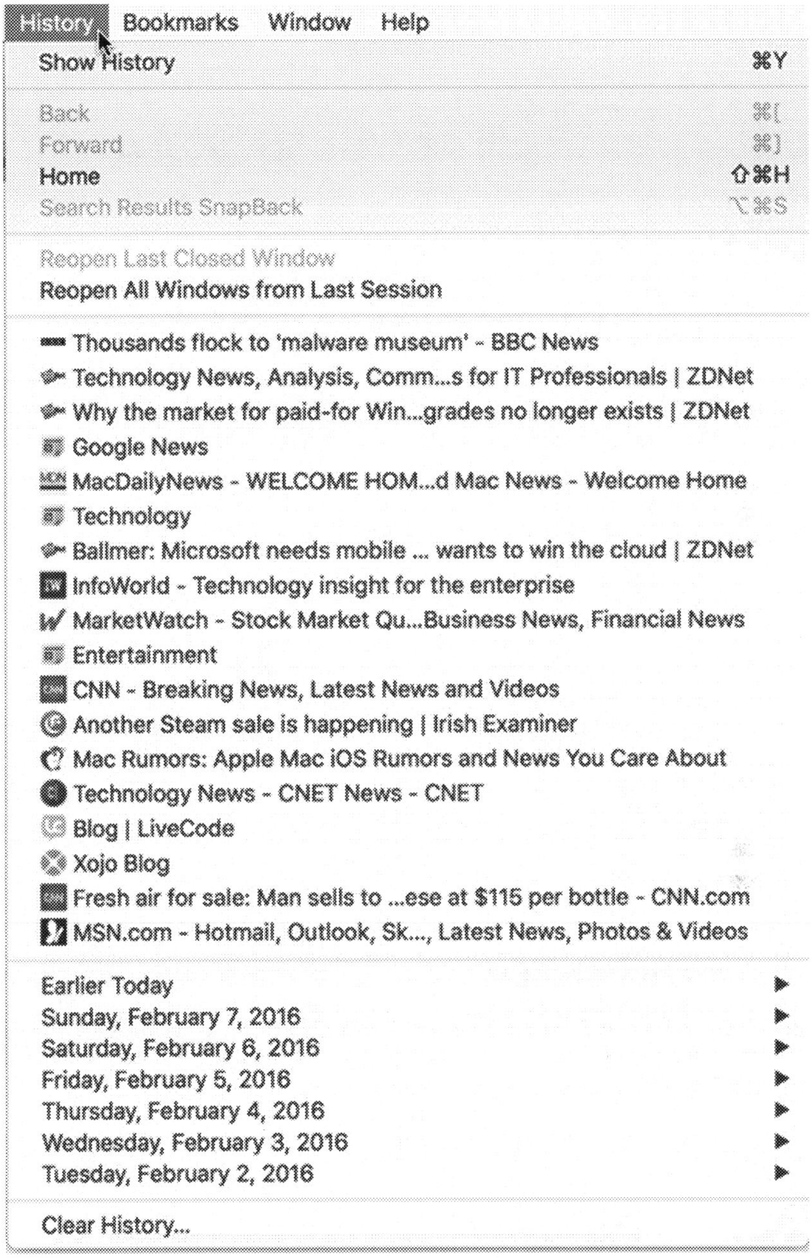
History
Bookmarks
Window
Help
Show History ⌘Y
Back ⌘[
Forward ⌘]
Home ⇧⌘H
Search Results SnapBack ⌥⌘S
Reopen Last Closed Window
Reopen All Windows from Last Session
Thousands flock to 'malware museum' - BBC News
Technology News, Analysis, Comm...s for IT Professionals | ZDNet
Why the market for paid-for Win...grades no longer exists | ZDNet
Google News
MacDailyNews - WELCOME HOM...d Mac News - Welcome Home
Technology
Ballmer: Microsoft needs mobile ... wants to win the cloud | ZDNet
InfoWorld - Technology insight for the enterprise
MarketWatch - Stock Market Qu...Business News, Financial News
Entertainment
CNN - Breaking News, Latest News and Videos
Another Steam sale is happening | Irish Examiner
Mac Rumors: Apple Mac iOS Rumors and News You Care About
Technology News - CNET News - CNET
Blog | LiveCode
Xojo Blog
Fresh air for sale: Man sells to ...ese at $115 per bottle - CNN.com
MSN.com - Hotmail, Outlook, Sk..., Latest News, Photos & Videos
Earlier Today
Sunday, February 7, 2016
Saturday, February 6, 2016
Friday, February 5, 2016
Thursday, February 4, 2016
Wednesday, February 3, 2016
Tuesday, February 2, 2016
Clear History...

***Figure 17-12.** The History menu lists previously viewed web sites*

3. Click a web site that appears in the History menu list.

Another way to use Safari's history list is to do one of the following:

- Click the History menu and choose Show History (History ➤ Show History)
- Press Command+Y

When you choose one of these two methods, Safari displays a detailed history list that displays the actual web site address in addition to the web site name, as shown in Figure 17-13.

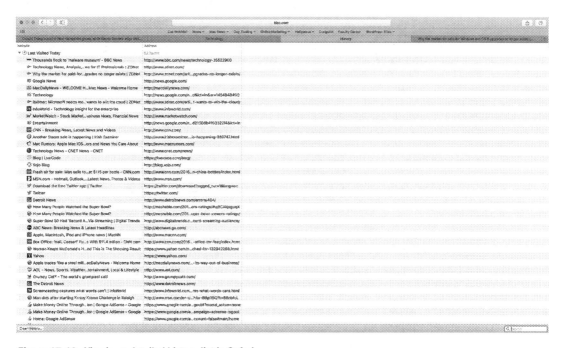

Figure 17-13. Viewing a detailed history list in Safari

To close this detailed history list, just press Command+Y or click the History menu and choose Hide History.

Protecting Your Privacy

One drawback of storing your browsing history is that you may not want anyone else to see which web sites you may have visited. Since you can't always keep people from away from your Mac, you can protect your privacy in two ways.

First, you can erase your browsing history. Second, you can use a special private browsing feature of Safari.

The drawback of erasing your browsing history is that you may delete a web site that you may want to visit later. If you use the private browsing feature of Safari, you can never go back to previously viewed web sites since Safari won't keep track of them.

When you erase your history, you have a choice of four options:

■   The last hour

■   Today

■   Today and yesterday

■   All history

Erasing Your Browsing History

To erase your history, follow these steps:

1. Start Safari.

2. Click the History menu and choose Clear History (History ➤ Clear History). A dialog asks how much of your browsing history you want to delete, as shown in Figure 17-14.

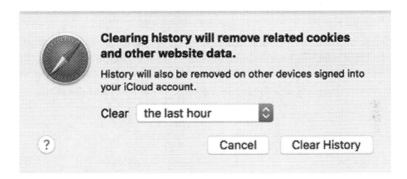

Figure 17-14. Deleting your browsing history in Safari

3. Click the Clear pop-up menu and choose how far back you want to delete your history, such as today or the last hour.

4. Click the Clear History button.

Because Safari originally saved your browser history, erasing it simply removes it from Safari but does not delete it from your hard disk. That means it's still possible to retrieve your browser history using special forensics tools.

If you really want to protect your privacy, use Safari's private browsing feature. This doesn't save any of your browsing history, so it's impossible to retrieve it later.

To use private browsing, click the File menu and choose New Private Window (File ➤ New Private Window), or press Shift+Command+N. Safari lets you know you're in a private browsing window by displaying the search text field with a dark background and by displaying a message near the top of the window, as shown in Figure 17-15.

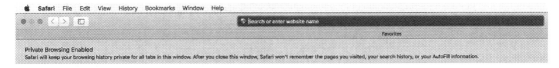

Figure 17-15. Viewing a private browsing window

A private browsing window lets you create additional tabs as well where each tab also lets you browse privately without saving your history. When you're done with a private browsing window, click the red dot (the close button) in the upper-left corner of the private browsing window.

Defining Browser Privacy Settings

When you browse the Internet, many web sites use small files known as cookies to track your behavior. In addition, some web sites can even identify your location. While this is handy in helping you find directions on a map, it can also be used to pinpoint your location, which you might not want.

To further protect your privacy, you can block cookies, location services, and tracking. It may not block particularly devious web sites, but it can provide an additional level of privacy.

The most secure setting is to always block cookies, deny all location services, and ask web sites not to track your activity.

If you always block cookies, you'll lose the convenience of web sites recognizing you when you return. If you block location services, you won't be able to get custom information from your area. You may want to experiment with different settings so that you can determine what trade-off between convenience and privacy you're willing to accept.

To define browser settings for Safari, follow these steps:

1. Start Safari.

2. Click the Safari menu and choose Preferences (Safari ➤ Preferences). The Preferences window appears.

3. Click the Privacy icon. Safari's Privacy settings appear, as shown in Figure 17-16.

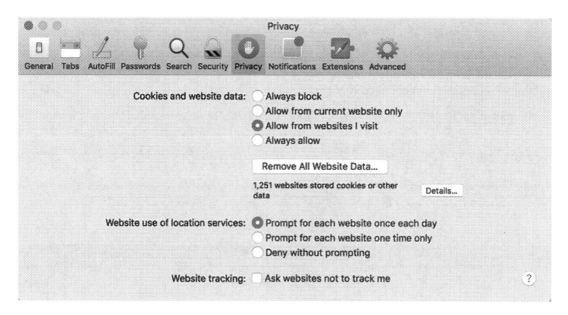

Figure 17-16. Safari's Privacy settings

4. Choose the options you want.

5. Click the red button (the close button) in the upper-left corner to make the Privacy window disappear.

Using Bookmarks

Jumping to a web site from your history list is convenient, but if there are web sites you visit frequently, it's far easier to save those web sites as bookmarks instead.

When you bookmark web sites, you can store those bookmarks in one of the following three places (and as shown in Figure 17-17):

- The Bookmarks menu

- The Bookmarks sidebar

- The Favorites bar

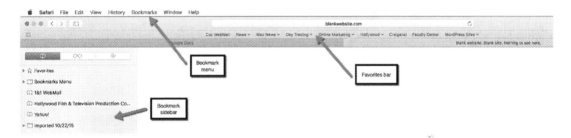

Figure 17-17. Places to store bookmarked web sites

Bookmarks are best for saving your favorite web sites. Now you can quickly access your favorite web sites with just one click of the mouse (or trackpad).

Bookmarking a Web Site

When you find a favorite web site, create a bookmark so that you'll always be able to find that web site again. When bookmark a web site, you can give it a descriptive name and choose where to store it.

To bookmark a web site, follow these steps:

1. Start Safari.

2. Open any web site that you want to visit repeatedly.

3. Click the Bookmark menu and choose Add Bookmark (Bookmark ➤ Add Bookmark). A dialog asks where you want to save your bookmark and what descriptive name you want to give it, as shown in Figure 17-18.

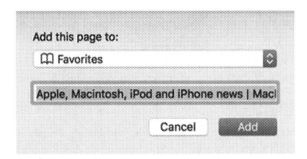

Figure 17-18. Defining a bookmark

4. Click in the Add this page to pop-up menu and choose a location where you want to save your bookmark.

5. Click in the bottom text field and edit or type a descriptive name for your bookmark.

6. Click the Add button.

Viewing Bookmarks

Once you've saved your bookmark, you'll eventually want to view it. To view bookmarks on the Bookmarks menu, just click the Bookmarks menu.

To view bookmarks in the Bookmarks sidebar, click the View menu and choose Show Bookmarks Sidebar (View ➤ Show Bookmarks Sidebar).

To view bookmarks in the Favorites bar, click the View menu and choose Show Favorites Bar (View ➤ Show Favorites Bar).

No matter where you've stored your bookmarks, you can click a bookmark to jump to the web site that it represents.

Creating Bookmark Folders

The more bookmarks you add, the more cluttered your bookmarks become until it's hard to find any particular bookmark. To organize your bookmarks, you can create bookmark folders. That way you can group related bookmarks together and avoid getting overwhelmed by a long list of bookmarks.

To create a bookmark folder, follow these steps:

1. Start Safari.

2. Click the Bookmark menu and choose Edit Bookmarks (Bookmark ➤ Edit Bookmarks). Safari displays all your bookmarks and the web site addresses stored in them, as shown in Figure 17-19.

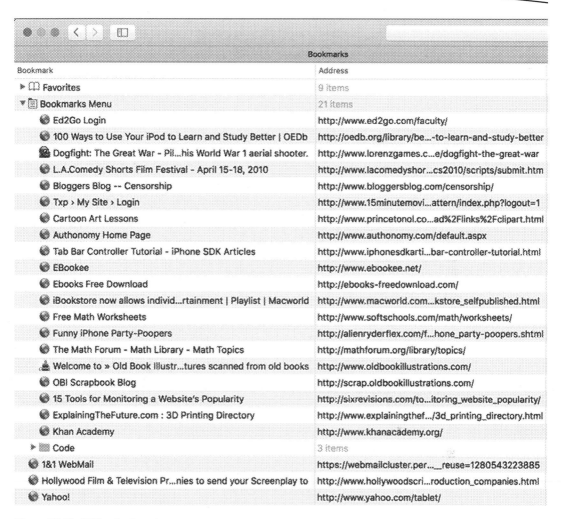

Bookmark	Address
▶ ◻ Favorites	9 items
▼ ▤ Bookmarks Menu	21 items
● Ed2Go Login	http://www.ed2go.com/faculty/
● 100 Ways to Use Your iPod to Learn and Study Better | OEDb	http://oedb.org/library/be...-to-learn-and-study-better
● Dogfight: The Great War - Pil...his World War 1 aerial shooter.	http://www.lorenzgames.c...e/dogfight-the-great-war
● L.A.Comedy Shorts Film Festival - April 15-18, 2010	http://www.lacomedyshor...cs2010/scripts/submit.htm
● Bloggers Blog -- Censorship	http://www.bloggersblog.com/censorship/
● Txp › My Site › Login	http://www.15minutemovi...attern/index.php?logout=1
● Cartoon Art Lessons	http://www.princetonol.co...ad%2Flinks%2Fclipart.html
● Authonomy Home Page	http://www.authonomy.com/default.aspx
● Tab Bar Controller Tutorial - iPhone SDK Articles	http://www.iphonesdkarti...bar-controller-tutorial.html
● EBookee	http://www.ebookee.net/
● Ebooks Free Download	http://ebooks-freedownload.com/
● iBookstore now allows individ...rtainment | Playlist | Macworld	http://www.macworld.com...kstore_selfpublished.html
● Free Math Worksheets	http://www.softschools.com/math/worksheets/
● Funny iPhone Party-Poopers	http://alienryderflex.com/f...hone_party-poopers.shtml
● The Math Forum - Math Library - Math Topics	http://mathforum.org/library/topics/
● Welcome to » Old Book Illustr...tures scanned from old books	http://www.oldbookillustrations.com/
● OBI Scrapbook Blog	http://scrap.oldbookillustrations.com/
● 15 Tools for Monitoring a Website's Popularity	http://sixrevisions.com/to...itoring_website_popularity/
● ExplainingTheFuture.com : 3D Printing Directory	http://www.explainingthef.../3d_printing_directory.html
● Khan Academy	http://www.khanacademy.org/
▶ ▦ Code	3 items
● 1&1 WebMail	https://webmailcluster.per..._reuse=1280543223885
● Hollywood Film & Television Pr...nies to send your Screenplay to	http://www.hollywoodscri...roduction_companies.html
● Yahoo!	http://www.yahoo.com/tablet/

Figure 17-19. Editing bookmarks

3. Click the Bookmarks menu and choose Add Bookmark Folder. Safari creates a folder called untitled folder.

4. Type a descriptive name for your bookmark folder.

5. Move the pointer over your newly created bookmark folder, hold down the left mouse button (or press a finger on the trackpad), and drag the bookmark folder where you want to store it, such as under the Bookmarks Menu or Favorites category.

6. Move the pointer over any bookmark, hold down the left mouse button (or press a finger on the trackpad), and drag the bookmark in your newly created bookmark folder.

Editing Bookmarks

After you've created a bookmark, you can always modify that bookmark later, such as changing its descriptive name or editing its web site address. Editing also lets you rearrange your bookmarks by dragging them with the mouse or trackpad.

To edit a bookmark, follow these steps:

1. Start Safari.

2. Click the Bookmark menu and choose Edit Bookmarks (Bookmark ➤ Edit Bookmarks). Safari displays all your bookmarks (see Figure 17-18).

3. Right-click the bookmark you want to edit. A pop-up menu appears, as shown in Figure 17-20.

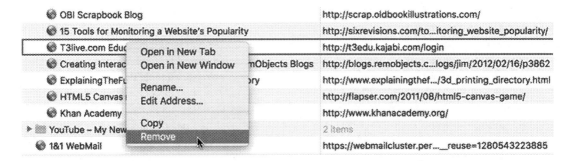

Figure 17-20. *Right-clicking a bookmark displays a pop-up menu*

4. Choose one of the following:

   a. Rename: Lets you rename the bookmark.

   b. Edit Address: Lets you edit the web site address stored in the bookmark.

   c. Remove: Lets you remove a bookmark from Safari.

Importing and Exporting Bookmarks

If you have a desktop and laptop Mac, you'll probably want to have the same bookmarks on both computers. To do this, you can export bookmarks from Safari and then import them on another computer.

If you've been using another browser, such as Chrome or Firefox, you can import bookmarks out of those browsers and import them into Safari. Or you can export bookmarks out of Safari and import them into a different browser.

Importing and exporting bookmarks just makes sure that you can use bookmarks on other computers or browsers. When you export bookmarks out of Safari, all of your bookmarks are saved in a single HTML (HyperText Markup Language) file that all browsers and computers can read.

To export a bookmark, follow these steps:

1. Start Safari.

2. Click the File menu and choose Export Bookmarks (File ➤ Export Bookmarks). A dialog asks for a name to give your bookmark file and a location to store it in.

3. Type a descriptive name for your bookmark file and choose a location to store it in.

4. Click the Save button.

To import a bookmark, follow these steps:

1. Start Safari.

2. Click the File menu and choose Import Bookmarks (File ➤ Import Bookmarks). A dialog asks for a bookmark file to import.

3. Click the bookmark file that you want to use and click the Import button.

Creating a Reading List

Bookmarks are meant to store web sites that you plan to visit regularly in the future. However, if you only want to save a web page to read but don't necessarily want to visit that site later, you can use Safari's reading list feature instead.

A reading list essentially acts like bookmarks. The only difference is that a reading list appears in a sidebar that you can hide or view at any time.

To place a web page on a reading list, follow these steps:

1. Start Safari.

2. Open a web page that you want to temporarily save to read later.

3. Click the Bookmarks menu and choose Add to Reading List (Bookmarks ➤ Add to Reading List). Safari adds the web page to the Reading List sidebar.

4. Click the View menu and choose Show Reading List Sidebar (View ➤ Show Reading List Sidebar). The reading list sidebar appears, as shown in Figure 17-21.

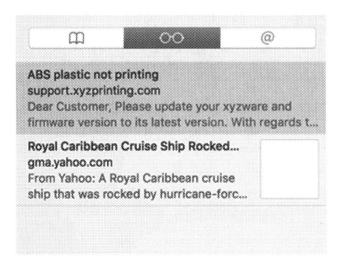

Figure 17-21. Right-clicking a bookmark displays a pop-up menu

5. Click any item in the reading list to view the contents of that web page.

To remove a web page from the reading list, right-click the web page that you want to remove. When a pop-up menu appears, as shown in Figure 17-22, choose either Remove Item or Clear All Items (to clear your entire reading list).

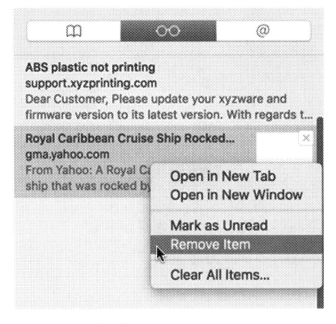

Figure 17-22. Right-clicking a reading list item displays a pop-up menu

Using AutoFill

If you often need to type the same information into different web sites, you may want to use AutoFill. AutoFill lets you store common information such as your name, street address, and credit card number. Now if you need to fill in this information on a web page, AutoFill can type all of this information for you automatically.

AutoFill can store four different types of information:

- Your contact information including your name, address, e-mail address, and phone number
- User names and passwords for different web sites
- Credit card numbers
- Additional sign-in information

> **Note**   For security, AutoFill does not save your credit card's security code. This prevents someone from accessing your Mac and using AutoFill to buy something with your stored credit card number.

The advantage of AutoFill is that it can simplify typing information needed to order products online or access different types of web sites, such as those that require a user name and password.

The disadvantage of AutoFill is if someone accesses your Mac without your permission, they could impersonate you by letting AutoFill automatically enter your personal data.

AutoFill works automatically as soon as it detects you're filling out a form in Safari, as shown in Figure 17-23.

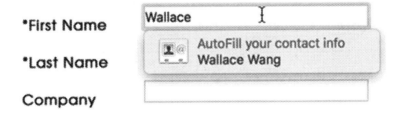

Figure 17-23. AutoFill appears automatically when you start filling out a form

If you click the AutoFill miniature window, Safari displays your saved information so that you can verify that it's correct. Then click the AutoFill button to automatically fill in the form.

To store and edit data for AutoFill to use, follow these steps:

1. Start Safari.

2. Click the Safari menu and choose Preferences (Safari ➤ Preferences).

3. Click the AutoFill icon. The AutoFill window appears, as shown in Figure 17-24.

Figure 17-24. The AutoFill window

4. (Optional) Select or clear the check boxes in front of each AutoFill web form option. If you don't want AutoFill to use your credit card information, clear the "Credit cards" check box.

5. Click the Edit button next to the AutoFill option that you want to modify. Depending on the option that you choose, a different window appears, letting you edit the saved data.

Muting Audio

If you visit some web sites, ads might start blaring right away. To avoid this nuisance of trying to find a way to lower or mute the volume, Safari offers a handy mute feature that appears on the right side of each tab.

Now if you visit a web site that blasts unwanted audio right away, you can quickly shut off the volume or turn it back on again just by clicking the volume icon on the tab, as shown in Figure 17-25.

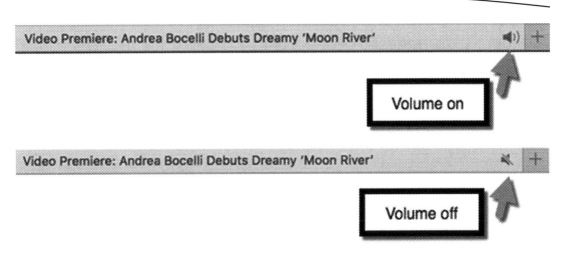

Figure 17-25. *The volume icon appears on the far right of each Safari tab*

Dealing with Unresponsive Web Pages

What's becoming an increasingly annoying problem is malicious web sites that lock up Safari and keep you from shutting down the window or tab. Typically, a booby-trapped web site locks up Safari and displays a warning message, as shown in Figure 17-26.

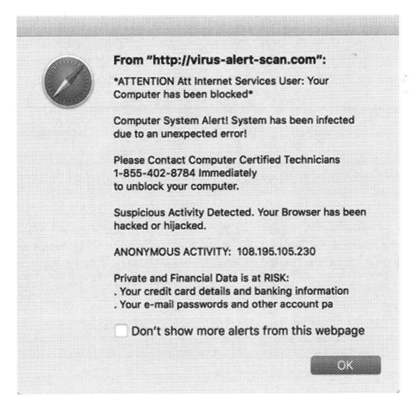

Figure 17-26. *A typical phony warning that freezes Safari*

Any time you see a web page warning of a computer infection that won't let you do anything with Safari, you likely visited a malicious web site.

To shut down Safari when it locks up, follow these steps:

1. Click the Apple menu in the upper-left corner of the screen.

2. Choose Force Quit. A Force Quit window appears, as shown in Figure 17-27.

Figure 17-27. The Force Quit window lets you shut down any unresponsive program

3. Click Safari.

4. Click the Force Quit button to shut down Safari.

5. Hold down the Shift key and open Safari again, such as clicking the Safari icon on the Dock or double-clicking the Safari icon in the Applications folder.

Normally, if you open Safari, it reopens all previously opened tabs and windows. By holding down the Shift key, you force Safari to just open a single window. This keeps Safari from reopening the malicious web site that originally locked up your browser.

Summary

Although you can always install and use any browser, such as Chrome or Firefox, Safari is optimized for OS X, especially on laptops that need to conserve power.

In Safari, you can browse web sites and save them later as bookmarks or part of a reading list. If you need to open and view multiple web sites at the same time, you can open them in separate windows or in multiple tabs within each window.

To protect your privacy, Safari offers a special privacy browsing window or you can define various privacy settings so that you control what web sites can track of your activities.

If you frequently fill out information such as your name, address, and credit card number, you can use Safari's AutoFill feature to automatically fill in information.

Safari acts as a gateway to the Internet, so be sure that you know how to use this program so that you can access information scattered all over the world.

Chapter 18

Using E-mail

Beyond browsing various web sites, the second most common use for the Internet is sending and receiving e-mail. To help you create and receive e-mail, OS X comes with a program called Mail.

Besides letting you send and receive text messages, e-mail also lets you send and receive files. This gives you a simple way to share files between two different computers as long as both computers can open that file.

There are two common ways to access an e-mail account:

- Through a browser
- Through an e-mail program

The advantage of accessing your e-mail account through a browser is that you can read messages using any computer connected to the Internet. The disadvantage of using a browser is that you can't read any messages if you don't have an Internet connection.

The advantage of using an e-mail program is that your messages will be stored on your computer so that you can read them any time that you want whether you have an Internet connection or not. The disadvantage is that your messages are stored on one computer so that you can't access those messages from another computer unless you copy or download them to another computer.

In this chapter, you'll learn how to use OS X's e-mail program called Mail. If you don't like Mail, you can always use a different e-mail program.

© Wallace Wang 2016
W. Wang, *Mac OS X for Absolute Beginners*, DOI 10.1007/978-1-4842-1913-3_18

Setting Up an E-mail Account

To send and receive e-mail, you need to create an e-mail account. You can create an e-mail account with major web sites (such as Google or Yahoo!), your Internet service provider, or your company. To set up an e-mail account, you need to know the following information:

- Your e-mail address (such as JohnSmith@mycompany.com): You can often choose the first part of your e-mail address (such as JohnSmith or JSmith) but the second part of your e-mail address will be defined by the e-mail provider such as Google (@gmail.com) or your Internet service provider, such as your cable company (@cox.net).

- Password: This is the password that gives you access to your account.

> **Note**   Make sure that you get all the information you need to set up an e-mail account or else you won't be able to send or receive e-mail.

Once you know all the information about your e-mail account, you can set up Mail to use that e-mail account. The Mail program can automatically set up e-mail accounts for popular e-mail services such as Google or AOL, but you might need to manually set up an account.

The first time you run the Mail program, it will guide you through the process of setting up an e-mail account. With e-mail providers like Google, Yahoo!, or AOL, you need to visit their web sites to set up an e-mail account.

When you set up an e-mail account through common e-mail providers like AOL or Google, you'll need to choose a user name and password. When you're done setting up an e-mail account, you can access your e-mail through a web page or download your e-mail to your computer using Mail.

To get an existing e-mail account to work within Mail, follow these steps:

1. Open the Mail program.

2. Click the Mail menu and choose Add Account. A list of e-mail providers appears, as shown in Figure 18-1. This list lets you choose a popular e-mail account that Mail can automatically help you set up.

Figure 18-1. The list of e-mail accounts that Mail can automatically recognize

3. Click an e-mail account provider, such as AOL or Google. If you don't see your e-mail account provider, click the Other Mail Account radio button.

4. Click the Continue button and follow the instructions on the screen.

5. If you choose one of the common e-mail providers, Mail asks you to sign into your account with your user name and password. Then Mail configures itself automatically so that you're able to send and receive e-mail from that account.

If you aren't using a common e-mail provider, you'll need to type additional information into Mail yourself, such as:

- Your e-mail account type: Common account types are IMAP and POP, but many corporations may use other e-mail account types, such as Microsoft Exchange.

- Incoming mail server name: The name of the computer that sends e-mail to you; it usually has a name like mail.server.com or pop.server.com, where server.com is the name of the mail server.

- Outgoing mail server name: The name of the computer that lets you send e-mail. It usually has a name like smtp.server.com, where server.com is the name of the mail server.

To get this information, you need to contact your e-mail provider.

> **Note** When you connect the Mail program to an e-mail account, you can access your e-mail through a browser or through the Mail program; you can use whichever method is most convenient.

Sending E-mail

Once you've set up an e-mail account, you'll likely want to send e-mail to other people. To create a new message, you need to define three items:

- An e-mail address: The e-mail address of the person you want to receive the message.

- A subject: This identifies the topic of your message.

- The message itself: This contains the text of your message, which can be as long or as short as you wish.

To create a new message and send it, follow these steps:

1. Open the Mail program.

2. Do one of the following to create a new message (also see Figure 18-2):

   a. Click the File menu and choose New Message (File ➤ New Message).

   b. Press Command+N.

   c. Click the New Message icon.

   A new message window appears.

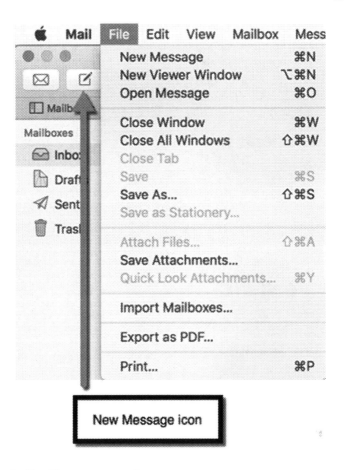

Figure 18-2. *Choosing the New Message command*

3. Click in the To: text field and type an e-mail address. (Make sure that you type the e-mail address correctly or else your message will not be sent to the person you want to receive it.)

4. Click in the Subject: text field and type the topic of your message.

5. Click in the message text box and type your message. (Remember, you can paste text in here from other programs, such as a word processor or spreadsheet.)

6. Click the Send icon, as shown in Figure 18-3, to send your message. To view all of your sent messages, click the Sent folder in the left pane of the Mail window.

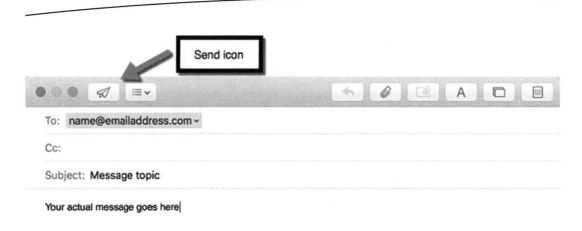

Figure 18-3. The Send icon appears in the upper-left corner of the message window

To send a message, you must have an e-mail address in the To: text field. If you want to send the same message to multiple people, you can use the carbon copy (cc:) or blind carbon copy (bcc:) feature.

Carbon copy means everyone who receives your message can see all the e-mail addresses of everyone who received the same message.

Blind copy means everyone who receives your message can only see your e-mail address but no one else's e-mail address. For privacy, use blind copy instead of carbon copy.

To add additional e-mail addresses to send a message to, click the View menu and choose Cc Address Field or Bcc Address Field (View ➤ Cc Address Field or View ➤ Bcc Address Field), as shown in Figure 18-4.

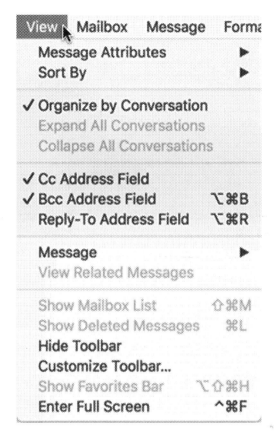

Figure 18-4. The View menu displays Cc Address Field and Bcc Address Field options

Once you've displayed the Cc or Bcc Address Field, you can type additional e-mail addresses into either of these fields to send the same message to multiple recipients.

Saving Drafts

Rather than write a message and send it off right away, you can save your message by clicking the file menu and choosing Save, or pressing Command+S. When you save a message without sending it, Mail stores the message in your Drafts folder that appears in the left pane of the Mail window, as shown in Figure 18-5.

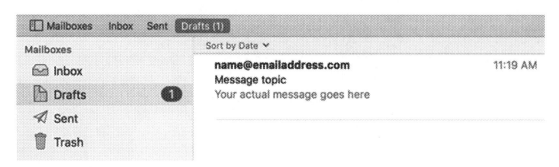

Figure 18-5. The Drafts folder

By saving messages as drafts, you can edit them later. To open a message stored in your Drafts folder, just click the Drafts folder and then double-click the message that you want to edit. Now you can edit your message and click the Send icon when you're ready to send it.

Formatting Text

Most people just type ordinary text in their e-mail messages. However, you may want to format text in fancy ways, such as choosing different fonts and font sizes, using bold or italics, or aligning text in the center or to the right.

To format text, you have two options. First, you can use the Format menu. Second, you can use the format bar that you can hide or display by clicking the Show/Hide format bar icon, as shown in Figure 18-6.

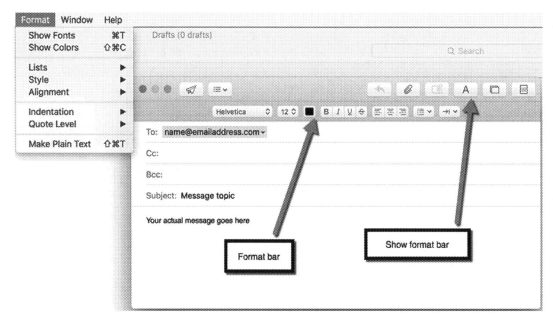

Figure 18-6. You can format text with the Format menu or format bar

Clicking the Show/Hide format bar icon toggles between showing and hiding the format bar. By default, the format bar is hidden.

Using Stationery

Formatting text can make your messages look prettier, but to make your messages look even better, you can use stationery. Stationery lets you choose from a template of different designs so that your message won't look like plain text but more colorful, as shown in Figure 18-7.

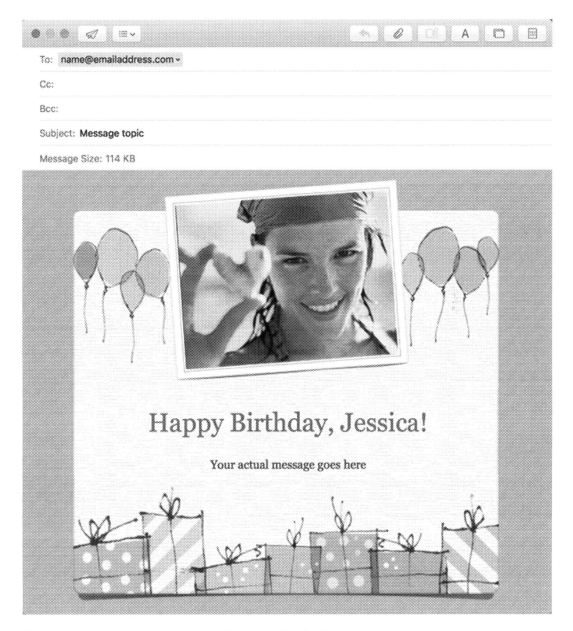

Figure 18-7. Stationery can make your e-mail messages look fancier

To use stationery, follow these steps:

1. Create a new message in the Mail program to open a message window.

2. Click the Show/Hide stationery pane icon to view a list of different stationery templates, as shown in Figure 18-8.

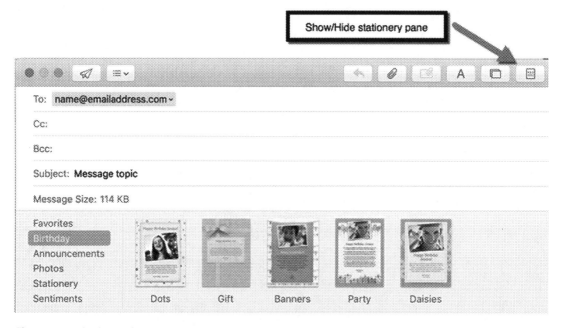

Figure 18-8. Viewing stationery templates

3. Click a stationery category, such as Photos or Sentiments.

4. Click the stationery template you want to use. Your chosen stationery template appears. At this point, you can customize the text and pictures by clicking the part you want to modify.

Attaching a File

Often times you may not just want to send text but an actual file as well such as a word processor document, a database file, or a spreadsheet. When you want to send someone a file created by another program, such as Microsoft Excel, you can attach a file to a message and send that file by e-mail.

Note   Depending on your e-mail provider, there may be a maximum file size limit you can send, such as 10MB.

You can attach multiple files of any type to a single message. However, if you plan to send multiple files, it's best to compress them by opening the Finder, selecting all the files you want to send, clicking the File menu and choosing Compress (File ➤ Compress).

Compressing creates a single ZIP file that you can attach to a message. If you receive a ZIP file, you can unzip it by double-clicking on the ZIP file to access the multiple files stored inside.

To attach a file to a message, follow these steps:

1. Create a new message in the Mail program to open a message window.

2. Click the Attach file icon, or click the File menu and choose Attach Files (File ➤ Attach Files), as shown in Figure 18-9. A dialog lets you choose a file to attach to your message.

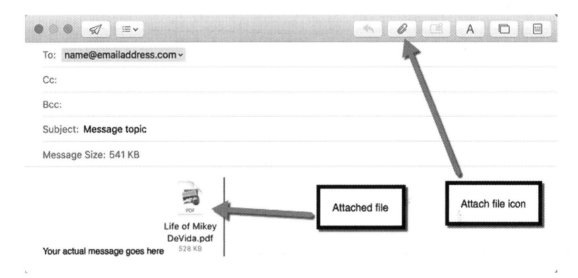

Figure 18-9. The Search text field appears at the top of the Safari window

3. Click a file to attach to your message and click the Choose File button. An icon representing your file appears in your message (see Figure 18-9). (You can click the attached file and press the Delete or Backspace key if you change your mind and don't want to attach the file to your message after all.)

Viewing Sent Messages

Whenever you send a message, the Mail program saves a copy of that message in its Sent folder, which appears in the left pane of the Mail program. If you click the Sent folder icon in the left pane, you can see a list of messages you've sent in chronological order.

If you click a specific message, you can read the contents of that message. Now you can review any of your past messages to see exactly what you sent and the time and date that you sent it.

Saving E-mail Addresses

Typing an e-mail address can get cumbersome because if you misspell one character, your e-mail won't go through. Rather than type an e-mail address in, it's far easier to type it once, save it, and then just click a saved e-mail address that you want to use.

To save e-mail addresses, you use the Contacts program. You can open the Contacts program through the Finder window and then manually type in someone's name and e-mail address.

To save e-mail addresses in the Contacts program, follow these steps:

1. Open the Contacts program in the Applications folder.

2. Click the File menu and choose New Card (or press Command+N). The Contacts program displays an empty card window, as shown in Figure 18-10.

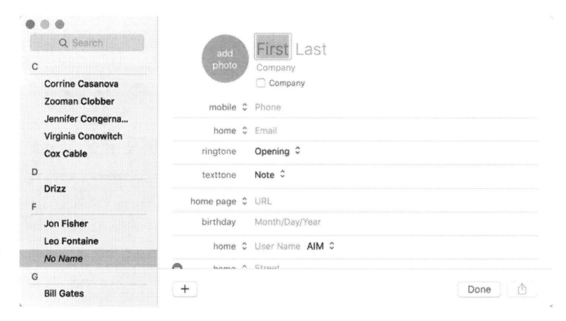

Figure 18-10. An empty card for filling in a person's name and e-mail address

3. Type a person's name and e-mail address.

4. Click the Done button when you've typed all the contact information about that person. You've now saved an e-mail address into the contacts program.

Once you've saved an e-mail address in the Contacts program, you can now retrieve that saved e-mail address when you create a new message in the Mail program.

To send a message to a saved e-mail address, follow these steps:

1. Create a new message in the Mail program to open a message window.

2. Click the plus (+) icon that appears on the far right in the To: text field. A pop-up window appears, as shown in Figure 18-11.

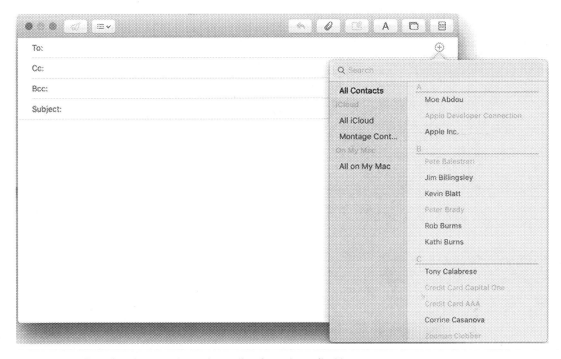

Figure 18-11. The + icon lets you choose from a list of saved e-mail addresses

3. Click a name that contains a saved e-mail address. (You can also type part or all of a name in the Search field to find a person's name and e-mail address faster.) Mail automatically types in the stored e-mail address for that person.

> **Note**   You can also use saved e-mail addresses in the Cc: and Bcc: text fields as well.

Manually typing an e-mail address into the Contacts program is one way to save e-mail addresses. Another way is to simply add the e-mail address of someone who sent you a message.

To add the e-mail address of a message to the Contacts program, follow these steps:

1. Start the Mail program and click a message that contains an e-mail address you want to save in the Contacts program. Mail displays the message contents in the right pane.

2. Move the pointer over the sender's e-mail address. Mail highlights the sender's e-mail address and displays a downward-pointing arrow to the right of that e-mail address.

3. Click the downward-pointing arrow to the right of the sender's e-mail address. A pop-up menu appears, as shown in Figure 18-12.

Figure 18-12. *Adding an e-mail address from a received message*

4. Choose one of the following:

    a. Add to Contacts: Saves your chosen e-mail address to your Contacts program so that you can use this saved e-mail address in the future.

    b. New E-mail: Creates a new message with the recipient's e-mail address automatically typed in the To: text field but does not save the e-mail address in the Contacts program.

Getting New Mail

Even if your Mac is connected to the Internet, you may still need to tell the Mail program to retrieve your messages from your e-mail account. To get any new e-mail messages, you can manually retrieve them or define settings that determine how often the Mail program automatically checks for messages.

To manually retrieve new e-mail messages, do one of the following (also see Figure 18-13):

*   Click the Mailbox menu and choose Get New Mail.

*   Click the Get New Messages icon in the upper-left corner of the Mail program.

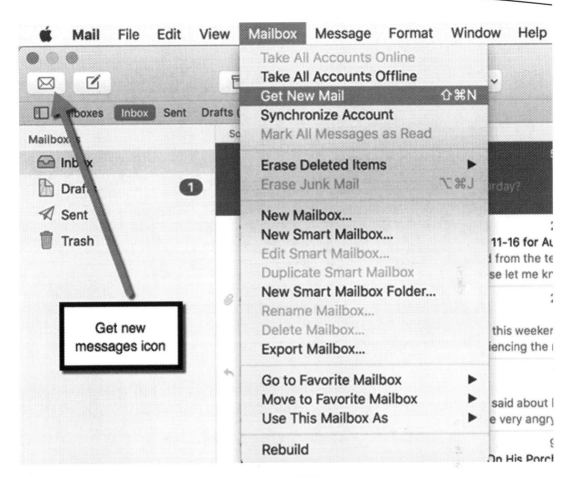

Figure 18-13. Manually retrieve new e-mail messages in the Mail program

Rather than manually retrieve new messages from your e-mail account, you can also define how often you want the Mail program do retrieve new e-mail. To define how often you want the Mail program to retrieve new e-mail, follow these steps:

1. Start the Mail program.

2. Click the Mail menu and choose Preferences (Mail ➤ Preferences). A Preferences window appears.

3. Click the General icon.

4. Click the "Check for new messages" pop-up menu and choose an option, as shown in Figure 18-14.

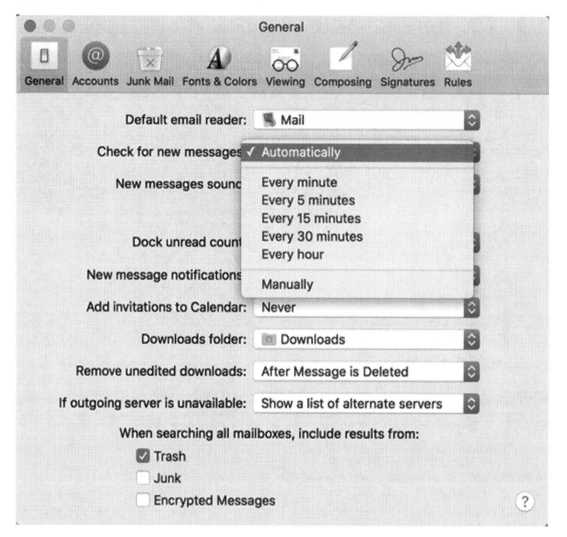

Figure 18-14. The Check for new messages pop-up menu lets you choose an option for retrieving e-mail automatically

5. Click the red dot (the close button) in the upper-left corner of the Preferences window to make it disappear.

Replying to Messages

When you receive messages, you can reply or create a new message altogether. When you reply to a message, you don't save the sender's e-mail address and you send the previous contents of the message for the recipient's reference.

For example, suppose you receive a message asking, "Are you coming to my birthday party this Saturday?"

If you reply to this message, Mail displays the message contents within your reply, as shown in Figure 18-15.

To: Wallace Wang ˅

Cc:

Bcc:

Subject: **Re: Birthday invitation**

On Feb 16, 2016, at 5:04 PM, Wallace Wang <mail@yahoo.com> wrote:

Are you coming to my birthday party this Saturday?

Figure 18-15. Replying to a message displays the contents of the received message

To make the previous message contents easy to find, the Mail program draws a vertical bar in the left margin and displays the previous message in a different color.

Each time you reference another previous message, the Mail program draws another vertical bar so that you can see the number of previous messages that you've references so far.

Mail gives you three ways to reply to a message:

- Reply: Lets you send a message back to the e-mail address of the person who sent the message.
- Reply All: Lets you send a message back to all e-mail addresses stored in the Cc: text fields.
- Forward: Lets you share a message with someone else, typically not the person who sent you the original message.

The main difference between Reply and Reply All is that Reply sends a message to one person while Reply All sends a reply to everyone who received the original message.

To reply to a message, follow these steps:

1. Start the Mail program.

2. Click the message that you want to reply to.

3. Do one of the following (also shown in Figure 18-16):

    a. Click the Message menu and choose Reply (Message ➤ Reply).

    b. Press Command+R.

    c. Click the Reply icon.

    d. Click the Reply to All icon.

    e. Click the Forward icon.

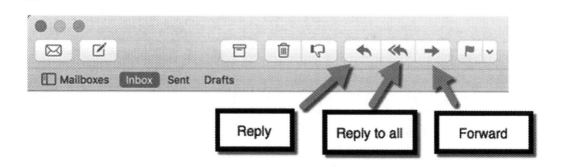

Figure 18-16. *The Reply, Reply All, and Forward icons*

4. Type a message and click the Send icon (it looks like a paper airplane) to send your reply.

Searching Messages

Normally, the Mail program lists your messages in chronological order that it receives them. This is fine when you know the date that you received a particular message. But what if you don't remember the exact date?

You can search for a particular message by the sender's name, e-mail address, subject, or any keyword in the message itself.

To search for a message, follow these steps:

1. Start the Mail program.

2. Click in the Search text field that appears in the upper-right corner of the Mail window.

3. Type part or all of the text that you want to find, such as a person's name, e-mail address, or subject. As you type, Mail displays a list of messages that match your criteria, as shown in Figure 18-17.

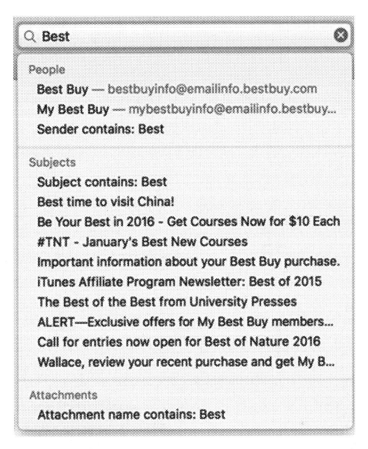

Figure 18-17. Searching messages in the Mail program

4. Click the message that you want to view. The Mail program displays all messages that match your search criteria.

5. Click the clear icon (it looks like an X inside a circle) that appears on the far right of the Search text field to clear out the Search text field, as shown in Figure 18-18. When you clear the Search text field, the Mail program displays all of your messages, not just the messages that match your search criteria.

Figure 18-18. The clear icon in the Search text

Organizing Messages with Smart Mailboxes

In most places, a mail carrier delivers letters to your home by placing them in your mailbox. When you open your mailbox, all of your mail is lumped in a pile.

Many people organize their mail in separate piles, where one pile might represent bills and another might represent messages from work.

The Mail program on the Mac works the same way. When you receive messages in your e-mail account, those messages appear lumped together, which can make finding a particular type of message difficult.

Just as you might sort your physical letters into separate piles, you can organize e-mail messages in separate piles. In the Mail program, you can organize your e-mail messages using Smart Mailboxes.

Smart Mailboxes automatically collect certain types of messages, such as work-related messages or messages from a specific person. With Smart Mailboxes, you can quickly find the type of messages you need without wading through your entire list of messages.

Creating and Using a Smart Mailbox

You can create as many Smart Mailboxes as you wish. Unlike sorting physical letters into separate piles, Smart Mailboxes allow the same messages to appear in multiple Smart Mailboxes.

For example, you might have a Smart Mailbox for messages related to a specific project and a second Smart Mailbox for messages from a certain person. So it's possible for a message to appear in two or more Smart Mailboxes at the same time.

When you create a Smart Mailbox, you must define rules that determine which types of messages appear in that Smart Mailbox. For example, you might only want to store messages from a certain person or messages on a specific type of subject.

You must define at least one rule, but you can define multiple rules. Multiple rules ensure that only certain types of messages appear in your Smart Mailbox, such as only messages from a certain person and related to a specific subject.

To create a Smart Mailbox, follow these steps:

1. Start the Mail prog]ram.

2. Click the Mailbox menu and choose New Smart Mailbox (Mailbox ➤ New Smart Mailbox). A dialog asks to name your Smart Mailbox and one or more rules to determine which types of e-mail messages are stored, as shown in Figure 18-19.

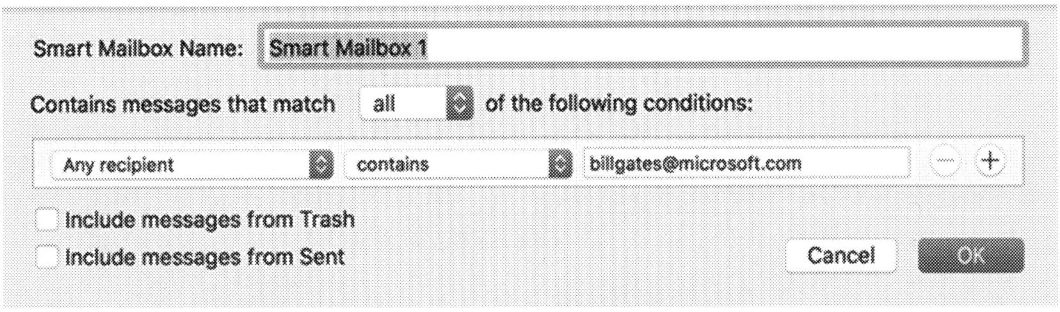

Smart Mailbox Name: Smart Mailbox 1

Contains messages that match   all   of the following conditions:

Any recipient   contains   billgates@microsoft.com   ⊖ ⊕

☐ Include messages from Trash
☐ Include messages from Sent   Cancel   OK

Figure 18-19. Defining a Smart Mailbox

3. Click in the Smart Mailbox Name text field and type a descriptive name.

4. Click in the left pop-up menu and choose criteria to store certain types of e-mail messages, such as "Any recipient" or Subject, as shown in Figure 18-20.

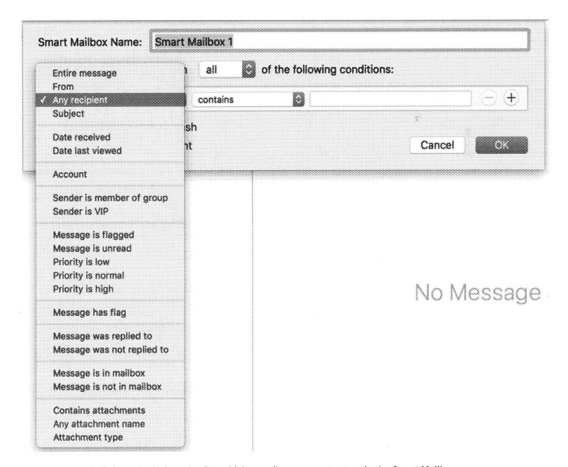

Figure 18-20. Defining criteria for selecting which e-mail messages to store in the Smart Mailbox

5. Click in the middle pop-up menu to define additional criteria.
    Depending on what you chose in the left pop-up menu, the middle
    pop-up menu may display different options, as shown in Figure 18-21.

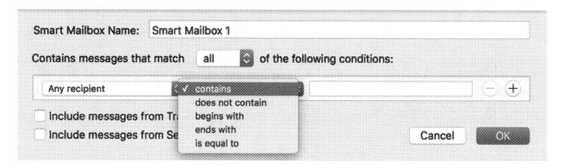

Figure 18-21. *The second pop-up menu lets you define your criteria for choosing messages*

6. Click in the text field and type any additional information necessary
    for your rule, such as defining an e-mail address or a subject title.

7. (Optional) Click the plus (+) icon on the right to create another rule.
    Then repeat steps 4-6.

> **Note**   After you define one or more rules to define the type of messages to appear in your Smart
> Mailbox, test it to make sure it works correctly.

When you create a Smart Mailbox, its name appears in the left pane of the Mail window,
under the Smart Mailboxes category, as shown in Figure 18-22.

Figure 18-22. *Smart Mailboxes appear in the left pane of the Mail window for easy access*

To view the contents of a Smart Mailbox, just click the Smart Mailbox name that you want to view.

To edit the criteria for a Smart Mailbox, right-click a Smart Mailbox name. When a pop-up menu appears, choose Edit Smart Mailbox.

If you want to delete a Smart Mailbox, right-click the Smart Mailbox name, and when a pop-up menu appears, choose Delete Mailbox. A warning asks if you really want to delete the Smart Mailbox, as shown in Figure 18-23.

Figure 18-23. You must confirm that you want to delete a Smart Mailbox

Note   Deleting a Smart Mailbox does not delete any messages displayed inside that Smart Mailbox.

Deleting Messages

When you're done reading a message and don't need to keep it for future reference, delete it. Each time you delete a message, the Mail program stores it in the Trash folder. This gives you one last chance to retrieve a message if you want.

To delete a message, follow these steps:

1. Start the Mail program.

2. Click a message that you want to delete.

3. Click the Edit menu and choose Delete (Edit ➤ Delete). Your chosen message now appears in the Trash folder.

Note   You can also right-click a message, and when a pop-up menu appears, choose Delete.

Retrieving Deleted Messages

If you delete a message by mistake, you can undo the delete command if you click the Edit menu and choose Undo (Edit ➤ Undo) or press Command+Z.

Unfortunately, the Undo command only works if you choose it immediately after deleting a message by mistake. If you deleted a message a long time ago and then suddenly decide you need it after all, you can undelete a message by retrieving it from the Trash folder.

To retrieve a message from the Trash folder, follow these steps:

1. Click the Trash folder in the left pane of the Mail window. The Mail program lists all messages that you deleted using the Delete command.

2. Click a message in the Trash folder that you want to retrieve.

3. Click the Message menu, choose Move To, and choose Inbox. Choose the inbox name to store the deleted message.

> **Note** You can right-click a message, and when a pop-up menu appears, choose Move To, choose Inbox, and then choose the inbox name to store the deleted message.

Erasing Deleted Messages for Good

You can always retrieve deleted messages no matter how long ago you deleted them. However, you may eventually want to delete messages for good to save space on your Mac and to avoid the risk of other people reading them if they ever gain access to your computer.

To erase deleted messages for good, follow these steps:

1. Start the Mail program.

2. Right-click the Trash folder in the left pane of the Mail program. A pop-up menu appears, as shown in Figure 18-24.

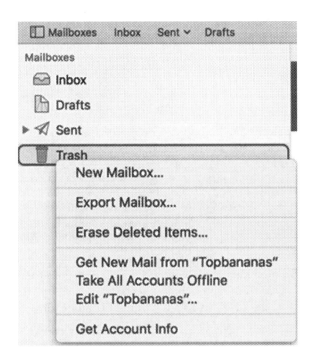

Figure 18-24. Right-clicking the Trash folder displays a pop-up menu

3. Choose Erase Deleted Items... A warning message appears, as shown in Figure 18-25, letting you know that if you erase items in the Trash folder, you won't be able to retrieve them later if you wish.

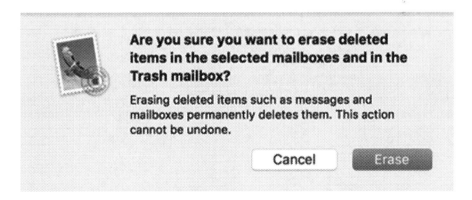

Figure 18-25. A warning message lets you know that erasing the Trash folder is a permanent action

4. Click the Erase button. The Mail program deletes all messages in the Trash folder.

Summary

The Mail program lets you retrieve messages from an e-mail account so that you can view and read them without connecting to the Internet. You can send messages by typing e-mail addresses each time, or store commonly used e-mail addresses in the Contacts program that you can use so that you don't have to type them again.

You can send a message to one e-mail address at a time, or send the same message to multiple e-mail addresses at once. When sending the same message to multiple people, you can use either Cc: (carbon copy) or Bcc: (blind carbon copy). Carbon copy lets everyone see all the e-mail addresses who received the same message while blind carbon copy does not.

To help you find a particular message, you can search for it. Another alternative is to set up Smart Mailboxes that automatically store messages based on certain criteria, such as the sender's e-mail address or message subject. Smart Mailboxes can help organize your messages automatically.

Once you delete a message, you can always retrieve it again from the Trash folder. To permanently delete a message, you must erase all deleted items in the Trash folder. Once you erase all deleted items in the Trash folder, you can never retrieve those deleted messages again.

The Mail program can connect to any e-mail account, such as Google or AOL. Use the Mail program as an alternative to reading your e-mail messages through a browser.

Chapter 19

Using Messages and FaceTime

With the introduction of high-speed Internet in most places around the world, people now have a new way to communicate with each other. Instead of sending e-mail and waiting for a response, you can now communicate in real-time using either Messages or FaceTime.

Messages essentially lets you send and receive text messages through your Mac. FaceTime lets you talk to other people, turning your Mac into a video telephone.

Both Messages and Facetime require an Internet connection to work. As long as you have an Internet connection and need to communicate with someone right away, you can choose which method is best for you.

Setting Up a Messages Account

Before you can chat with Messages, you need to set up a Messages account. Your account determines how people can reach you to send a message.

The three most common types of accounts are Google, Yahoo!, and AOL e-mail addresses. If you aren't using one of these services for e-mail, you can also connect Messages to an AIM (AOL Instant Messenger) or Jabber account.

AIM and Jabber are two popular instant messaging programs, so you can share text messages with people who may not be using the Messages program.

The Messages program can automatically recognize e-mail addresses from Google, Yahoo!, and AOL, but if you have an e-mail address with a different e-mail provider, you'll need to define the settings yourself.

© Wallace Wang 2016
W. Wang, *Mac OS X for Absolute Beginners*, DOI 10.1007/978-1-4842-1913-3_19

If you set up a Messages account to work with your iPhone number, you can receive messages on your iPhone and your Mac. To link your Messages account to your mobile phone number or additional e-mail addresses, follow these steps:

1. Open the Messages program.

2. Click the Messages menu and choose Preferences. A Preferences window appears.

3. Click the Account icon and choose the additional e-mail addresses or mobile phone numbers that you want to link to your Messages account.

4. Click the red dot (the close button) in the upper-left corner to make the Preferences window disappear.

To set up a Messages account, follow these steps:

1. Open the Messages program.

2. Click the Messages menu and choose Add Account. A list of e-mail providers appears, as shown in Figure 19-1. This list lets you choose a popular e-mail account that Mail can automatically help you set up.

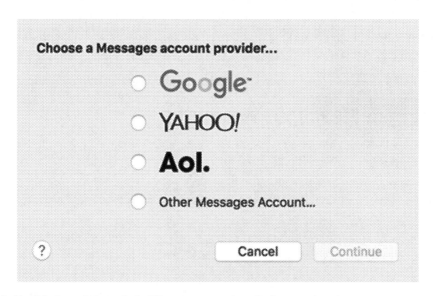

Figure 19-1. The list of e-mail accounts that Messages can automatically recognize

3. Click an e-mail account provider, such as AOL or Google. If you don't see your e-mail account provider, click the Other Messages Account radio button and then you can choose an AIM or Jabber account, as shown in Figure 19-2.

Figure 19-2. Choosing Other Messages Account lets you select an AIM or Jabber account

4. Click the Continue button and follow the instructions on the screen.

5. No matter which option you choose, you'll need to type your user name and password.

Sending a Message

Once you've set up Messages to use an existing e-mail, AIM, or Jabber account, you can send messages to other people as long as you know their e-mail address, AIM name, Jabber account name, or mobile phone number.

To create and send an instant message, follow these steps:

1. Open the Messages program.

2. Do one of the following methods to create a new message:

    a. Click the File menu and choose New Message (File ➤ New Message).

    b. Press Command+N.

    c. Click the New Message icon, as shown in Figure 19-3.

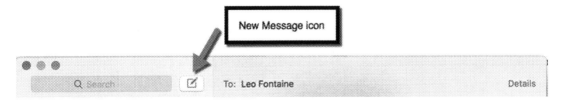

Figure 19-3. Choosing the New Message command

3. Click in the To: text field and type one of the following: an e-mail address, an AIM or Jabber account name, or a mobile phone number. (Make sure that you type everything correctly, otherwise your message will not be sent to the person that you want to receive it.)

4. (Optional) As an alternative to typing a recipient's contact information, click the plus sign (+) icon at the far right of the To: text field. This displays a list of names saved in the Contacts program, as shown in Figure 19-4. If you click saved contact information under a particular name, you can enter the contact information automatically into the To: text field.

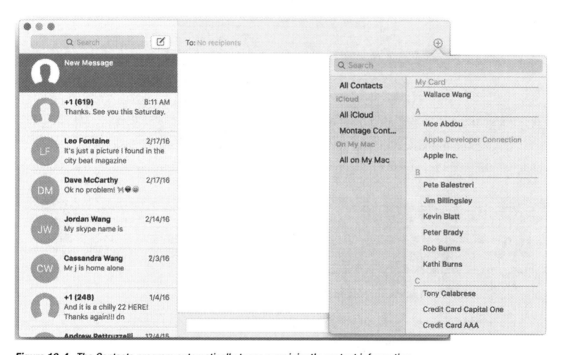

Figure 19-4. The Contacts program automatically types a recipient's contact information

5. Click in the message text field at the bottom of the Messages window and type your message.

6. (Optional) Click the Emoticon icon, as shown in Figure 19-5, to add an emoticon to your message.

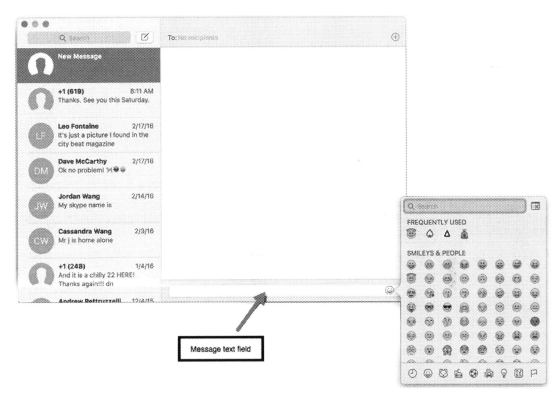

Figure 19-5. The Message text field and Emoticon icon lets you create a message to send to others

7. Press Return to send your message.

Reading Messages

Each time someone sends you a text message, the Messages program groups those messages under the sender's name or contact information (such as the sender's mobile phone number) in the left pane of the Messages window (see Figure 19-5).

To read messages, follow these steps:

1. Open the Messages program.

2. Click a name, mobile phone number, or e-mail address of a person in the left pane of the Messages window. Messages lists all the messages you've sent and received from that person, as shown in Figure 19-6.

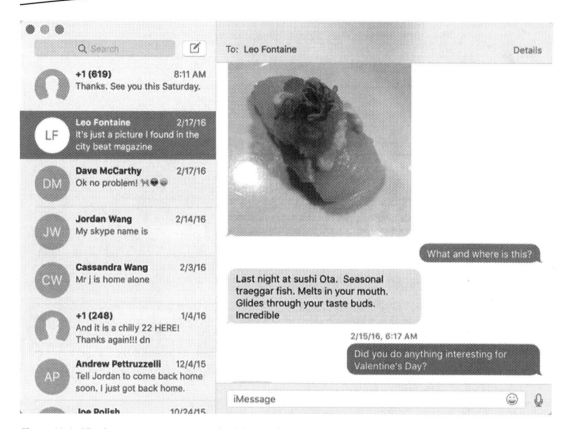

Figure 19-6. Viewing messages sent or received from a single person

Sending Audio as a Message

Typing is troublesome for some people, so as an alternative to typing a message, you may find it easier to record your voice instead. When you capture a spoken message, you can send it as an audio file that someone else can listen to.

To capture and send an audio file, follow these steps:

1. Open the Messages program.

> **Note** If you've already started a conversation with someone, you can just click that person's name in the left pane of the Messages window, and skip steps 2 and 3.

2. Do one of the following methods to create a new message:

   a. Click the File menu and choose New Message (File ➤ New Message).

   b. Press Command+N.

   c. Click the New Message icon.

3. Type a recipient's contact information (e-mail address, AIM/Jabber account name, mobile phone number) in the To: text field.

4. Click the microphone icon that appears to the right of the message text field, as shown in Figure 19-7.

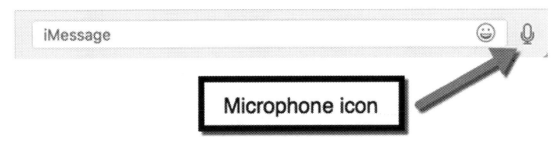

Figure 19-7. The microphone icon lets you record audio to send as a message

5. Speak your message. The built-in microphone on your Mac records your audio. The bottom of the Messages window shows you the time length of your audio file. There is also a Stop button, as shown in Figure 19-8.

Figure 19-8. Recording your audio

6. Click the red Stop button when you're done recording your message. The bottom of the Messages window displays your audio message and its time length, as shown in Figure 19-9.

Figure 19-9. Getting ready to send an audio file

7. Click the Send button to send your audio (or click the Cancel button if you don't want to send the audio file).

Deleting Messages

If you don't need to review past messages, you can delete them. There are two ways to delete messages. First, you can delete individual messages. Second, you can delete an entire person's message conversation, which means you could wipe out all messages you've sent to a person and all messages that person has sent to you.

To delete individual messages, follow these steps:

1. Open the Messages program.

2. Click a name, e-mail address, or mobile phone number that appears in the left pane of the Messages window. Messages shows all the messages that you've sent to that person and all messages that you've received from that person (see Figure 19-6).

3. Click the message that you want to delete.

4. Click the Edit menu and choose Delete (Edit ➤ Delete). (You can also right-click a message and choose Delete from the pop-up menu.) A warning dialog appears, letting you know that if you delete a message, you won't be able to retrieve it later.

5. Click the Delete button.

Deleting an individual message leaves the rest of your message conversation intact. If you would rather delete an entire conversation (all messages sent and received from a specific person), follow these steps:

1. Open the Messages program.

2. Click a name, e-mail address, or mobile phone number that appears in the left pane of the Messages window. Messages shows all the messages that you've sent to that person and all the messages that you've received from that person (see Figure 19-6).

3. Do one of the following:

    a. Move the pointer over a name, e-mail address, or mobile phone number, and then click the X icon that appears.

    b. Move the pointer over a name, e-mail address, or mobile phone number, and then swipe two fingers to the left to reveal a red Delete button. Click the Delete button, as shown in Figure 19-10.

    A warning dialog appears to let you know that if you delete an entire conversation of messages, you can't retrieve those deleted messages later.

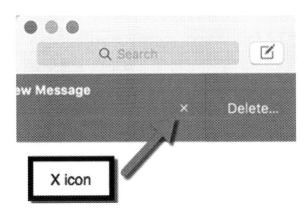

Figure 19-10. *Deleting all messages in a conversation*

4. Click the Delete button.

Using FaceTime

The Messages program is best for sending and receiving text. If you want to chat in real-time using either audio or video, you need to use FaceTime.

> **Note**   To use FaceTime, both people need a fast and reliable Internet connection and an Apple device that supports FaceTime, such as a Mac or iPhone.

To use FaceTime, you need an Apple ID so that you can assign an e-mail address to your FaceTime account. That way if someone wants to reach you, they just need to know your e-mail address.

If you set up a FaceTime account to work with your iPhone phone number, you can receive messages on your iPhone and your Mac. To link your FaceTime account to your mobile phone number or additional e-mail addresses, follow these steps:

1. Open the FaceTime program.

2. Click the FaceTime menu and choose Preferences. A Preferences window appears.

3. Click the Settings tab and choose additional e-mail addresses or mobile phone numbers that you want to link to your FaceTime account.

4. Click the red dot (the close button) in the upper-left corner to make the Preferences window disappear.

After you've set up FaceTime with your Apple ID and e-mail address or mobile phone number, you can start using FaceTime. FaceTime gives you the option of making an audio call (like a telephone) or a video call (where you can see the other person). You can choose which type of call to make by clicking the Video or Audio tab.

Note   Video calls require a faster Internet connection, so if either person on the FaceTime call has a slow or less reliable Internet connection, they will likely experience audio and/or video issues.

To make a FaceTime call, follow these steps:

1. Start the FaceTime program.

2. Click the Video or Audio tab.

3. Do one of the following to contact someone:

    a. Click in the text field that displays the text "Enter a name, e-mail, or number" and type an e-mail address or mobile phone number, as shown in Figure 19-11.

    b. Click a name, e-mail address, or mobile phone number that appears in the left pane of the FaceTime window. This lists people you've contacted through FaceTime in the past, so if you haven't used FaceTime yet, this left pane will be empty.

    c. Click the plus (+) icon that appears on the far right of the text field that displays "Enter a name, e-mail, or number." This displays a list of names stored in the Contacts program. Now click a name to contact that person.

Figure 19-11. *FaceTime lets you type in the e-mail address or mobile phone number of someone that you want to contact*

When someone receives a call through FaceTime, a FaceTime notification window appears, displaying an Accept or Decline button, as shown in Figure 19-12.

Figure 19-12. *FaceTime displays a small notification window to let you know that someone is trying to reach you*

Blocking Callers in Messages and FaceTime

You may have chatted with someone through Messages or FaceTime in the past, but now your relationship with that person has ended. You may not want that person to contact you or to see their attempts to reach you. Fortunately, both the Messages and FaceTime programs offer ways to block a specific e-mail address or mobile phone number. When you block someone in Messages or FaceTime, your Mac completely ignores any contact requests from that person.

To block a caller in Messages, follow these steps:

1. Start the Messages program.

2. Click the Messages menu and choose Preferences. A Preferences window appears.

3. Click the Accounts icon.

4. Click the Blocked tab, as shown in Figure 19-13.

Figure 19-13. Defining the name of someone to block automatically in Messages

5. Click the plus (+) icon that appears in the lower-left corner underneath the "Enter iMessage addresses to block in the list below:" text field. A list of names stored in the Contacts program appears.

6. Click a name in the Contacts program that you want to block.

7. Click the red dot (the close button) in the upper-left corner of the Accounts window to make it disappear.

To block a caller in FaceTime, follow these steps:

1. Start the FaceTime program.

2. Click the FaceTime menu and choose Preferences. A Preferences window appears.

3. Click the Blocked tab, as shown in Figure 19-14.

Figure 19-14. Defining the name of someone to block automatically in FaceTime

4. Click the plus (+) icon that appears in the lower left corner underneath the "Enter iMessage addresses to block in the list below" text field. A list of names stored in the Contacts program appears.

5. Click a name in the Contacts program that you want to block.

6. Click the red dot (the close button) in the upper-left corner of the Preferences window to make it disappear.

Summary

When sending and receiving e-mail is too slow, you can communicate in real-time using text, audio, or video. The Messages program lets you type and send text messages to another person using a computer or smartphone.

FaceTime lets you chat with someone using audio or video. To use FaceTime, both people need an Apple product that supports FaceTime (such as a Mac or an iPhone). Audio calling in FaceTime is like making a telephone call. Video calling in FaceTime lets you talk and see someone at the same time.

Messages lets you communicate with others using different types of computers. FaceTime only works with Apple products, so if someone doesn't have an Apple product capable of using FaceTime, you won't be able to chat using FaceTime.

With both Messages and FaceTime, you can communicate with anyone around the world absolutely free just as long as both of you have an Internet connection.

Chapter 20

Using iCloud

In the old days, every computer was an island. Anything you created on one computer would have to be copied and moved to another computer. If you forget to copy a file from your desktop to your laptop, you might travel to another city only to realize that you're missing several crucial files.

Fortunately, there's a better solution. Rather than try to keep your files synchronized on multiple computers, you can just use iCloud. The main idea behind iCloud is that you have storage space on the Internet, otherwise known as the "cloud."

The advantage of iCloud is that you'll always be able to access your files on any device you wish as long as you have Internet access. The disadvantage is that if you happen to be somewhere without Internet access, you won't be able to access your files.

Since Internet access is so readily available in many places, using iCloud can help you keep track of your files in one place so that you'll never be without them again.

Setting Up an iCloud Account

To use iCloud, you must create an Apple ID and then turn on iCloud for your Mac. Initially, Apple gives you 5GB of storage space, but you can buy more storage space if you wish.

Once you turn on iCloud, you can choose various options for choosing which programs can store data on and retrieve data from iCloud.

To set up an iCloud account, follow these steps:

1. Click the Apple menu to display a pull-down menu.

2. Choose System Preferences. The System Preferences window appears.

3. Click the iCloud icon. The iCloud window appears, as shown in Figure 20-1.

© Wallace Wang 2016
W. Wang, *Mac OS X for Absolute Beginners*, DOI 10.1007/978-1-4842-1913-3_20

Figure 20-1. *The iCloud window lets you define which programs can access iCloud*

4. Make sure that the iCloud Drive check box is selected.

5. Select or clear the check boxes to the left of each program. If a check box is clear, then that program won't be able to share data with other devices—such as an iPhone or iPad—that you may also own.

Once you have set up iCloud Drive, you can access it through the Finder as if it were just another drive physically attached to your Mac. To make the iCloud Drive appear in the Finder, follow these steps:

1. Click the Finder icon on the Dock. The Finder window opens.

2. Click the Finder menu and choose Preferences. The Preferences window appears.

3. Click the Sidebar icon. A list of items that can appear in the left sidebar pane of the Finder appears, as shown in Figure 20-2.

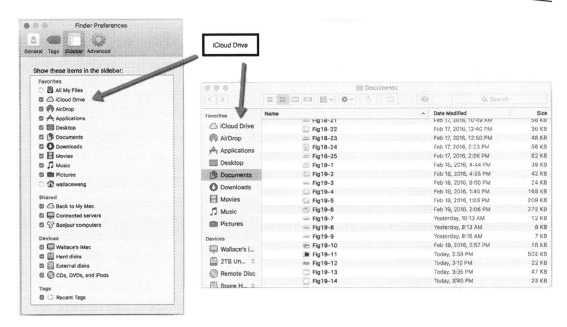

Figure 20-2. Selecting the iCloud Drive check box makes the iCloud Drive visible in the Finder

4.   Select the iCloud Drive check box. The iCloud Drive icon now appears in the left sidebar pane of the Finder window. Now you can copy and paste files from your Mac to your iCloud Drive (and vice versa).

Moving Files to and from iCloud

When you drag and drop a file in the Finder, you either copy or move a file. If you drag and drop a file on the same drive, dragging and dropping moves the file.

If you drag and drop a file from one drive to another (such as from a flash drive to a hard drive), dragging and dropping copies a file. So when you drag and drop a file to or from iCloud, you're moving a file from one location to another.

Since moving a file from iCloud keeps any other device from accessing that file, the Finder displays a warning dialog, as shown in Figure 20-3.

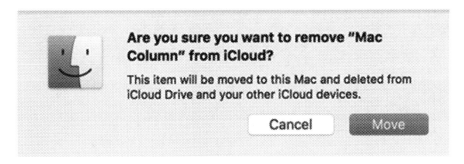

Figure 20-3. A warning dialog appears to let you know the consequences of moving a file off iCloud

If you're sure that you no longer want that file to be accessible over the Internet, click the Move button. Otherwise, click the Cancel button to keep the file on iCloud.

One way to use iCloud is to store critical files there. If anything happens to your computers, your files are always safe. However, if you store multiple files or large files, storing files on iCloud can get expensive because you may need to pay for extra storage space.

A second way to use iCloud is to temporarily store files that you need to access on different devices. When you're sure that you won't need to use these files any more, move them from iCloud to conserve space.

> **Note**   Apple only gives you 5GB of free storage, so if you need more storage, you'll have to pay extra for it.

Accessing iCloud from a Browser

You can access iCloud from the Finder (as long as you have an Internet connection) or you can access iCloud through a browser, such as Safari. Accessing iCloud through the Finder makes it easy to move files from a Mac to iCloud. Accessing iCloud through a browser is handy when you're using a different computer, such as a Windows or Linux PC.

When you access iCloud through a browser, you can create and delete folders to organize your files. You can also delete or rename files, or upload new files. When you need to access your iCloud files without a Mac, you can do it through any computer with a browser and an Internet connection.

To access iCloud through a browser, follow these steps:

1. Open a browser on any computer and visit www.icloud.com. The iCloud web site appears.

2. Type your Apple ID and password. The iCloud web site displays program icons that you can access over the Internet, such as Pages or Photos, as shown in Figure 20-4.

Figure 20-4. *The iCloud web site displays the iCloud Drive icon*

3. Click the iCloud Drive icon. The iCloud web site now displays the contents of your iCloud.

Once you access your iCloud Drive from your browser, you can create new folders, upload new files, download files, or delete files and folders, as shown in Figure 20-5.

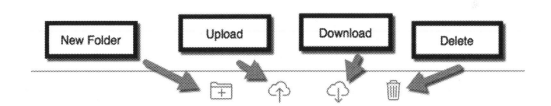

Figure 20-5. *iCloud Drive lets you modify files and folders*

Using iWork for iCloud

Accessing iCloud from any browser gives you access to your files on any computer. However, what if you want to edit a file stored on iCloud?

One solution is to download the file from iCloud to your computer, modify that file, and then upload the modified version back to iCloud. While this can work, it's clumsy and risks creating multiple versions of the same file stored in different locations (one copy on iCloud and another copy stored on your computer).

To solve this problem, you can use Apple's office suite, called iWork, directly on iCloud. This lets you modify files on iCloud directly.

The three iWork programs are Pages (a word processor), Numbers (a spreadsheet), and Keynote (a presentation program). Best of all, Pages can import and export Microsoft Word documents, Numbers can import and export Microsoft Excel files, and Keynote can import and export Microsoft PowerPoint files. By using iWork, you can share common office files with other people, even if they're not using a Mac.

By using iWork in your browser, you can use a full office suite on any computer, whether you're using a Mac, a Windows PC, or an Android tablet. This lets you edit and create files on any computer that has a browser and an Internet connection.

There are several ways to access the iWork programs with a browser. If you access the iCloud web site, you can click a program icon, such as Pages, Numbers, or Keynote (see Figure 20-4).

If you have already opened your iCloud Drive, you can click a program icon by clicking the iCloud Drive label in the upper-left corner of the iCloud Drive window. This displays a menu that shows different program icons, such as Pages, Numbers, or Keynote, as shown in Figure 20-6.

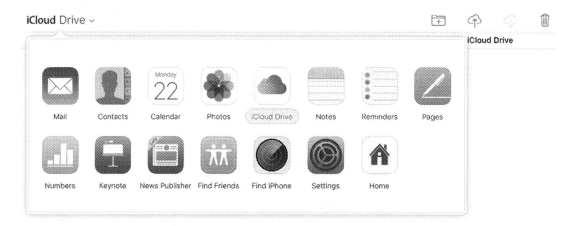

Figure 20-6. Accessing the iWork program icons within iCloud Drive

If you already have iWork files stored in iCloud Drive, you can also open Pages, Numbers, or Keynote by clicking an iWork file.

Although iWork for iCloud looks and works like the iWork programs on the Mac, there are some minor differences. First, iWork programs on the Mac display pull-down menus at the top of the screen, whereas iWork for iCloud displays icons that let you access most (but not all) of the features found on iWork on the Mac, as shown in Figure 20-7.

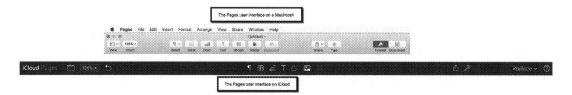

Figure 20-7. The user interface of iWork programs on the Mac look slightly different from iWork programs on iCloud

The iWork user interface on iCloud is much simpler than the iWork user interface on the Mac. As a result, iWork for iCloud is meant for performing common tasks, whereas iWork on the Mac offers more sophisticated features, such as creating a table of contents automatically in a word processor document.

Because of its simplified user interface, iWork for iCloud forces you to click icons to access commands instead of using pull-down menus. To help you identify the purpose of each icon, just move the mouse pointer over an icon, and after a few seconds, a brief explanation of that icon's function appears, as shown in Figure 20-8.

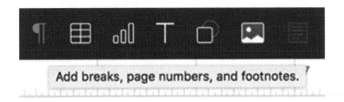

Figure 20-8. You can identify the purpose of icons by moving the mouse pointer over that icon

Opening a File in iWork for iCloud

To open an iWork file stored on iCloud, you must first double-click the appropriate program icon (such as clicking the Pages, Numbers, or Keynote icon). As soon as you load an iWork for iCloud program, a list of files stored on iCloud appears, as shown in Figure 20-9.

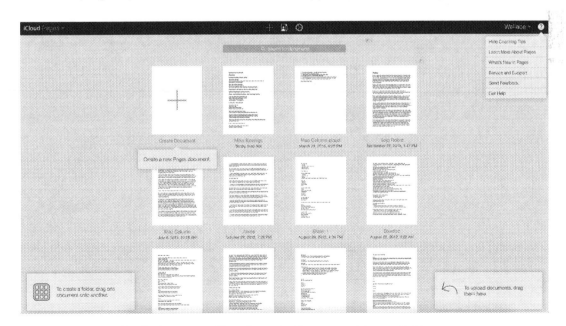

Figure 20-9. You can identify the purpose of icons by moving the mouse pointer over that icon

Just click the file that you want to open, or click the Create Document icon that displays a plus sign (+) in the middle. As soon as you choose a file to open, you can start editing that file within iWork for iCloud.

Downloading Online Files

When you create files using iWork for iCloud, your files are saved on iCloud. If you want a copy of the file on your own computer, you need to download a copy of that file.

To download a file from iWork for iCloud to your Mac, follow these steps:

1. Open an iWork for iCloud file, such as Pages or Keynote.

2. Click the Tools icon (it looks like a wrench) in the upper-right corner of the screen, as shown in Figure 20-10.

Figure 20-10. *The Tools icon*

3. Choose Download a Copy. A dialog asks you to choose a file format, as shown in Figure 20-11. Depending on whether you're using Pages, Numbers, or Keynote, these file format options will be different.

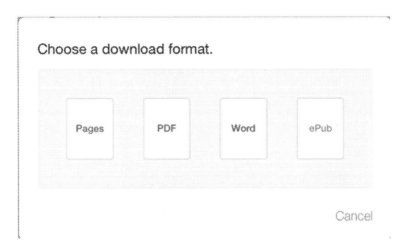

Figure 20-11. *Choosing a file format for the downloaded file*

    4.   Click a file format. Your file appears on your Mac.

Collaborating Online

One unique feature that iWork for iCloud offers is the ability to share and collaborate on files over the Internet. When you share an iCloud file, you have two options.

First, you can let another person view the file but not edit it. Second, you can let another person edit the file using iWork for iCloud.

To send someone a link to an iCloud file, follow these steps:

    1.   Open an iWork for iCloud file, such as Pages or Keynote.

    2.   Click the Share icon, as shown in Figure 20-12. A dialog asks how you want to share the file, as shown in Figure 20-13.

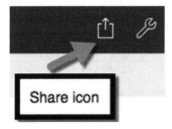

Figure 20-12. *The Share icon lets you share an iCloud file with others*

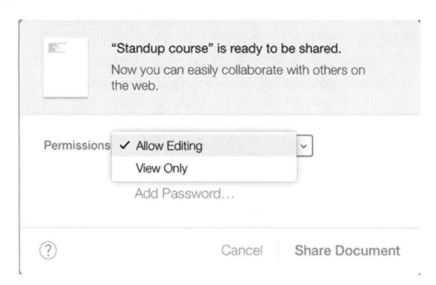

Figure 20-13. Choosing how to share an iCloud file

3.   Click the Permissions pop-up menu and choose Allow Editing or View Only.

4.   Click Share Document. A dialog displays the link to your file, which you can copy and send to others, as shown in Figure 20-14.

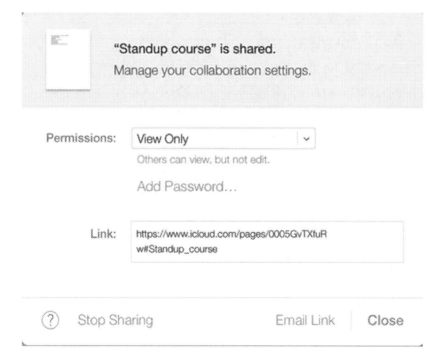

Figure 20-14. iCloud creates a link to your file that you can send to others

5. (Optional) Click Email Link. This lets you send an e-mail directly from your iCloud e-mail account, if you have set up one. Otherwise, you can copy the link and paste it into an e-mail message using another program, such as Mail.

6. Click Close.

When you share a link to an iCloud file, the Share icon changes into a Collaboration icon that looks like a person's silhouette, as shown in Figure 20-15.

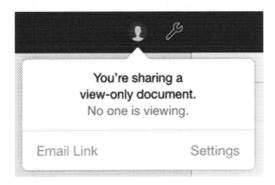

Figure 20-15. The Collaboration icon replaces the Share icon to let you know when you've shared a file

To stop sharing an iCloud file, follow these steps:

1. Open the iWork for iCloud file that you shared previously.

2. Click the Collaboration icon. A pop-up menu appears (see Figure 20-15).

3. Click Settings. A dialog appears, displaying the link to your iCloud file (see Figure 20-14).

4. Click Stop Sharing.

Exiting from iCloud

When you're done using iCloud, you need to sign out. Signing out closes your iCloud session. If you fail to sign out, it's possible that someone else could get on your Mac and visit your browser history to access your iCloud files.

To sign out from iCloud, click your name in the upper-right corner. When a menu appears, choose Sign Out, as shown in Figure 20-16.

Figure 20-16. *The Sign Out option appears on a menu that appears when you click your name*

Summary

If you have a reliable Internet connection, you can take advantage of iCloud. Apple gives you free 5GB of storage, but you can purchase more if you need it.

With iCloud, you can store crucial files that you can access on any Apple device, including a Mac, an iPhone, or an iPad. If you occasionally use a non-Apple device such, as an Android tablet or a Windows PC, you can still access your files on iCloud. (Just be aware that you may need to convert files to a format that another computer can recognize.)

If you want to modify iCloud files without copying them to your own computer, you can use iWork for iCloud, which lets you use Pages, Numbers, or Keynote to create or edit files. Best of all, you can use iWork for iCloud using any computer, such as a Windows or Linux PC, just as long as you have an Internet connection.

Think of iCloud as an extension of your computer. You can store files online, share files with others, and even create and edit files online, whether you have a Mac or another type of computer. By using iCloud, your Mac becomes even more versatile.

Part V

Getting Work Done

No matter how much you may like playing with your Macintosh, eventually you may need to get some work done. Fortunately, using a Macintosh doesn't have to be drudgery. In fact, you may find that working on a Macintosh can make any work-related task easier and even more enjoyable.

To help you keep track of important people in your life, you can use the Contacts program so that you never lose track of someone's phone number or e-mail address again.

To help you keep track of random thoughts and ideas, you can use the simple Notes program that lets you organize related ideas in folders for quick access. If you need constant reminders of something, you can create electronic sticky notes that you can paste on your screen so you'll always see them.

If you receive important forms or documents stored as PDF files, you can fill them in without printing them out, and even add your own signature to an electronic form.

More importantly, you can synchronize data between a Macintosh and an iPhone or iPad; that way, you can access your crucial information whenever you need it.

Chapter 21

Keeping Track of Contacts

Everyone needs to keep track of people, whether for business or for personal reasons. After all, you probably don't want to memorize someone's street address or e-mail address.

In the past, people stored contact information in Rolodex files or black books. To make it easier to store names, addresses, and other information about people, OS X comes with a simple database called Contacts.

The advantage of using Contacts is that you can search for specific names, you can group names in categories, and then contact people directly through FaceTime or Messages. If you have an iPhone or an iPad, you can share and synchronize contact information between your Mac and iPhone or iPad using iCloud (see Chapter 20) so that you always have the latest contact information at all times.

Storing Data

The Contacts program lets you store a name and additional information, such as e-mail address, phone number, or street address. For some people, you might only store a name and street address. For others, you might store a name, street address, e-mail address, Twitter name, web site address, and anything else that provides a way to contact that person.

The Contacts program acts like an electronic version of a Rolodex file, storing the name of one person on a card or window. Unlike physical Rolodex cards, a Contacts card can contain as much or as little information as you like.

To store a name and additional contact information in the Contacts program, follow these steps:

1. Open the Contacts program in the Applications folder.

2. Click the File menu and choose New Card (File ➤ New Card) or press Command+N. A new blank card appears, as shown in Figure 21-1.

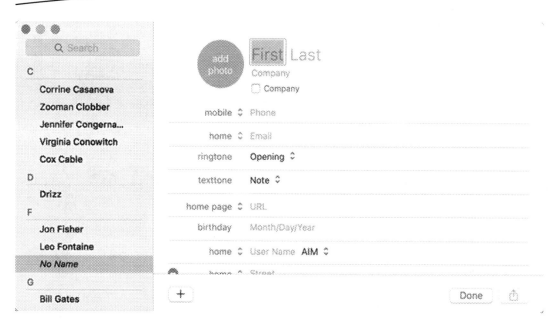

Figure 21-1. *A new card contains blank fields for storing contact information about a person*

3. Click in the First text field and type the person's first name.

4. Click in the Last text field and type the person's last name.

5. Click the Add Photo circle to add the person's photo or an image that reminds you of that person, as shown in Figure 21-2. You can choose to add a picture from a list of different images, from your iCloud Photos account, from the Faces category in Photos, or from your Mac's camera.

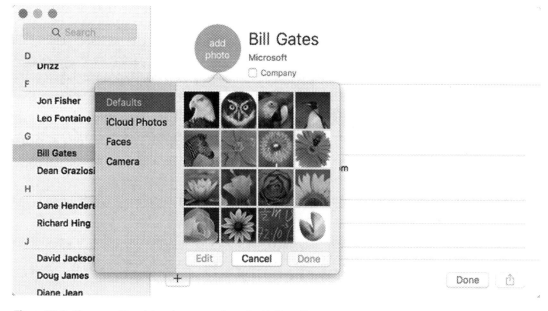

Figure 21-2. *You can add a picture to a person's contact information*

6. Click in any additional fields and type information in there, such as that person's mobile phone number, company name, or birthday.

7. (Optional) Click the plus sign icon (+) in the lower-left corner if you need to add additional fields, as shown in Figure 21-3.

Figure 21-3. Clicking the + icon lets you add more fields to store information

8. Click the Done button when you're finished adding information.

Once you've added information to a card in the Contacts program, you can always edit that information later. To edit a person's contact information, follow these steps:

1. Open the Contacts program

2. In the left pane, click the name of the person whose information you want to edit.

3. Click the Edit button in the bottom-left corner. Any currently stored information appears with a red circle and a white dash to the left of it, as shown in Figure 21-4.

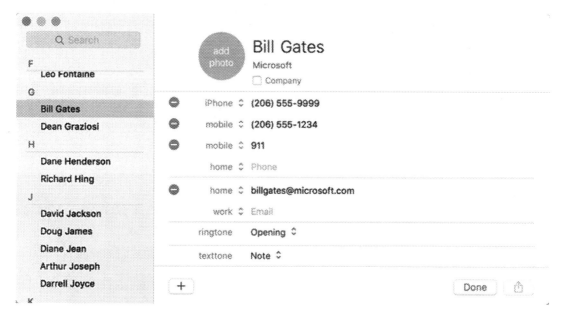

Figure 21-4. You can delete or edit data

4. Click in any existing data. Use the arrow keys and Backspace key to edit the existing data.

5. Click the red circle with the white dash that appears to the left of any data that you want to delete completely.

6. Click the Done button when you're finished.

Searching for a Name

The Contacts program lists names alphabetically by last name. When you have a small number of stored names, you can easily find a name just by scrolling through the name list. However, once you start storing large numbers of names, scrolling through the alphabetic list can get cumbersome.

That's why Contacts provides a search field. Just like searching on the Internet with a search engine, the search field lets you type part or all of the information that you want to find, such as part of a person's last name, telephone number, e-mail address, or street address. Just as long as you know some bit of information about someone, and that information is stored in the Contacts program, you'll be able to search and find it.

To search for a name in the Contacts program, follow these steps:

1. Open the Contacts program.

2. Click in the search field that appears in the upper-left corner of the Contacts window.

3. Type whatever contact information you recall, such as the city where the person lives or their mobile phone number, and press Return. The Contacts program only lists names matching your criteria.

4. Click the close icon (it looks like an X in a circle) that appears to the right of the search field to clear it and display all names in the Contacts program once more.

Grouping Names

The Contacts program organizes people alphabetically by last name. While this can help you find a particular person if you know their last name, it's not the most convenient way to find everyone or groups of people; for example, the names of co-workers or people associated with a particular group, such as your daughter's Girl Scouts organization. The Contacts program normally sorts all of these people in alphabetical order, but you can create groups.

A group is simply a subset of names that are related based on your own criteria. You can add or remove names to a group at any time, and names can appear in more than one group if you wish. There are three ways to do this:

▩ Create a group and then copy names into it

▩ Select the names that you want to put in a group and then create a group that contains only those names

▩ Create a smart group that automatically adds names to it

Creating a Group

The most straightforward way to create a group is to define it with a descriptive name and then copy names into that group. To create a group, follow these steps:

1. Open the Contacts program.

2. Click the File menu and choose New Group (File ➤ New Group). An untitled group appears in the left pane of the Contacts window, as shown in Figure 21-5.

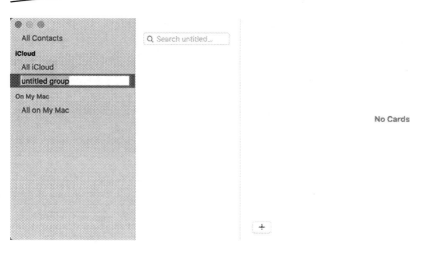

Figure 21-5. Group names appear in the left pane

3. Type a descriptive name for your group and press Return. The Contacts program creates a new group that's initially empty.

4. In the left pane, click All Contacts. This displays all names stored in the Contacts program.

5. Move the pointer over a name. Then drag and drop that name on the group name in the left pane to add it to the group, as shown in Figure 21-6.

> **Note**   You can place the same name in more than one group.

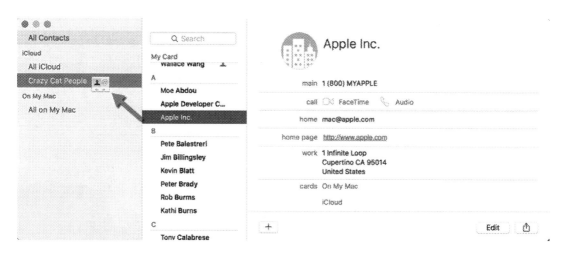

Figure 21-6. To store a name in a group, drag and drop it on a group name

Selecting Names to Put in a Group

Creating groups and then dragging names into that group can be tedious. To store names in groups more quickly, select multiple names and then tell the Contacts program to create a new group that includes all the names that you've selected.

To select multiple names and automatically store them in a group, follow these steps:

1. Open the Contacts program.

2. In the left pane, click All Contacts to view all the names stored in the Contacts program.

3. Hold down the Command key and click each name that you want to store in a group.

4. Click the File menu and choose New Group From Selection (File ➤ New Group From Selection). Your chosen names automatically appear in a group that appears in the left pane, as shown in Figure 21-7.

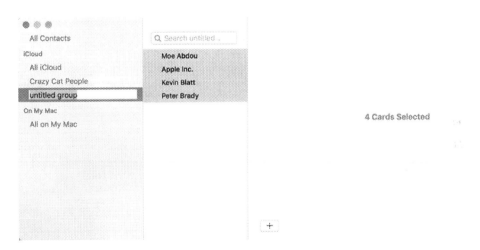

Figure 21-7. Contacts creates a generic group that automatically includes the names you selected

5. Type a descriptive name for your group and press Return.

Creating a Smart Group

There's one problem with creating a group and manually selecting the names to appear in that group. Each time you add a new name to the Contacts program, you need to decide whether that name belongs in one of your existing groups. If you forget to do this, your groups won't contain all the right names.

That's the purpose of smart groups. Smart groups use criteria that you define to determine which names should automatically appear in a group, such as names with certain e-mail addresses or company names.

To create a smart group, follow these steps:

1. Open the Contacts program.

2. Click the File menu and choose New Smart Group (File ➤ New Smart Group). The Contacts program displays a window in which you can define criteria for adding names automatically, as shown in Figure 21-8.

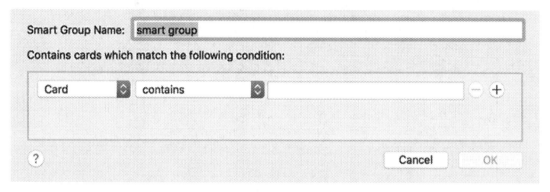

Figure 21-8. Defining criteria for a smart group in the Contacts program

3. Type a descriptive name for your smart group in the Smart Group Name text field.

4. Click in the first pop-up menu and choose an option, such as Card, Company, or Department, as shown in Figure 21-9.

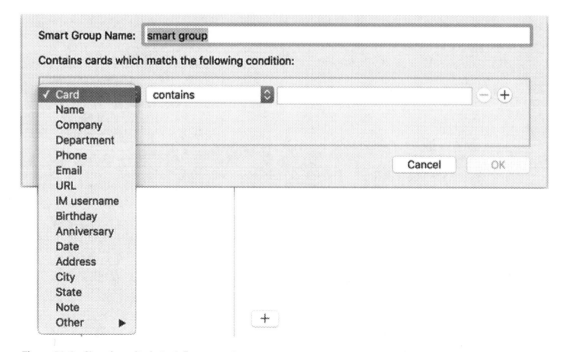

Figure 21-9. Choosing criteria to define a smart group

5. Click in the second pop-up menu and choose an option, such as "contains" or "is member of" (see Figure 21-10). Depending on the option you chose in step 4, the options listed in the second pop-up menu may be different.

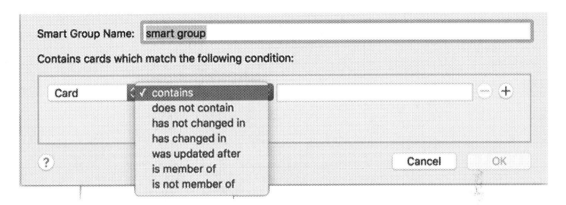

Figure 21-10. Specifying the details of an option

6. Click in the text field and type text to complete your criteria. For example, your criteria might list "Card contains Acme Corporation," which means any new name that you add to the Contacts program that includes the Acme Corporation is automatically included in the smart group.

7. (Optional) Click the plus (+) button on the far right to define an additional rule. If you click the minus (–) button, you can delete any rules you may have created.

8. Click the OK button. Your smart group appears in the left pane under the Smart Group category, as shown in Figure 21-11.

Figure 21-11. Smart groups appear under the Smart Group category to easily identify them from other groups

Renaming a Group

Once you've created a group, you can always rename it later. The only exception is that you cannot rename the All Contacts group. To rename a group, follow these steps:

1. Open the Contacts program.

2. In the left pane, click the group that you want to rename.

3. Click the Edit menu and choose Rename Group (Edit ➤ Rename Group). Your chosen group name appears highlighted.

4. Type or edit a new name and press Return when you're done.

Removing Names from a Group

If you created an ordinary group (not a smart group), you can remove names from a group. When you remove a name, you have two options.

First, you can completely delete the name from your Contacts program. Second, you can simply remove the name from a group but keep it saved in your Contacts program.

To remove a name from a group, follow these steps:

1. Open the Contacts program.

2. In the left pane, click the group that contains a name that you want to remove. A list of names in that group appears.

3. Click the Edit menu and choose Remove From Group (Edit ➤ Remove From Group).

Deleting a Group

Eventually you may want to delete a group. When you delete a group, you do not delete the names that appeared inside it. Any names that appear in the group that you want to delete also appears in the All Contacts group.

To delete a group, follow these steps:

1. Open the Contacts program.

2. In the left pane, click the group that you want to delete.

> **Note**   You cannot delete the All Contacts group.

3. Click the Edit menu and choose Delete Group (Edit ➤ Delete Group). A message asks if you're sure that you want to delete the group.

4. Click the Delete button (or Cancel if you don't want to delete the group).

Deleting Names

Although it's easy to add names, eventually you may want to delete names. You can delete names from the All Contacts group or from within another group you created.

When you delete a name from a group you've created, you have a choice of deleting the name completely or just removing the name from the group.

To delete a name, follow these steps:

1. Open the Contacts program.

2. In the left pane, click the group that contains a name you want to remove. If you click the All Contacts group name, you'll completely delete the name from the Contacts program.

3. Click the Edit menu and choose Delete Card (Edit ➤ Delete Card). A message asks if you're sure that you want to delete the name.

4. Click the Delete button (or Cancel if you don't want to delete the group).

Merging Names

Trying to keep track of so many names can be difficult, which means you may accidentally enter the same person's name in twice. To avoid storing duplicate information, the Contacts program finds duplicate names and merges the information.

To merge duplicate names, follow these steps:

1. Open the Contacts program.

2. Click the Card menu and choose Look for Duplicates (Card ➤ Look for Duplicates). If the Contacts program finds any duplicate names, a dialog asks if you want to merge the entries together, as shown in Figure 21-12.

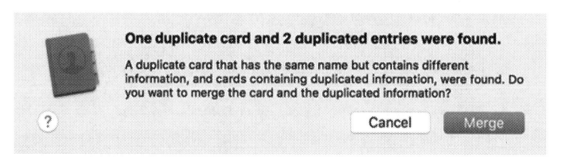

Figure 21-12. You can find and merge duplicate names

3. Click the Merge button

Sharing Contact Information

If you want to share contact information with others, you can save it as one of the following types of files:

- Contacts Archive: This file can only be read by someone using the Contacts program on another Mac.

- vCard: A standard format for storing contact information. Use the vCard format when you need to share contact information with people using other programs.

- PDF: Data stored as a Portable Document Format file. The receiver of this file needs to copy this data and paste it into another program if they wish to use it.

To share contact information, follow these steps:

1. Open the Contacts program.

2. Click the name that you want to share.

3. Do one of the following:

    a. Click the File menu and choose Export as PDF (File ➤ Export as PDF).

    b. Click the File menu, choose Export, and then choose Export vCard or Contacts Archive.

Summary

The Contacts program is especially handy if you use iCloud and have an iPhone. You can synchronize your contact list between both your iPhone and your Mac. Even if you're just using a Mac, the Contacts program is a convenient place to store the names and contact information of family members, friends, and business associates.

To help you organize your list of names, you can create groups. You can manually add names to a group or create a smart group that does this for you automatically based on criteria that you define.

The Contacts program is nothing more than a simple database for helping you keep track of the people in your life who are most important to you.

Chapter 22

Using Notes, Stickies, and the Calendar

One way to keep track of random information is to write it down on sticky notes and stick them on the side of your monitor. Another way is to have a calendar on your desk where you can easily jot down important appointments. Yet another way is to jot down ideas on napkins, envelopes, or other random pieces of paper and stack them in a pile on your desk.

While such paper solutions may work, they can be clumsy and messy. A far better solution is to store everything electronically on your Mac using one or more of the following programs:

- Notes: A simple word processor for jotting down quick thoughts and ideas.

- Stickies: An electronic version of sticky notes that appear on your screen so that you can't miss them.

- Calendar: An electronic calendar that keeps track of important dates and appointments.

By using any of these three programs by themselves or together, you can keep track of important information that you need to save and find at a glance.

Jotting Down Notes

You can use a word processor like Pages to capture ideas, but it often offers more features than you need, such as formatting or a table of contents. With the Notes program, you can create brief amounts of text that you can quickly browse.

Unlike a word processor, the Notes program stores all your notes together so you can easily find them. To organize your notes, the Notes program window displays three panes, as shown in Figure 22-1.

© Wallace Wang 2016
W. Wang, *Mac OS X for Absolute Beginners*, DOI 10.1007/978-1-4842-1913-3_22

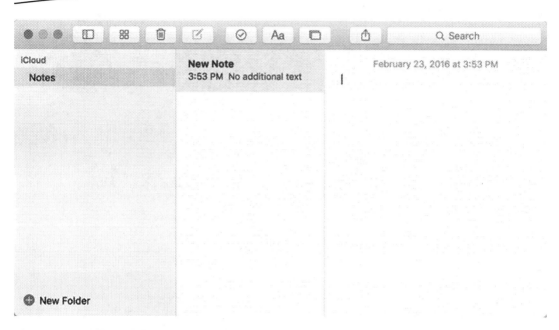

Figure 22-1. The Notes window consists of three panes

The left pane displays folders. Each folder can store any number of notes.

The middle pane displays one or more note titles. The first sentence you type in your note becomes its title, so type a descriptive title to help you identify a note's contents.

The right pane displays the actual contents of each note. This right pane is where you can view and edit text stored in a note.

Creating a New Note

To create a new note, follow these steps:

1. Open the Notes program in the Applications folder. The Notes window appears (see Figure 22-1).

2. Click the folder where you want to store your note.

3. Click the File menu and choose New Note, or press Command+N. The middle pane displays your new note.

4. Click in the right pane and type your text. Notice that as you type, the Notes program uses the first sentence to define the title of the note, as shown in Figure 22-2.

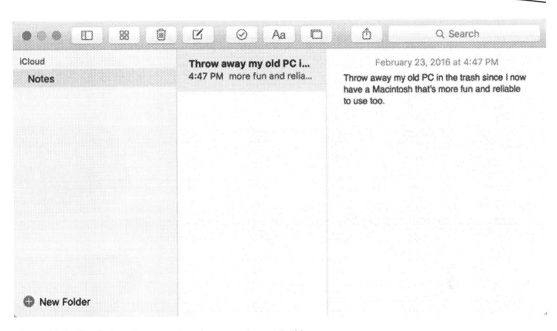

Figure 22-2. The first sentence you type becomes the note's title

Creating a New Folder

If you just have a handful of notes, you can easily find the one you want. However, once you start collecting large numbers of notes, you may want to organize related notes in a group. By creating multiple groups, you can keep your notes separated into different categories to easily find them again.

To create a folder, follow these steps:

1. Open the Notes program.

2. Click the File menu and choose New Folder (File ➤ New Folder). The new folder appears in the left pane, as shown in Figure 22-3.

Figure 22-3. A new folder appears in the left pane of the Notes window

3. Type a descriptive name for your folder and press Return.

Searching for a Note

When you've created multiple notes, you can search for them manually. However, it's faster and more accurate to search by entering a word or phrase that appears within a note.

To making searching for a note more accurate, use keywords in certain types of notes. For example, for work-related notes, add your company name or project name. For personal notes, type in a topic such as "dieting" or "real estate". If you do this consistently with all notes, then searching for your keywords can help you find your notes quickly.

To search for a note, follow these steps:

1. Open the Notes program.

2. Click in the Search field that appears in the upper-right corner of the Notes window.

3. Type part or all of a word or phrase that is contained in the note you want to find. A list of all notes that contain your search criteria appears. The search criteria is highlighted in the text, as shown in Figure 22-4.

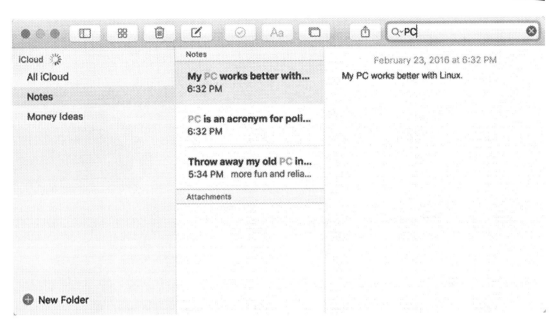

Figure 22-4. Notes highlights the search criteria in each note that matches

4.   Click the close icon (the X in the gray circle) that appears in the right of the Search field to clear it and view all of your notes once more.

Sharing Notes

Once you've created a note, you may want to share it with others. The simplest way to share a note is to copy the text in the Notes program and paste it in another program, such as an e-mail message. Notes lets you share a note in several ways, including as an e-mail message, as a text message in the Messages program, or as a note in Twitter, LinkedIn, or Facebook.

To share a note, follow these steps:

1.   Open the Notes program.

2.   Click the note that you want to share.

3.   Click the File menu and choose Share (File ➤ Share). A pop-up menu of ways to share the note appears, as shown in Figure 22-5. (You can also click the Share icon.)

Figure 22-5. Choosing how to share a note

4. Choose the way that you want to share your note. Each method of sharing works slightly differently. It helps to be familiar with each method, such as Twitter or Messages, to share a note successfully.

Renaming a Folder

A folder's name should be descriptive. If you don't like the name you initially gave a folder, you can always change it later. (The only folder than you cannot rename is the Notes folder.) To rename a folder, follow these steps:

1. Open the Notes program.

2. In the left pane, right-click the group that you want to rename. A pop-up menu appears, as shown in Figure 22-6.

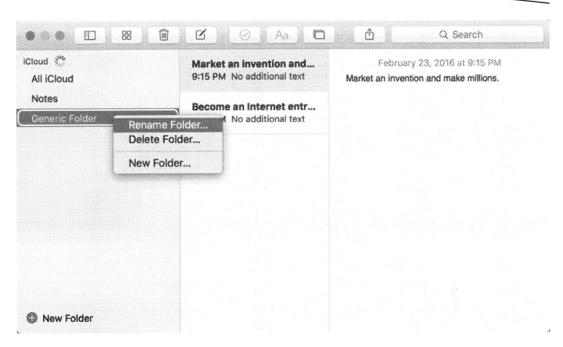

Figure 22-6. Renaming a folder

3. Choose Rename Folder. The current folder name appears selected.

4. Edit the existing folder name or type a new folder name and press Return when you're done.

Deleting Folders and Notes

Notes are often temporarily, which means that you'll eventually want to delete a note. You can delete notes individually or delete an entire folder of notes.

To delete an individual note, follow these steps:

1. Open the Notes program.

2. Click the note that you want to delete.

3. Click the Edit menu and choose Delete (Edit ➤ Delete). Your chosen note disappears.

Note   If you delete a note by mistake, just click the Edit menu and choose Undo (Edit ➤ Undo) or press Command+Z. This Undo command only works if you choose it immediately after deleting the note.

To delete an entire folder, follow these steps:

1. Open the Notes program.

2. Click the folder you want to delete.

3. Click the Edit menu and choose Delete (Edit ➤ Delete). A warning appears to let you know that deleting a folder will also delete all notes stored in that folder, as shown in Figure 22-7. Remember, you cannot delete the Notes folder because it contains all notes stored in the program.

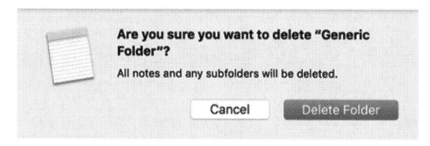

Figure 22-7. A warning message appears when you try to delete a folder

4. Click the Delete Folder button.

Note When you delete notes, the Notes program actually retains deleted notes for up to 30 days. To see deleted notes, click the Recently Deleted group in the left pane of the Notes program, as shown in Figure 22-8.

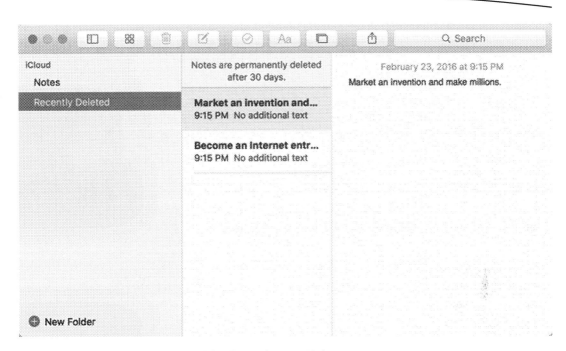

Figure 22-8. *The Notes program stores deleted notes for up to 30 days*

Using Stickies

The Notes program is a handy place to capture ideas and thoughts; you always know where to find them. Another way to capture your ideas is to use the Stickies program.

The main difference between the Notes program and the Stickies program is that the Notes program lets you organize notes into folders but the Stickies program lets you display a Stickies window on the screen at all times to mimic pasting a paper sticky note on the front of your computer screen.

Because the Stickies program displays miniature windows all over the screen, it's meant to store a handful of Stickies windows. If you store too many sticky notes, they will eventually clutter the screen.

Creating a Sticky Note

To type text into the Stickies program, follow these steps:

1.   Open the Stickies program.

2.   Click the File menu and choose New Note (File ➤ New Note). The Stickies program creates a new Stickies window, as shown in Figure 22-9.

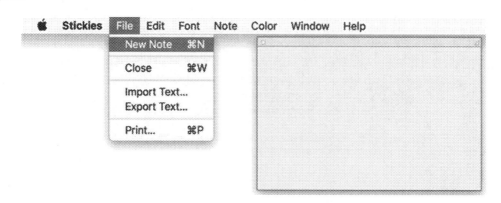

Figure 22-9. A new Stickies note

3. Type any text you wish into the Stickies window.

Once you've created a sticky note, you can move or resize it on the screen to make it easier to see. To move a sticky note, follow these steps:

1. Open the Stickies program.

2. Move the pointer over the horizontal bar at the top of the Stickies window, as shown in Figure 22-10.

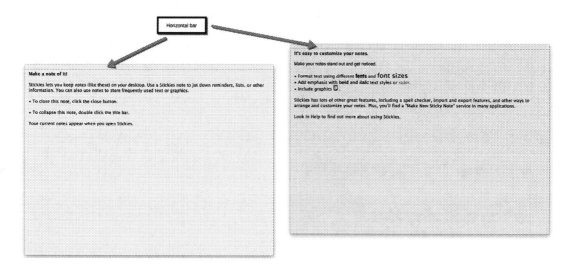

Figure 22-10. A new Stickies note

3. Hold down the left mouse button (or press a finger on the trackpad) and move the mouse or slide your finger on the trackpad to move the Stickies window on the screen.

Another way to make sticky notes easier to see is to resize them. Just like resizing any window on the screen, you can resize a Stickies window by moving the pointer over the edge or corner of a Stickies window until the pointer turns into a two-way pointing arrow.

Then drag the mouse or trackpad to resize the window. If you move the pointer to a corner of a Stickies window, you can resize both the width and height of the window at the same time.

Making a Sticky Note Easy to See

Whenever you start the Stickies program, all of your sticky notes appear on the screen. That's why the Stickies program is best for storing a small number of notes: because too many notes just clutters the screen.

Moving and resizing sticky notes keeps them organized on your screen, but the Stickies program offers two additional ways to make sticky notes easier to see.

First, you can turn a sticky note into a floating window. Normally, if you switch to a different program, all of your Stickies windows are hidden underneath other program windows. A floating window means that a Stickies window always appears on the screen, even if you switch to another program. This mimics slapping a physical sticky note on your screen.

Second, you can change the color of a sticky note. By using different colors for different topics, you can make it easy to find a particular sticky note.

To turn a sticky note into a floating window, follow these steps:

1.   Open the Stickies program.

2.   Click the sticky note that you want to turn into a floating window.

3.   Click the Note menu and choose floating Window (Note ➤ Floating Window). Your chosen Stickies window now appears on the screen at all times unless you exit out of the Stickies program.

> **Note**   Repeat the preceding steps to turn off a floating window so that it doesn't always appear on the screen.

To change the color of a sticky note, follow these steps:

1.   Open the Stickies program.

2.   Click the sticky note that you want to change to a different color.

3.   Click the Color menu and choose a color, as shown in Figure 22-11.

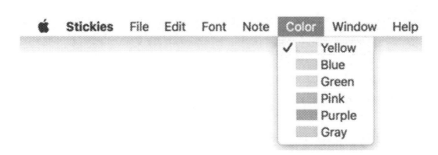

Figure 22-11. *The Color menu lets you choose a different sticky note background color*

Importing and Exporting Text into a Sticky Note

Normally, you just type text into a sticky note. However, if you have text stored in an ordinary text file (not a word processor file, such as a Pages or Microsoft Word file), you can import that text file onto a sticky note.

Since Stickies windows are fairly small, you don't want to import large amounts of text, but importing a small text file lets you display important information on a sticky note.

To import text onto a sticky note, follow these steps:

1. Open the Stickies program.

2. Click the File menu and choose Import Text (File ➤ Import Text). An Open dialog appears.

3. Click the text file that contains text you want to display on a sticky note and click the Open button. The Stickies program creates a new sticky note with the contents of your chosen text file.

If you've created an important sticky note, you can save it as a text file. When you export a sticky note, you can save the text as plain text with no formatting, or as Rich Text Format (RTF), which preserves formatting.

To export text from a sticky note, follow these steps:

1. Open the Stickies program.

2. Click the sticky note that contains the text that you want to save.

3. Click the File menu and choose Export Text (File ➤ Export Text). An Export dialog appears, as shown in Figure 22-12.

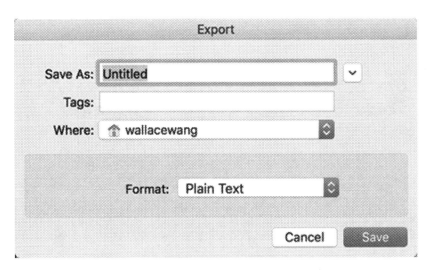

Figure 22-12. *The Export dialog lets you define a file name, a location, and a file format*

4. Type a descriptive name for your file in the Save As text field.

5. Click the Where pop-up menu and choose a folder to store your file.

6. Click in the Format pop-up menu and choose a file format, such as Plain Text or RTF (Rich Text Format), which retains any formatting in your text.

7. Click the Save button.

Deleting a Sticky Note

No matter how useful a sticky note might be, eventually you'll want to get rid of it. To delete a sticky note, follow these steps:

1. Open the Stickies program.

2. Click the sticky note that you want to delete.

3. Click the close icon in the upper-left corner of the sticky note, as shown in Figure 22-13. A warning dialog appears to let you know that if you delete a sticky note, you'll lose the contents of that note.

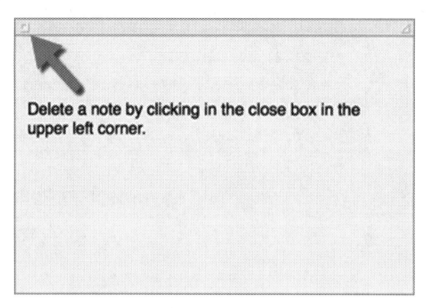

Delete a note by clicking in the close box in the upper left corner.

Figure 22-13. The close icon appears in the upper-left corner of sticky notes

4. Click the Don't Save button. (If you click the Save button, you have the opportunity to export your sticky note text to a file.)

Using the Calendar

The Calendar program helps you keep track of appointments on a particular date. You can look at your calendar from a yearly, monthly, weekly, or daily view. You can spot appointments far in advance, or check your daily schedule to see your appointments and how long they should take.

Changing the Calendar View

With a paper calendar, you're stuck with viewing a monthly, a weekly, or a daily view. With the Calendar program, you can switch views any time by choosing one of the following (also see Figure 22-14):

- Year: View ➤ By Year; press Command+4; or click the Year icon.
- Month: View ➤ By Month; press Command+3; or click the Month icon.
- Week: View ➤ By Week; press Command+2; or click the Week icon.
- Day: View ➤ By Day; press Command+1; or click the Day icon.

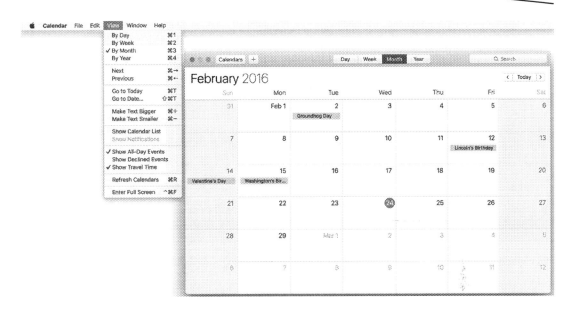

Figure 22-14. Switching calendar views

Setting an Appointment

No matter which calendar view you choose, you can create an appointment, also known as an *event*, for a particular date. To create an appointment, follow these steps:

1. Open the Calendar program.

2. Click the File menu and choose New Event (File ➤ New Event), press Command+N, or click the plus sign (+) icon in the upper-left corner of the Calendar window. A Create Quick Event window appears, as shown in Figure 22-15.

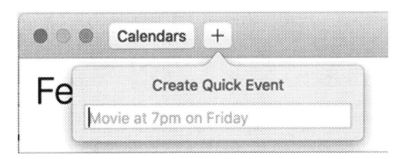

Figure 22-15. Creating an appointment

3. Click in the Create Quick Event text field, type your appointment, and press Return. As you type, the Calendar program tries to identify times and dates automatically, such as April 12 or next Friday. The Calendar program places your appointment on the current date and displays a window in which you can modify that appointment, as shown in Figure 22-16.

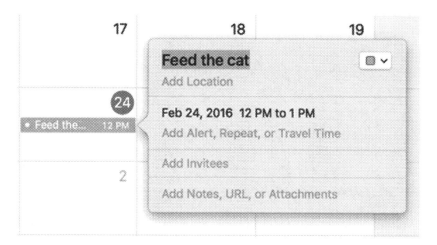

Figure 22-16. A pop-up window shows details of an appointment

4. Click the date of your appointment to modify it. A new pop-up window appears, as shown in Figure 22-17.

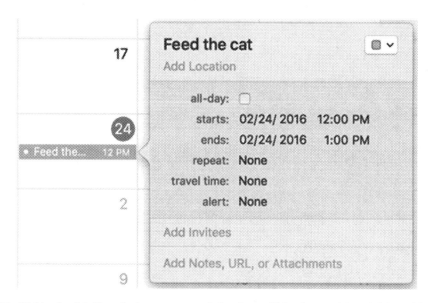

Figure 22-17. Clicking the date/time displays a pop-up window for modifying the appointment date and time

5. Do one or more of the following:

   a. Click the "all-day" check box to set the appointment for the entire day.

   b. Click "starts" and "ends" date and time to define the starting/ending date and time, as shown in Figure 22-18.

   c. Click "repeat" to define whether this appointment occurs every day, week, month, or year.

   d. Click "travel time" to define the travel time needed to get to your appointment.

   e. Click "alert" if you want the Calendar program to alert you ahead of time, such as 10 or 30 minutes before your appointment.

Figure 22-18. Defining a different starting/ending date for an appointment

6. Click anywhere away from this pop-up window to make it disappear.

Deleting an Appointment

When you're done with an appointment, you can delete it from your calendar. To delete an appointment, follow these steps:

1. Open the Calendar program.

2. Click the appointment that you want to delete.

3. Click the Edit menu and choose Delete (Edit ➤ Delete).

> **Note** If you accidentally delete an appointment, you can retrieve it by immediately choosing the Edit ➤ Undo command or by pressing Command+Z.

Summary

When you have fleeting thoughts that you want to capture, store them in the Notes or Stickies programs. The Notes program is useful for storing large numbers of ideas that you can organize into related groups.

The Stickies program is useful for storing a small number of brief ideas that you can also keep floating on the screen so that they're always visible, like a real sticky note.

You can use the Calendar program to keep track of your schedule and plan your day, week, month, or year.

By using the Notes, Stickies, and Calendar programs, you can turn your Mac into an electronic desk organizer. You'll always have all the information you need at your fingertips just as long as you have your Mac.

Chapter 23

Modifying PDF Files

Many businesses and government agencies store crucial forms and documents as PDF (Portable Document Format) files because anyone can open and view a PDF file on nearly any type of computer. Best of all, PDF files retain all formatting, so you can print a form, fill it out by hand, and mail it.

Although printing a PDF form and filling it out by hand is one way to use a PDF file, another way is to modify it directly. By doing so, you can type or add comments into a PDF file. For example, let's suppose that someone sent you a PDF file to review. You could type your comments directly in the form and send the modified PDF file back to the other person.

In the past, you needed to buy expensive software to modify PDF files, but OS X comes with a free program called Preview that can modify PDF files. By using the Preview program, you can both view and modify PDF files.

Rearranging Pages

Most PDF files have multiple pages. With the Preview program, you can rearrange the order of the pages, delete pages, or insert a PDF file within the pages of another PDF file.

To rearrange the pages of a PDF file, follow these steps:

1. Open the Preview program.

2. Click the File menu and choose Open (File ➤ Open). Choose the PDF file whose pages you want to rearrange.

3. Click the View menu and choose Thumbnails (View ➤ Thumbnails) so that a check mark appears to the left of the Thumbnails command. The Preview window displays thumbnail images of each page in the PDF file, as shown in Figure 23-1.

© Wallace Wang 2016
W. Wang, *Mac OS X for Absolute Beginners*, DOI 10.1007/978-1-4842-1913-3_23

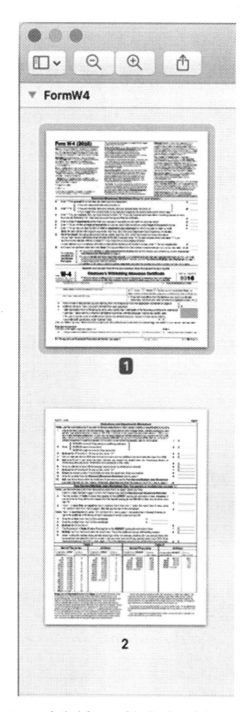

Figure 23-1. Thumbnails of pages appear in the left pane of the Preview window

4. Move the pointer over a thumbnail image of a page and drag it up or down to a new position so that the existing thumbnail pages make room for it.

5. Release the left mouse button or trackpad when the thumbnail page is in the location that you want.

6. Click the File menu and choose Save (File ➤ Save) to save the rearranged pages in the PDF file.

Adding Pages

It's possible to add graphic images or even another PDF file inside an existing PDF file. To insert a graphic image or another PDF file, follow these steps:

1. Open the Preview program and the PDF file that you want to modify.

2. Make sure that thumbnail views appear in the left pane of the Preview window.

3. Click a thumbnail page. Any graphic images or PDF files that you add now appear after this thumbnail page.

4. Click the Edit menu, choose Insert, and choose Page from File (Edit ➤ Insert ➤ Page from File). A dialog appears.

> **Note**   If you choose Edit ➤ Insert ➤ Blank Page, you can insert a blank page in your PDF file.

5. Click the PDF file or graphic image that you want to add to the currently open PDF file. Click the Open button. The graphic image or PDF file appears in the current PDF file.

6. Click the File menu and choose Save (File ➤ Save) to save the added pages in the PDF file.

Deleting Pages

Besides adding new pages to a PDF file, you can also delete pages by following these steps:

1. Open the Preview program with the PDF file that you want to modify.

2. Make sure that thumbnail views appear in the left pane of the Preview window.

3. Click a thumbnail page. If you hold down the Command key, you can click to select more than one thumbnail page.

4. Press the Delete button on the keyboard.

> **Note**   If you accidentally delete a page, press Command+Z or click Edit ➤ Undo.

5. Click the File menu and choose Save (File ➤ Save) to save the rearranged pages in the PDF file.

Marking Up Text

While you can't physically edit the text or graphics stored in a PDF file, you can highlight text, such as changing the text background to yellow (to mimic highlighting with a yellow marker), underlining text, or striking through text.

To mark up text, follow these steps:

1. Open the Preview program with the PDF file that you want to modify.

2. Click the Tools menu and choose Annotate (Tools ➤ Annotate). A submenu appears, as shown in Figure 23-2.

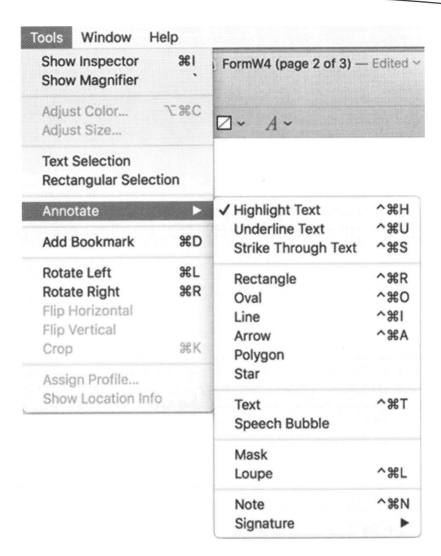

Figure 23-2. *The Annotate submenu lets you mark up text in a PDF file*

3. Choose one of the following:

   a. Highlight Text

   b. Underline Text

   c. Strike Through Text

4. Select the text in the PDF file that you want to modify, as shown in Figure 23-3.

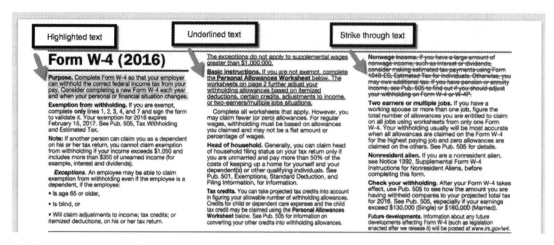

Figure 23-3. *Three different ways to annotate text in a PDF file*

5. Click the File menu and choose Save (File ➤ Save) to save the modified pages in the PDF file.

Adding Text

Although you can't edit text displayed in a PDF file, you can add your own text and place it on a PDF file. This can be especially useful for filling out forms.

In the past, you would have to print a PDF file and fill it the blanks by hand. With the Preview program, you can type text inside of boxes and move those boxes over the appropriate places in a PDF file. This lets you fill out a form stored as a PDF file, including typing your name, address, or phone number.

To add text to a PDF file, follow these steps:

1. Open the Preview program with a PDF file that you want to modify.

2. Click the Tools menu, choose Annotate, and then choose Text (Tools ➤ Annotate ➤ Text). A text box appears, as shown in Figure 23-4.

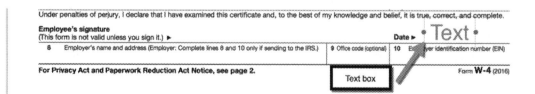

Figure 23-4. *Adding a text box to a PDF file*

3. Do one or more of the following to modify the text box:

    a. Double-click inside the text box and type anything you want to appear on the PDF file, such as your name or the date.

    b. Move the pointer over the text box handle (little circles on the left and right edges of the text box) and drag the mouse to resize the text box.

    c. Move the pointer over the text box so that it turns into a hand pointer, and then drag the mouse to move the text box to a new location in the PDF file.

4. Click the Text Style icon to display a formatting pop-up window that lets you do such things as change the text color or font (see Figure 23-5).

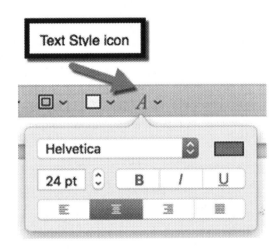

Figure 23-5. Formatting text in a text box

Besides using text boxes, another way to add text to a PDF file is through speech bubbles, which look like the dialogue bubbles used in comic books. The main purpose of a speech bubble is to type a comment and have the speech bubble point to a specific part of a PDF file.

By pointing a speech bubble at a particular place in a PDF file, you can add a comment about specific items in the PDF file, such as pointing out an error or missing information. A speech bubble is basically a different type of text box with a border that makes it easy to spot.

To add a speech bubble, follow these steps:

1. Open the Preview program with a PDF file that you want to modify.

2. Click the Tools menu, choose Annotate, and then choose Speech Bubble (Tools ➤ Annotate ➤ Speech Bubble). A speech bubble appears, as shown in Figure 23-6.

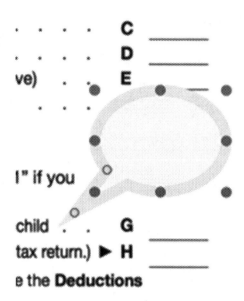

Figure 23-6. Adding a speech bubble to a PDF file

3. Do one or more of the following to modify the speech bubble:

  a. Double-click inside the speech bubble and type a comment.

  b. Move the pointer over the text box handle (little circles around the edges of the speech bubble) and drag the mouse to resize the speech bubble.

  c. Move the pointer over the speech bubble so that it turns into a hand pointer, and then drag the mouse to move the speech bubble to a new location in the PDF file.

  d. Move the pointer over the handle (a clear circle) near the pointer of the speech bubble and drag the mouse to move the pointer to a new location.

You can modify the border or interior of a text box or speech bubble by clicking either the Border Color or Fill Color icon, as shown in Figure 23-7.

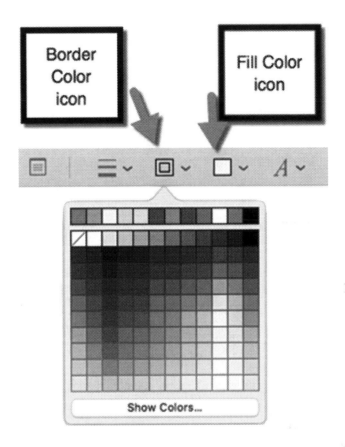

Figure 23-7. Coloring a text box or speech bubble with the Border Color or Fill Color options

Adding Signatures

In the past, one of the biggest problems with PDF files was adding a signature. That's why most people simply printed out a PDF file, filled it out by hand, and signed it before mailing or faxing it to someone else.

While you can still sign a PDF file by printing it out, you can also sign a PDF file by either using a trackpad (if you have one) or the camera on your Mac (if your Mac has a built-in camera).

With a trackpad, you can use your finger to sign your name. With a camera, you can sign your name on a sheet of white paper and then take a picture of your signature.

With either method, you can then save your signature in Preview. Whenever you need to add a signature to a PDF file, you can use your saved signature to paste it in the appropriate spot on the PDF file.

Capturing a Signature with a Trackpad

If you have a trackpad, you can capture your signature by following these steps:

1. Open the Preview program.

2. Click the Tools menu, choose Annotate, Signature, and then Manage Signatures (Tools ➤ Annotate ➤ Signature ➤ Manage Signatures). Another way is to click the View menu and choose Show Markup Toolbar (View ➤ Show Markup Toolbar), and then click the Sign icon.

3. Click the Trackpad tab, as shown in Figure 23-8.

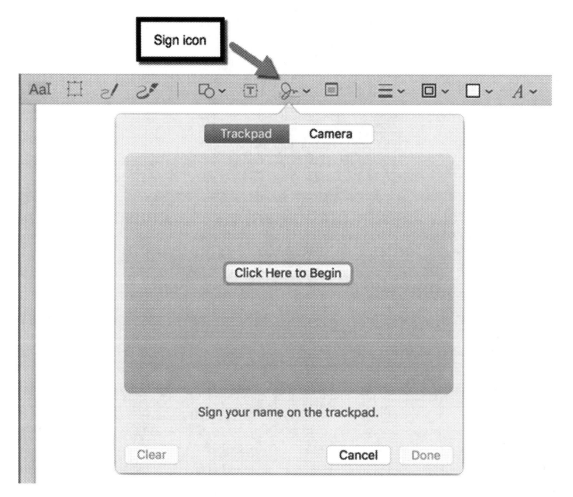

Figure 23-8. Writing a signature with a trackpad

4. Click the Click Here to Begin button.

5. Sign your name with your finger on the trackpad and press any key when you're done. If you want to try again, click the Clear button and sign your name again.

6. Click the Done button. The Preview program stores your signature under the Sign icon, as shown in Figure 23-9. You can store as many signatures as you wish.

Figure 23-9. Stored signatures appear under the Sign icon

Capturing a Signature with the Mac Camera

Almost all Mac models (except for the Mac mini) come with a built-in camera, thus another way to capture a signature is to take a picture of it. Just sign your name on a white sheet of paper and then hold your signature up to the camera to capture it.

To capture your signature with the camera, follow these steps:

1. Open the Preview program.

2. Write your signature on a white sheet of paper.

3. Click the Tools menu, choose Annotate, Signature, and then Manage Signatures (Tools ➤ Annotate ➤ Signature ➤ Manage Signatures). Another way is to click the View menu and choose Show Markup Toolbar (View ➤ Show Markup Toolbar), and then click the Sign icon.

4. Click the Camera tab.

5. Hold up your written signature to the camera and click the Done button.

Placing a Signature in a PDF File

Once you've captured one or more signatures using either the trackpad or camera, you can place that signature on a PDF file by following these steps:

1. Open the Preview program and open the PDF file in which you want to add a signature.

2. Click the View menu and choose Show Markup Toolbar (View ➤ Show Markup Toolbar) to make the markup toolbar appear. (If the markup toolbar is already visible, skip this step.)

3. Click where you want to add the signature on the page.

4. Click the Sign icon. A list of stored signatures appears, as shown in Figure 23-10.

Figure 23-10. Your saved signatures appear in a menu

5. Click the signature that you want to use. The Preview program places your signature in the PDF file, as shown in Figure 23-11.

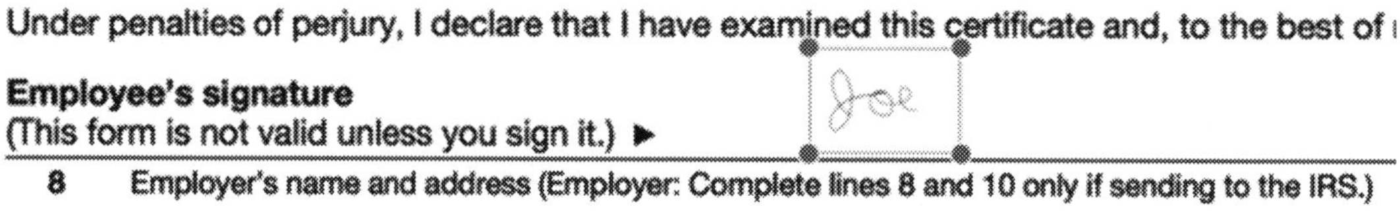

Under penalties of perjury, I declare that I have examined this certificate and, to the best of

Employee's signature
(This form is not valid unless you sign it.) ▶

8   Employer's name and address (Employer: Complete lines 8 and 10 only if sending to the IRS.)

Figure 23-11. A signature appears in a box that you can move or resize

6. Do one or more of the following to modify the signature box:

   a. Move the pointer over the box handle (little circles around the corners) and drag the mouse to resize the signature box.

   b. Move the pointer over the signature box so that it turns into a hand pointer, and then drag the mouse to move the signature box to a new location in the PDF file.

> **Note**   Anyone with access to your Mac could potentially use your saved signature, so guard against access by unauthorized users.

Deleting a Signature

Eventually, you may want to delete a saved signature. Deleting your saved signature makes sure that no one else can access it to impersonate you.

To delete a signature, follow these steps:

1. Open the Preview program.

2. Click the View menu and choose Show Markup Toolbar (View ➤ Show Markup Toolbar) to make the markup toolbar appear. (If the markup toolbar is already visible, skip this step.)

3. Click the Sign icon to view a list of saved signatures.

4. Move the mouse pointer over the signature that you want to delete. A close icon (an X inside a gray circle) appears to the right of the signature, as shown in Figure 23-12.

Figure 23-12. A close icon appears when the pointer is over a signature

5. Click the close icon next to the signature that you want to delete.

Saving Changes to a PDF File

If you've modified a PDF file in any way, remember to save your changes. To save a PDF file in the Preview program, click the File menu and choose Save, or press Command+S.

Summary

PDF files are convenient for sharing data, but you can modify them with the Preview program. The simplest way to modify a PDF file is to add, delete, or rearrange its pages.

A more common way to modify a PDF file is to mark up in the PDF file, such as highlighting, underlining, or striking through existing text. These features let you edit text in a PDF file so that others can see your suggestions.

When you need to add text, you can choose between a text box and a speech bubble. A text box lets you fill out a form stored in a PDF file, whereas a speech bubble is more useful for pointing out certain text and offering your comments.

If you need to sign forms, you can capture and save your signature to add it to the file without physically printing the form and signing it by hand.

No matter how you modify a PDF file, always remember to save your changes using the Save command.

Chapter **24**

Capturing Screenshots and Video

In the business world, many people give presentations using programs like Microsoft PowerPoint or Apple's Keynote. Usually such presentations consist of text and graphics, but sometimes you might need to capture images from your screen. Such images can be static (known as a *screenshot*) or video, such as showing the steps for using a particular program.

Capturing images from the screen used to require buying specialized software, but OS X includes several ways to capture screenshots and video. By capturing images directly from the screen, you can show people your computer display rather than try to describe it to them.

There are three ways to capture screenshots on a Mac. First, you can use the screen-capturing feature in OS X. Second, you can use a separate program called Grab. Third, you can use the Preview program

The main difference between these three methods is that the OS X screen capture saves screenshots in the PNG file format and automatically stores them on your desktop. Any time you're using your Mac, you can capture a screenshot with the OS X screen capture feature.

On the other hand, to capture a screenshot with the Grab program, you must specifically load the Grab program. The Grab program does let you capture a timed screenshot in which you can set a delay before capturing it. The Grab program also saves screenshots in the .tiff file format, which takes up more space.

The Preview program captures and saves screenshots as graphic images (PNG or JPG files), or as PDF files. Depending on which type of file format you need, you can choose the best screen-capturing method for your needs.

© Wallace Wang 2016
W. Wang, *Mac OS X for Absolute Beginners*, DOI 10.1007/978-1-4842-1913-3_24

Capturing Screenshots with OS X

To capture a screenshot with OS X, you must use one of the following keystroke combinations:

- Command+Shift+3: Captures the entire screen

- Command+Shift+4: Captures part of the screen

- Command+Shift+4: Captures a window

When you want to capture the whole screen, press Command+Shift3. When you want to capture part of the screen (either a portion you define or a specific open window), press Command+Shift+4.

Capturing the Whole Screen

To capture the whole screen, press Command+Shift+3. OS X then stores your screenshot on the desktop as a PNG file with a generic name that includes the date and time it was captured, as shown in Figure 24-1.

Figure 24-1. A screenshot contains the date and time of its capture

Capturing Part of the Screen

You may not always want to capture the entire screen, so OS X gives you the option to capture just part of the screen. You can either define the area to capture or capture a single window on the screen.

To capture part of the screen that you define, follow these steps:

1. Press Command+Shift+4. The pointer turns into a crosshair.

2. Move the crosshair pointer where you want to start capturing part of the screen.

3. Hold down the left mouse button (or press on the trackpad) and move the mouse (or slide your finger on the trackpad) to define a gray rectangular area to capture, as shown in Figure 24-2.

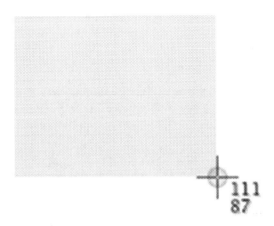

Figure 24-2. Dragging the mouse (or trackpad) can capture part of the screen

4. Release the left mouse button (or trackpad). Your screenshot appears on the desktop.

Capturing a Window

If you just want to capture an open window on the screen, you could manually drag the mouse around the window boundaries, but it's faster and more accurate to let OS X capture the entire window instead.

To capture a single open window on the screen, follow these steps:

1. Press Command+Shift+4. The pointer turns into a crosshair.

2. Press the spacebar. The crosshair pointer changes into a camera pointer.

3. Move the pointer over the open window that you want to capture. The currently selected window appears highlighted so that you know which window you're about to capture.

4. Click the mouse (or trackpad). Your screenshot appears on the desktop.

Using the Grab Program

Using the OS X screen-capturing feature is fast and simple, but if you want the flexibility to delay capture for a few seconds, then you might want to use the Grab program.

The Grab program is stored in the Utilities folder inside the Applications folder. Like the OS X screen-capturing features, the Grab program can also capture the entire screen, part of the screen, or a single open window on the screen.

When using the Grab program, you must manually save any screenshots by clicking the File menu and choosing Save, or by pressing Command+S.

To capture the whole screen, follow these steps:

1. Open the Grab program stored in the Utilities folder (inside the Applications folder).

2. Click the Capture menu and choose Screen (Capture ➤ Screen), or press Command+Z. A dialog appears, as shown in Figure 24-3.

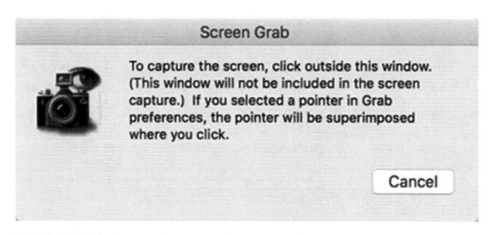

Figure 24-3. The Grab dialog appears when you want to capture an entire screen

3. Click anywhere outside the Screen Grab window. The Grab program captures the screen and displays it on the screen.

4. Click the File menu and choose Save (File ➤ Save) or press Command+S. A dialog appears, asking where you want to save the screenshot and what name you want to give it.

To capture part of the screen, follow these steps:

1. Open the Grab program stored in the Utilities folder (inside the Applications folder).

2. Click the Capture menu and choose Selection (Capture ➤ Selection). A dialog appears, as shown in Figure 24-4.

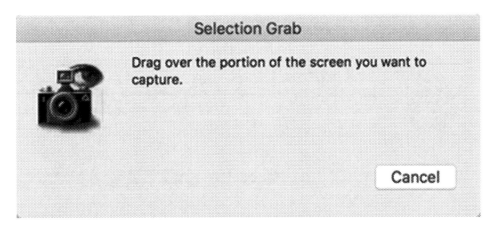

Figure 24-4. The Grab dialog appears when you want to capture part of a screen

3. Hold down the left mouse button (or press a finger on the trackpad) and move the mouse (or slide your fingertip on the trackpad) to define the area that you want to capture, which appears in a red rectangular box.

4. Release the mouse (or trackpad) when you're done defining the area that you want to capture. The Grab program displays your screenshot in a window.

5. Click the File menu and choose Save (File ➤ Save), or press Command+S. A dialog asks where you want to save the screenshot and what name you want to give it.

To capture a single open window on the screen, follow these steps:

1. Open the Grab program stored in the Utilities folder (inside the Applications folder).

2. Click the Capture menu and choose Window (Capture ➤ Window). A dialog appears, as shown in Figure 24-5.

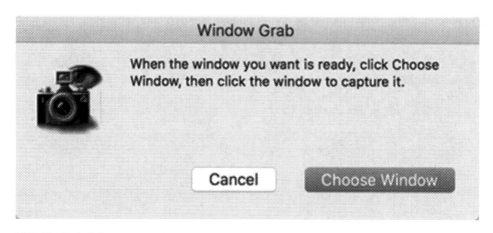

Figure 24-5. The Grab dialog appears when you want to capture a window on the screen

3. Click the Choose Window button.

4. Click the window that you want to capture. The Grab program
    displays your screenshot in a window.

5. Click the File menu and choose Save (File ➤ Save), or press
    Command+S. A dialog asks where you want to save the screenshot
    and what name you want to give it.

Capturing a Timed Screen

One unique feature of the Grab program is its ability to capture a timed screen. That means
the Grab program delays capturing the screen for a few seconds. This gives you a chance to
set up your screen the way you want before capturing it.

When capturing a timed screen, you can only capture the entire screen, not just part of it.

To use the timed screen feature, follow these steps:

1. Open the Grab program in the Utilities folder (inside the Applications
    folder).

2. Click the Capture menu and choose Timed Screen (Capture ➤ Timed
    Screen). A dialog appears, as shown in Figure 24-6.

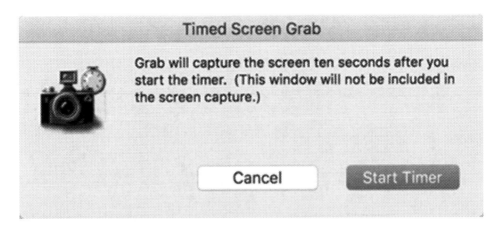

Figure 24-6. The Grab dialog appears when you want to capture a timed screen

3. Click the Start Timer screen.

4. The Timed Screen Grab dialog shows you the amount of time left before the Grab program captures the entire screen. Eventually, the Grab program displays your screenshot in a window.

5. Click the File menu and choose Save (File ➤ Save), or press Command+S. A dialog asks where you want to save the screenshot and what name you want to give it.

Capturing the Pointer

The Grab program gives you the option of capturing screens with or without the pointer. Sometimes you may want the pointer to appear to show exactly what the screen looks like, but other times the pointer simply gets in the way.

To determine how to capture the pointer in a screenshot, follow these steps:

1. Open the Grab program in the Utilities folder (inside the Applications folder).

2. Click the Grab menu and choose Preferences (Grab ➤ Preferences). A Preferences window appears, as shown in Figure 24-7.

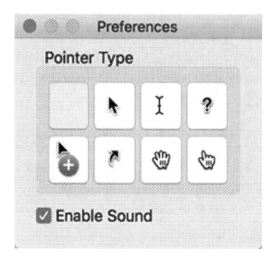

Figure 24-7. *The Grab Preferences window lets you choose how the pointer appears in a screenshot*

3. Click a pointer type. If you don't want the pointer to appear at all, click the blank option.

4. Click the red dot (the close button) in the upper-left corner of the Preferences window to make it disappear. From now on, every time that you capture a screenshot with the Grab program, the pointer will appear the way you chose in step 3.

Capturing Screenshots with the Preview Program

Yet another way to capture screenshots is with the Preview program. You can capture all or part of a screen, or capture just a single window on the screen.

You can then save captured screenshots as individual files or as part of an existing file.

To capture a screenshot with the Preview program, follow these steps:

1. Open the Preview program.

2. Click the File menu and choose Take Screenshot (File ➤ Screenshot). A submenu appears, as shown in Figure 24-8.

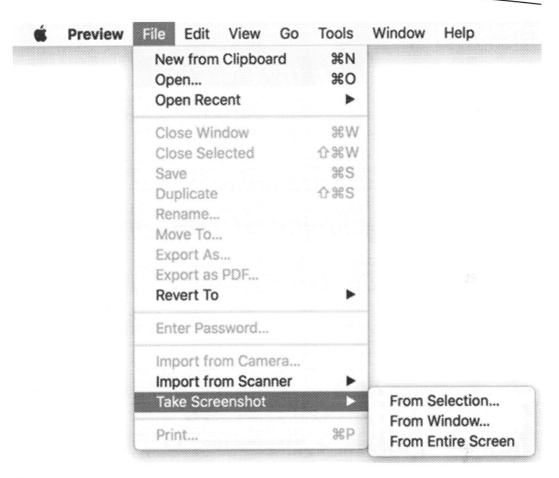

Figure 24-8. The Take Screenshot submenu

3. Choose one of the following:

    a. From Selection: Drag the mouse to define a rectangular area of the screen to capture.

    b. From Window: Click a window to capture.

    c. From Entire Screen: Capture the entire screen.

    The Preview program displays your captured screenshot in a window.

4. Click the File menu and choose Save (File ➤ Save). A Save dialog appears, as shown in Figure 24-9.

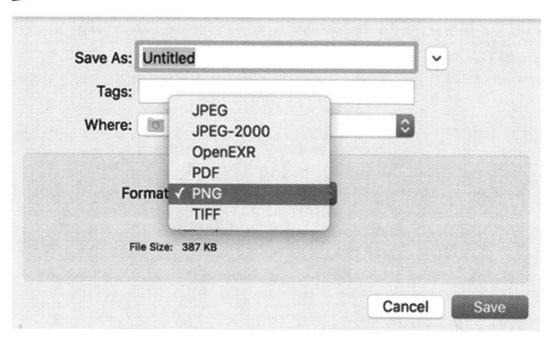

Figure 24-9. The Save dialog lets you define a file format to save your screenshot in

5. Click in the Save As text field and type a descriptive name for your file.

6. Click in the Where pop-up menu and choose a folder to store your file.

7. Click in the Format pop-up menu and choose a file format (such as PDF or PNG) to store your screenshot.

8. Click the Save button.

Capturing Video and Audio

Capturing screenshots can show someone else images from your Mac. For greater impact, you might prefer to capture video of your screen. Such a video can demonstrate how to perform a task so that others can see exactly which steps they need to follow.

When you capture video, you can also capture the audio that plays out of your Mac's speakers. The program for capturing video is called the QuickTime Player.

The QuickTime Player can capture three types of recordings:

- Audio Recording: Captures only audio from the Mac's built-in microphone

- Screen Recording: Captures the video and audio from what appears on the screen

- Movie Recording: Captures video from the built-in camera on the Mac

Capturing an Audio Recording

Capturing audio is useful when you're dictating a message. Once you've captured an audio file, you can then send it to someone else through an e-mail file attachment.

To capture audio, follow these steps:

1. Open the QuickTime Player program.

2. Click the File menu and choose New Audio Recording (File ➤ New Audio Recording). An audio recording window appears.

3. (Optional) Click the downward-pointing arrow to the right of the red Record button. A menu appears, letting you choose which microphone to use (if there is more than one) and the quality of the audio that you want to record, as shown in Figure 24-10.

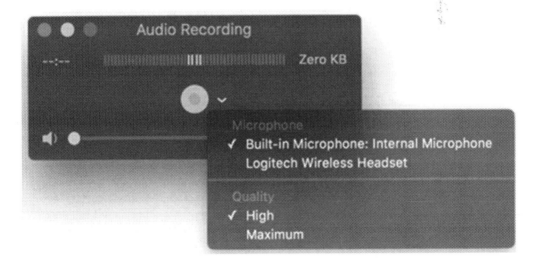

Figure 24-10. The Audio Recording window

4. Click the red Record button and start talking. The Record button turns into a Stop button.

5. Click the Stop button when you're done recording. The QuickTime Player displays the audio file so that you can listen to it, as shown in Figure 24-11.

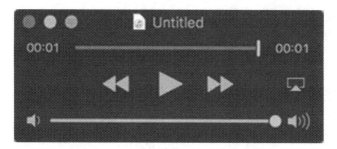

Figure 24-11. *After recording audio, you can listen to it before saving it to a file*

6. Click the Play button to hear your captured audio file.

7. Click the File menu and choose Save (File ➤ Save) to save your file as an .m4a audio file. A dialog appears.

8. Click the folder in which you want to save your file and type a descriptive name for your audio file.

9. Click the Save button.

Capturing a Screen Recording

A screen recording captures everything that appears on the screen. Screen recordings are handy for creating software tutorials to show someone how to perform a specific task on the computer.

When you capture a screen recording, you can also capture audio through the built-in microphone on the Mac. If anything on your Mac plays audio (such as music), then the audio is only captured from outside the speakers. As a result, the audio may sound muffled and less than perfect.

When recording a screen, you can record the entire screen or just part of the screen.

To capture a screen recording, follow these steps:

1. Open the QuickTime Player program.

2. Click the File menu and choose New Screen Recording (File ➤ New Screen Recording). A screen-recording window appears.

3. Click the Record button. A dialog appears, giving you instructions for how to capture all or part of a screen, as shown in Figure 24-12.

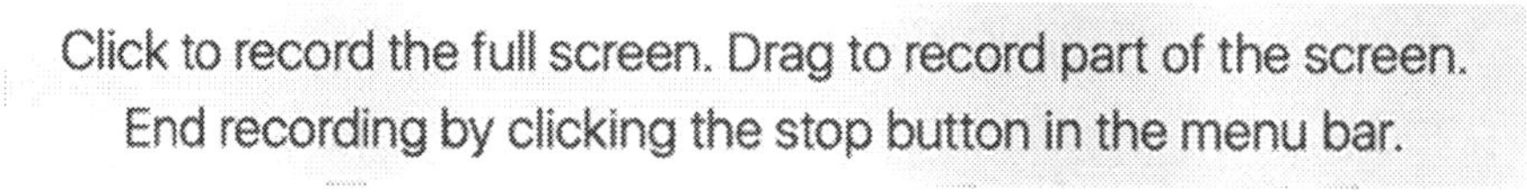

Click to record the full screen. Drag to record part of the screen.
End recording by clicking the stop button in the menu bar.

Figure 24-12. *Instructions for recording the screen*

4. Do one of the following to start capturing all or part of the screen:

    a. Click outside the dialog (see Figure 24-10) to record the entire screen.

    b. Drag the mouse (or trackpad) to define a rectangular portion of the screen that you want to record.

5. Click the Stop button on the menu bar in the upper-right corner of the screen to stop recording. The QuickTime Player displays a window of your screen recording.

6. Click the Play button to review your screen recording.

7. Click the File menu and choose Save (File ➤ Save). A dialog appears.

8. Click the folder where you want to save your screen recording as a .mov QuickTime video file and type a descriptive name for your file.

9. Click the Save button.

Capturing a Movie Recording

A movie recording captures everything from your Mac's built-in webcam. This lets you record yourself or whoever (or whatever) happens to be in front of your computer's webcam. On most desktop and laptop Mac computers, the webcam appears in the middle near the top of the monitor. When the webcam is recording, a green light appears.

To capture a movie recording, follow these steps:

1. Open the QuickTime Player program.

2. Click the File menu and choose New Movie Recording (File ➤ New Movie Recording). A movie-recording window appears, showing everything that the webcam sees.

3. Click the Record button. QuickTime Player starts recording everything that the webcam sees.

4. Click the Stop button to stop the recording. QuickTime Player displays a window of your recorded movie.

5. Click the Play button to review your recorded movie.

6. Click the File menu and choose Save (File ➤ Save). A dialog appears.

7. Click the folder where you want to save your screen recording as a .mov QuickTime video file and type a descriptive name for your file.

8. Click the Save button.

Summary

Capturing static or video images on your screen can help you show others how to use a computer or how to use a particular feature in a program. By capturing screenshots or videos, you can create tutorials to show people exactly what they should see on their own Mac.

You can capture screenshots in three different ways: with OS X keystroke commands, with the Grab program, or with the Preview program.

Capturing screenshots with OS X keystroke commands is fast and simple.

Capturing screenshots with the Grab program gives you the option of capturing screenshots after a fixed amount of time.

Capturing screenshots with the Preview program lets you define a graphic or PDF file format to save your images.

The QuickTime Player program lets you capture audio, screen recordings, or movie recordings. Audio only captures audio through the built-in microphone of the Mac.

Screen recordings only capture video and audio from the screen. If your Mac plays any audio, that audio gets captured through the Mac's built-in microphone, so the sound may be muffled.

Movie recordings only capture video and audio from a webcam. Movie recordings are best for capturing video of whoever happens to be sitting in front of your Mac.

With so many different ways to capture screenshots, audio, and video, you can find the way that you like best and capture screenshots or entire movies that you can share with others.

Chapter 25

Syncing a Mac with an iPhone or iPad

If you're happy with your Mac, chances are good that you have an iPhone or iPad as well. Since many of the programs on the Mac have equivalent apps on the iPhone and iPad, you can store data on one device and transfer it to another.

For example, you might enter an appointment in your Calendar app on the iPhone, and then transfer it to your Mac so that you see the same appointment on all of your calendars.

You might also have music or an e-book that you put on your Mac but you want to read on your iPad. Whenever you put data on one device, you can seamlessly transfer it to another device so that you always have your data when you need it, whatever Apple product you are using.

The following are some of the programs and data that you can share between a Mac and an iPhone or iPad:

- Calendar: Appointments
- Contacts: Names, addresses, and other contact information
- Notes: Ideas and random thoughts
- Photos: Digital photographs
- iBooks: PDF files and e-books
- iTunes: Audio and video files

By synchronizing data between your Mac and your iPhone or iPad, you can always have the most up-to-date data that you need wherever you go.

© Wallace Wang 2016
W. Wang, *Mac OS X for Absolute Beginners*, DOI 10.1007/978-1-4842-1913-3_25

Connecting a Mac to an iPhone or iPad

There are two ways to connect a Mac to an iPhone or iPad. The most straightforward way is to plug the USB charging cable that comes with every iPhone or iPad into both the Mac and the iPhone or iPad.

Another way to connect a Mac to an iPhone or iPad is through a Wi-Fi network. No matter which method you choose, you can then synchronize data between your Mac and iPhone or iPad using the iTunes program on your Mac.

To synchronize a Mac with an iPhone or iPad, follow these steps:

1. Plug the USB charging cable into both your Mac and your iPhone or iPad.

2. Open iTunes on your Mac. A Device icon appears in the upper-left corner of the iTunes window, as shown in Figure 25-1.

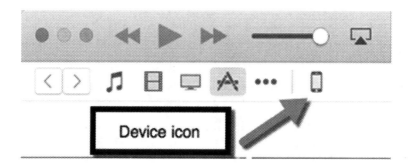

Figure 25-1. The Device icon appears when iTunes recognizes an iPhone or iPad connected to your Mac

3. Click the Device icon. iTunes shows information about the connected iPhone or iPad, as shown in Figure 25-2.

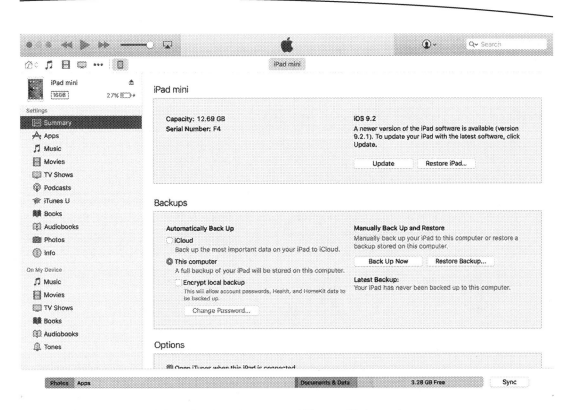

Figure 25-2. iTunes displays information about the connected iPhone or iPad

4. Click Summary in the left pane of the iTunes window.

5. (Optional) Scroll down to the Options category and select the "Synchronize with this iPhone or iPad over Wi-Fi" check box, as shown in Figure 25-3. Click the Apply button in the bottom-right corner of the iTunes window.

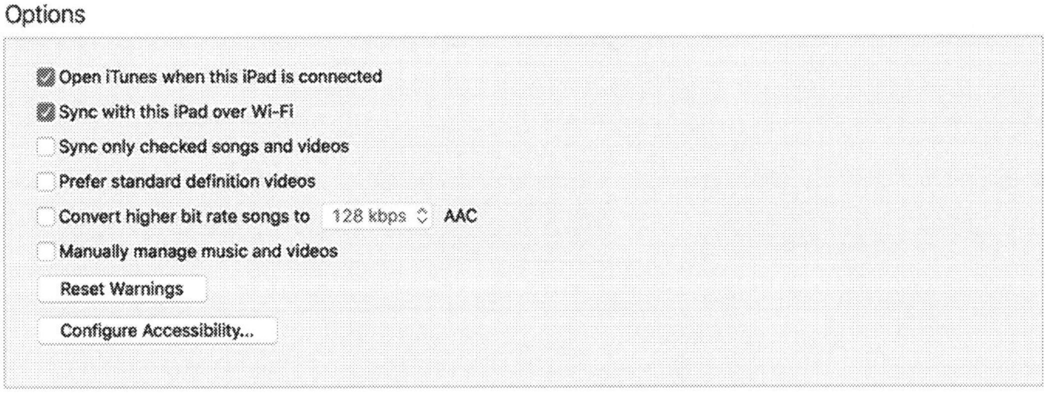

Options

- ☑ Open iTunes when this iPad is connected
- ☑ Sync with this iPad over Wi-Fi
- ☐ Sync only checked songs and videos
- ☐ Prefer standard definition videos
- ☐ Convert higher bit rate songs to   128 kbps ◇ AAC
- ☐ Manually manage music and videos

  Reset Warnings

  Configure Accessibility...

Figure 25-3. Selecting to synchronize over Wi-Fi

If you have turned on Wi-Fi synchronization, it only occurs when both your Mac and iPhone or iPad use the same Wi-Fi network. Synchronization occurs automatically whenever iTunes is open on your Mac and your iPhone or iPad is charging.

Backing Up Your iPhone or iPad

One critical reason to synchronize your Mac with your iPhone or iPad is to back up your iPhone or iPad data. If you've created data or taken pictures on your iPhone or iPad, you risk losing all that important data if you lose your iPhone or iPad.

You can back up your iPhone or iPad to iCloud or to your Mac. That way, if you lose your iPhone or iPad, you can get another one, retrieve your backups, and essentially clone your old iPhone or iPad onto your new one.

To back up your iPhone or iPad to your Mac, follow these steps:

1. Plug the USB charging cable into both your Mac and your iPhone or iPad.

2. Open iTunes on your Mac. A Device icon appears in the upper-left corner of the iTunes window (see Figure 25-1).

3. Click the Device icon. iTunes shows you information about your connected iPhone or iPad (see Figure 25-2).

4. Click Summary on the left pane of the iTunes window.

5. Click the "This computer" radio button under the Backups category, as shown in Figure 25-4.

Figure 25-4. The Backup options in iTunes

6. (Optional) Select the "Encrypt local backup" check box. You need to type a password use this backup in the future. Encrypting your backup protects your data so that someone else can't retrieve it if they get access to your Mac.

7. Click the Back Up Now button.

Syncing Through iCloud

You can synchronize an iPhone or iPad with your Mac every time you connect them (through the USB cable or Wi-Fi). However, most people don't synchronize their iPhone or iPad with their Mac every time they change data on one device or the other.

That's why it's much faster and convenient to synchronize your Mac with your iPhone or iPad through iCloud. This means that every time you change data on one device (provided it has an Internet connection at the time), the changed data gets stored on iCloud and then synchronized back with your other device the next time it connects to the Internet.

For example, you might type in the name of a new person you've met into the Contacts app on an iPhone. That new person's name becomes synchronized in iCloud and stored on the Contacts program on your Mac. By using iCloud, you never have to worry about keeping your data synchronized yourself.

To synchronize through iCloud, you need to define the iCloud settings on both your Mac and on your iPhone or iPad. Make sure that you define the same iCloud settings for each device.

So if you want to synchronize your Contacts data, make sure that you give the Contacts program access to iCloud on both your Mac and your iPhone or iPad.

To define iCloud settings on your Mac, follow these steps:

1. Click the Apple menu and choose System Preferences. The System Preferences window appears.

2. Click the iCloud icon.

3. Select (or clear) the check boxes for the programs that you want to synchronize through iCloud, as shown in Figure 25-5.

Figure 25-5. Defining program settings for iCloud

4. Click the red dot (the close button) in the upper-left corner of the iCloud window to make it disappear.

Once you've defined which programs to synchronize on iCloud, you need to do the same thing with your iPhone or iPad. To define iCloud synchronization options on an iPhone or iPad, follow these steps:

1. Tap the Settings icon. The Settings screen appears.

2. Tap iCloud. The iCloud screen appears, as shown in Figure 25-6.

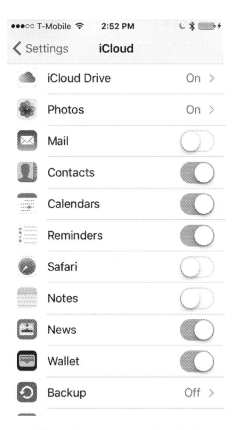

Figure 25-6. The iCloud screen lets you define which apps can synchronize data

3. Turn the options on or off for different apps. Make sure that the apps you choose on your iPhone or iPad are the same ones you chose for your Mac.

Syncing Through iTunes

Keeping your appointments, contacts, and notes updated on multiple devices is critical. That's why it's important to synchronize this type of data on iCloud; it's always current as long as you have regular Internet access.

However, other types of data are far less time-sensitive, such as your favorite songs, e-books, or movies. To synchronize less important data, you can use iTunes every time you connect your iPhone or iPad to your Mac.

When synchronizing data between your Mac and iPhone or iPad, you can either choose all the data or individually choose which items to synchronize. For example, if you click Music in the Settings category, you can choose to copy all of your music from your Mac to your iPhone or iPad, or just choose individual songs.

To synchronize your Mac with your iPhone or iPad through iTunes, follow these steps:

1. Connect your iPhone or iPad to your Mac with the USB cable.

2. Open the iTunes program on your Mac.

3. Click the Device icon in the upper-left corner of the iTunes window (see Figure 25-1). iTunes displays a list of categories under the Settings heading, as shown in Figure 25-7.

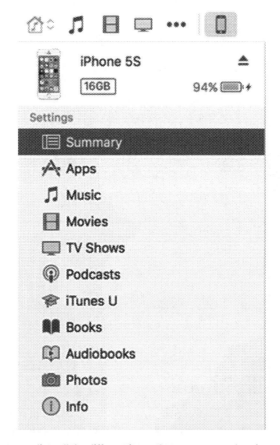

Figure 25-7. The Settings category lists all the different items that you can synchronize

4. Click a category under the Settings heading, such as Music or Podcasts. A list of items appears that you can select or clear, as shown in Figure 25-8.

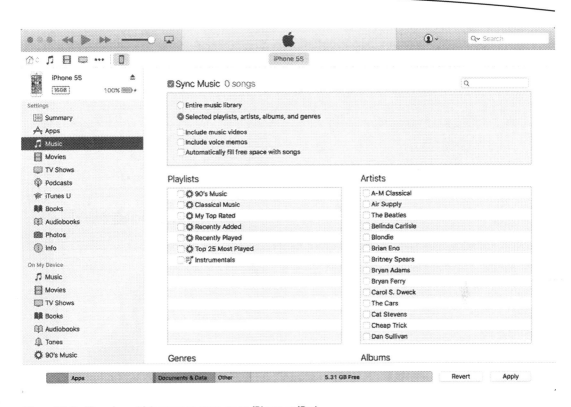

Figure 25-8. Choosing which songs to store on an iPhone or iPad

5. Select (or clear) the options that you want.

6. Click the Apply button.

Disconnecting an iPhone or iPad

When you're done synchronizing data between your Mac and iPhone or iPad, don't disconnect the USB cable just yet; you have to eject the iPhone or iPad first.

Ejecting the iPhone or iPad gives your Mac a chance to make sure that there are no open files on the iPhone or iPad so that you can safely disconnect and remove the device.

To disconnect an iPhone or iPad from a Mac, follow these steps:

1. Open the iTunes program.

2. Click the Eject button, as shown in Figure 25-9.

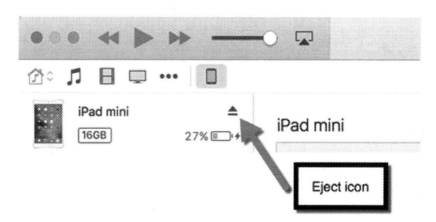

Figure 25-9. The Eject button lets you safely disconnect an iPhone or iPad from a Mac

3. Disconnect your iPhone or iPad form the USB cable.

Summary

Your data is important to you, so it's crucial that you have access to your important data whether you're using a Mac, an iPhone, or an iPad. By synchronizing your data, your data essentially follows you, whichever device you happen to be using at the time.

For synchronizing critical information such as contacts and appointments, use iCloud. Through iCloud and regular access to the Internet, your data is synchronized instantly. For less time-sensitive data, such as e-books or music, you can synchronize data manually.

Besides synchronizing your data, iTunes can also be used to back up your iPhone or iPad. By doing this, you'll never risk losing data on your iPhone or iPad again.

With an iPhone or iPad and a Mac, you'll be able to work anywhere you have an Apple device, whether it's at a desk or on the road.

VI

Useful Macintosh Information

A surprisingly large amount of information about using a computer is often passed around by word of mouth but rarely printed in a book. That's why this part of the book includes useful information known by experienced Macintosh users. By reading this part of the book, you'll learn what experienced Macintosh users have known for years.

First, you'll learn about simple disk maintenance tasks that you can perform to tune up your computer any time it starts acting erratically.

Second, you'll learn how to protect your Macintosh from malware. Although the malware threat isn't as severe as the one that Windows PC users face every day, malware is slowly coming to the Macintosh, so you need to know how to identify the threats and protect your computer as much as possible.

Third, you'll eventually need to buy a new computer one day, so you need to know the best ways to buy another computer without spending too much to do it.

By reading this part of the book, you'll learn hidden secrets that have taken most people years to gather on their own.

Chapter 26

Protecting Your Data

Computers are like cars because they only work if you properly maintain them. While it's nice to think that your Mac will work all the time, whenever you *need* it, the reality is that your Mac may eventually fail if you don't take care of it. Perhaps the most important way to maintain your Mac and all of your critical data is to maintain your disk.

Older Mac computers have physical hard disks, whereas newer Mac models use solid-state drives that act like USB flash drives in that they have no moving parts. While solid-state drives are much faster than mechanical hard drives, they are prone to failure too. One of the most common ways disks can fail is by corrupting or losing data.

Losing or corrupting data may never happen to you, but it's not a surprise when it does occur. That's because OS X isn't perfect and it's possible that, through no fault of your own, OS X will simply fail to correctly save a file in the right location, overriding or destroying other files that you've saved.

Ultimately, maintaining your disk is really about protecting your files. Two common ways to lose a file are deleting it by mistake or OS X corrupting it.

Retrieving Deleted Files

When you delete a file, OS X doesn't physically erase the file. Instead, it stores the file in the Trash folder. As long as a file appears in the Trash folder, you'll be able to retrieve it. That means that if you delete a file today and peek in your Trash folder five years from now, you'll be able to find your file safe and sound. The only way you ever risk losing a file is if you dump it in the Trash folder and then empty the Trash folder.

The moment that you empty the Trash folder, OS X pretends that the file never existed. However, the file still physically exists on your hard disk, which means that if you buy special file-recovery software, you may still be able to retrieve previously deleted files. However, the longer you wait to retrieve a deleted file, the lower your chances of actually recovering it.

© Wallace Wang 2016
W. Wang, *Mac OS X for Absolute Beginners*, DOI 10.1007/978-1-4842-1913-3_26

If you haven't emptied the Trash folder, you can recover a deleted file by following these steps:

1. Right-click the Trash icon on the Dock. A pop-up menu appears, as shown in Figure 26-1.

Figure 26-1. Right-clicking the Trash icon displays a pop-up menu

2. Choose Open. The Finder window lists all the deleted files still in the Trash folder.

3. Right-click the file that you want to retrieve. A pop-up menu appears, as shown in Figure 26-2.

Figure 26-2. Right-clicking a file displays a pop-up menu with the Go Back command

4. Choose the Put Back command. The Finder moves your file back to its original location.

Using Time Machine

Retrieving files from the Trash folder works if you haven't emptied the Trash folder. The moment you empty the Trash folder, you're unable to retrieve any previously deleted files without buying special file-recovery software.

Of course, you have to empty your Trash folder periodically; otherwise, all of your deleted files will take up space until you have so many deleted files on your computer that you can't store anything else. That's why you need to empty the Trash folder periodically, but only after you're sure that you will never need any of those deleted files again.

If you want the option of retrieving deleted files in the future, then another solution is to use Time Machine, which is a free backup program included with every Mac.

To use Time Machine, you need an external hard disk that's connected to your Mac at all times. The most common way to connect an external hard disk to a Mac is through a USB cable, but some external hard disks (such as Apple's Time Capsule) can connect to a Mac through a Wi-Fi network. Connecting an external hard disk wirelessly can be especially convenient with laptops, such as the MacBook, which lacks a traditional USB port.

Once you have an external hard disk, you need to configure Time Machine to work with that external hard disk. Ideally, you should only use that external hard disk solely for backing up your Mac on Time Machine.

Configuring an External Hard Disk with Time Machine

Once you have an external hard disk connected to your Mac, you need to configure Time Machine to work with that external hard disk.

To configure a hard disk to work with Time Machine, follow these steps:

1. Click the Apple menu. A pull-down menu appears.

2. Choose System Preferences. The System Preferences window appears.

3. Click the Time Machine icon. A Time Machine window appears, as shown in Figure 26-3.

Figure 26-3. The Time Machine window

4. Click the On/Off switch to On.

5. Click the Select Backup Disk button. A window appears, listing all the available hard disks that you can use, as shown in Figure 26-4.

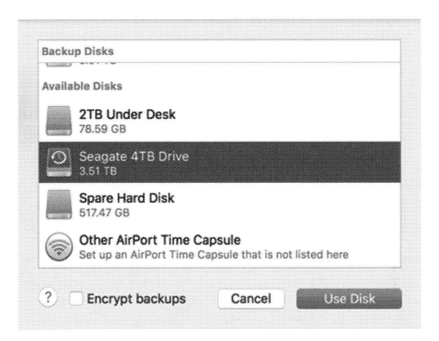

Figure 26-4. Choosing a hard disk to use with Time Machine

6. Click the hard disk that you want to use for Time Machine and click the Use Disk button.

7. (Optional) Select (or clear) the "Show Time Machine in menu bar" check box. Putting the Time Machine icon on the menu bar lets you easily access Time Machine, as shown in Figure 26-5.

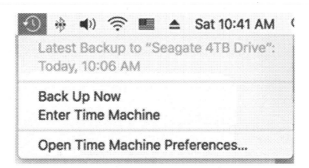

Figure 26-5. The Time Machine icon on the menu bar displays a pull-down menu for accessing Time Machine

8. Click the red dot (the close button) in the upper-left corner of the Time Machine window to make it disappear.

Retrieving Deleted Files with Time Machine

Time Machine backs up your entire Mac every hour, including files, programs, and settings. Once Time Machine fills up an external hard disk, it starts erasing the oldest backup and replaces it with the latest backup.

Because of this, you want the largest external hard disk you can afford. If you get a small external hard disk, Time Machine won't be able to store backups from too far in the past. If you get a large external hard disk, you'll be able to retrieve files from longer in the past, such as several months or even several years ago.

The moment that you realize you need a file that you once had, you don't have to panic or frantically search through your computer to see if another copy still exists. Instead, you can just load Time Machine, go back to a specific time in the past when you know the file existed, and retrieve the file.

To retrieve a file saved by Time Machine, follow these steps:

1. Open Time Machine by either double-clicking the Time Machine icon in the Applications folder or by clicking the Time Machine icon on the menu bar (see Figure 26-5) and choosing Enter Time Machine. The Time Machine window appears, as shown in Figure 26-6.

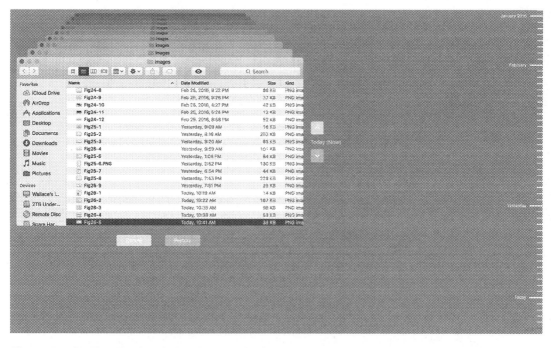

Figure 26-6. The Time Machine window displays a timeline on the right edge of the screen

2. Click the timeline to a point in the past when you know a certain file existed.

3. Navigate in the Finder window until you find the file that you want to retrieve.

4. Click the file that you want to retrieve.

5. Click the Restore button. Time Machine retrieves your file and displays it in the Finder window.

Using the Disk Utility Program

The Trash folder and Time Machine are handy for retrieving files that you may have deleted by mistake. However, sometimes your hard disk might simply fail, either from mechanical problems or from problems with OS X. If you try to access a hard disk and get error messages, you might need to use the Disk Utility program to fix your hard disk.

The Disk Utility program is stored in the Utilities folder inside the Applications folder. The Disk Utility can't recover corrupted or deleted files, but it can fix the way that files are stored on the hard disk, so you might be able to retrieve files off that disk again.

To use the Disk Utility program to fix your hard disk, follow these steps:

1. Open the Disk Utility program inside the Utilities folder (which is inside the Applications folder). The Disk Utility window appears, as shown in Figure 26-7.

Figure 26-7. The Disk Utility window

2. In the left pane, click the name of the disk that you want to fix.

3. Click the First Aid icon in the top middle portion of the Disk Utility window, or click the File menu and choose Run First Aid (File ➤ Run First Aid). A dialog asks if you want to run First Aid, as shown in Figure 26-8.

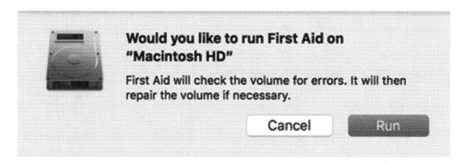

Figure 26-8. *The Disk Utility program asks if you want to run First Aid*

4. Click the Run button.

5. (Optional) Click the Show Details disclosure triangle to see what First Aid has examined on your hard disk, as shown in Figure 26-9.

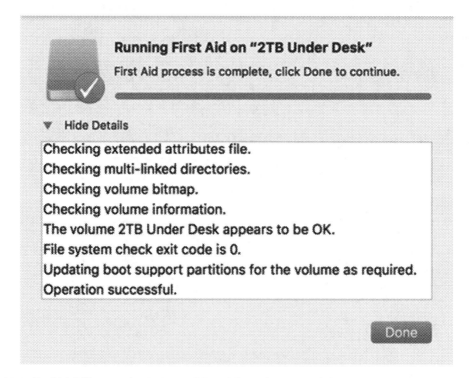

Figure 26-9. *The Disk Utility program displays additional information on what it has done*

6. Click the Done button.

7. Click the Disk Utility menu and choose Quit Disk Utility (Disk Utility ➤ Quit Disk Utility), or press Command+Q.

Note   If Disk Utility can't fix a problem, you may need to use a more extensive disk utility repair program.

Summary

The two most common ways to a lose file are through user error or computer failure. If you accidentally delete a file, you might be able to retrieve it from the Trash folder, provided you didn't empty the Trash folder.

If you did empty the Trash folder and you still need to retrieve a lost file, you might still be able to recover that file if an external hard disk was connected to your Mac and you used the Time Machine backup program.

With Time Machine, you can retrieve files from days, weeks, months, or even years ago. Of course, Time Machine can only protect your files if you set it up long before you actually need it.

If your hard disk is acting erratically, you may need to repair it. Sometimes hard disks fail because of mechanical errors, but most of the time hard disks fail because OS X can no longer recognize the files on that particular hard disk.

When this occurs, you can often fix these software errors by using the Disk Utility program, which comes in the Utilities folder inside the Applications folder. Disk utility can repair OS X problems to correctly recognize the files stored on a hard disk again.

Chapter 27

Protecting a Mac from Malware

Malware is a category of software known as malicious software or viruses. Most malware can only attack specific operating systems. Since Windows PCs were once the dominant computers in the world, most malware targets Microsoft Windows.

With the growing popularity of the Mac, more and more malware now targets OS X. No matter what type of computer you use, it is always possible to become infected with malware.

There are two ways to guard against malware. The most common way is to rely on technological solutions such as antivirus software. Unfortunately, technological solutions can never provide 100-percent protection. That's because the weakest link in any computer's security is always the user.

If users fail to turn on or use technological solutions, then those technological solutions are useless. Even worse, users can often be tricked into installing malware. Ultimately, no amount of technological solutions can ever protect your computer. You also need a basic understanding of computer security so that you don't accidentally infect your computer by mistake.

Malware can only infect your computer if it can access it. The following are some of the ways that malware can get into a computer:

- Inserting an infected USB flash drive into the USB port of your computer
- Downloading an infected file attachment sent to you by e-mail
- Visiting a malicious web site

Ultimately, the best defense against malware is knowing the types of threats that may attack your computer and avoiding falling prey to their traps.

© Wallace Wang 2016
W. Wang, *Mac OS X for Absolute Beginners*, DOI 10.1007/978-1-4842-1913-3_27

Password Protecting a Mac

Beyond physically locking your Mac behind a door, the next best way to block access to your Mac is to provide password protection. When you first set up your Mac, you have to choose a password, but you can always change it later.

> **Note**   The best passwords contain random letters, numbers, and symbols.

Besides changing your password periodically, there are the following two other options to consider:

* Requiring a password after a fixed amount of inactivity: Password protects your Mac if you step away for a moment

* Disabling automatic login: Requires a password to log in

To change the password settings on your Mac, follow these steps:

1. Click the Apple menu. A pull-down menu appears.

2. Choose System Preferences. The System Preferences window appears.

3. Click the Security & Privacy icon. The Security & Privacy window appears.

4. Click the General tab (see Figure 27-1).

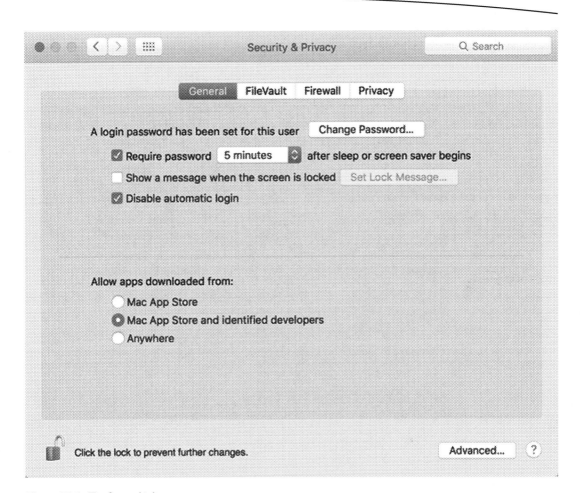

Figure 27-1. *The General tab*

5. Select (or clear) the "Require password" check box. Click in the pop-up menu to define a time, such as 15 minutes or 1 hour. Selecting this option gives you greater security.

6. Select (or clear) the "Disable automatic login" check box. Selecting this option gives you greater security.

7. Click the Change Password button if you want to change your password. (Generally, you should change your password periodically for greater security.)

8. Click the red dot (the close button) in the upper-left corner to make the Security & Privacy window disappear.

Turning on the Firewall

If your Mac is connected to the Internet, it's vulnerable. Every time you connect to the Internet, you're an open target for anyone around the world to hack into your computer.

To protect yourself when you're on the Internet, you need to turn on the *firewall*. A firewall essentially acts like a locked door that keeps hackers on the Internet from getting into your computer. Without a firewall, anyone on the Internet can get into your computer, so it's crucial that you turn on your firewall.

Generally, if you turn on your firewall, you'll rarely have a reason to turn it off; so once you turn on the firewall, leave it on.

To turn on the firewall, follow these steps:

1. Click the Apple menu. A pull-down menu appears.

2. Choose System Preferences. The System Preferences window appears.

3. Click the Security & Privacy icon. The Security & Privacy window appears.

4. Click the Firewall tab. (If a green dot appears next to the "Firewall: On" label, your firewall is already turned on, so you don't need to follow the remaining steps.)

5. Click the Lock icon in the bottom-left corner. A dialog appears for you to type your password.

6. Type your password and click the Unlock button.

7. Click the Turn On Firewall button (see Figure 27-2).

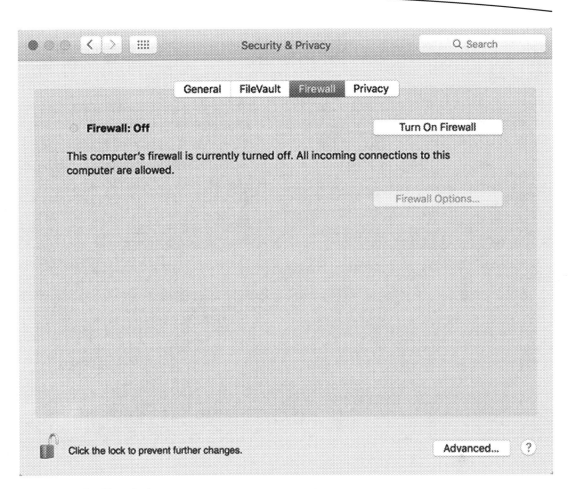

Figure 27-2. The Firewall tab

8. Click the Firewall Options button. A window lists the programs that have access to the Internet, as shown in Figure 27-3.

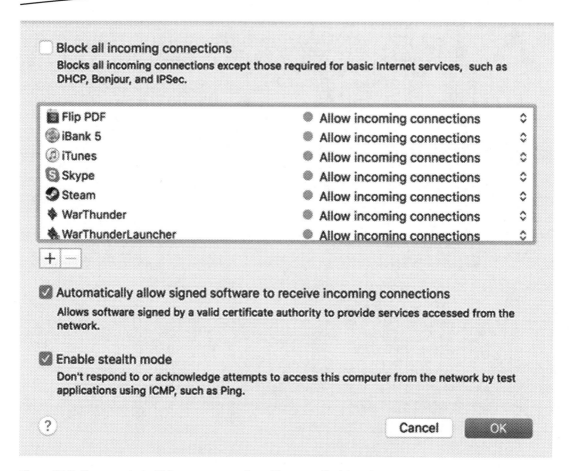

Figure 27-3. You can select which programs are allowed to access the Internet

9. Select (or clear) the "Block all incoming connections" check box. Selecting this check box provides greater security. If this check box is clear, you can individually block certain programs from accessing the Internet by clicking the pop-up menu to the right of each program name and choose "Allow or Block incoming connections". Ideally, you want to allow incoming connections for programs that you recognize, and block incoming connections for programs that you don't recognize.

10. Select (or clear) the "Automatically allow signed software to receive incoming connections" check box. Selecting this check box provides greater security because signed software represents software that a third party has verified, much like a driver's license represents that a government agency has verified your identity (although, like a driver's license, signed software can also be faked).

11. Select (or clear) the "Enable stealth mode" check box. Stealth mode hides your computer from hackers trying to find it on the Internet. Selecting this check box provides greater security.

12. Click OK.

13. Click the red dot (the close button) in the upper-left corner to close the Security & Privacy window.

Protecting Safari

Every time that you use a browser like Safari, you're at risk of visiting a malicious web site. Such malicious web sites often contain misspelled domain names.

For example, instead of typing the correct *microsoft.com*, you might misspell it, such as *mircosoft.com*. Because it's so easy to misspell a domain name, many hackers set up malicious web sites using similar domain names as well-known sites.

The best way to protect yourself from such malicious web sites is to type a domain address carefully and check its spelling before visiting the site. Then, if it's a site you plan on visiting often, bookmark the site so that you can safely visit that site in the future.

Of course, it's not always possible to avoid malicious web sites because sometimes hackers booby-trap legitimate web sites as well. Because you can never be too safe on the Internet, you need to take precautions with your browser.

Since most hackers know that Mac users rely on Safari as their main browser, one trick is to use a less popular browser, such as Opera. Malware designed to trick Safari may not be able to trick another browser, like Opera.

If you're going to use Safari, you need to make sure that you have turned on additional security measures.

Defining "Safe" Files to Download

By default, Safari defines common files as "safe" for downloading, such as PDF files. In reality, PDF files along with movie files are often specifically infected with malware because so many people think these types of files are safe. While it's convenient to let these types of files be freely downloaded, it does open up a huge security hole in your Mac, so you need to decide if convenience is worth the security risk.

Many times, hackers disguise malware as seemingly innocent file attachments. For example, one trick is to send an e-mail message supposedly from Federal Express or UPS, claiming the service tried to drop off a package and you now need to download and open a file attachment.

Sometimes hackers even hijack a friend's e-mail account and send messages from a friend's e-mail address. Once again, assume that anything from the Internet is not what it seems until you can prove otherwise. That might mean contacting your friend in a different way (such as through text messaging on a smartphone) to verify that he or she really did send you a file (or did not if you receive a suspicious message from a "friend" claiming to be trapped in a foreign country and needing you to send money to a strange address overseas right away).

Another trick is to booby-trap ads on legitimate web sites. Visiting a web site might display a warning message that asks you to take some kind of action, such as clicking a link. When in doubt, don't believe anything on the Internet and play it safe by only downloading files you absolutely trust.

To define whether to allow downloading PDFs, movies, and other common types of files from the Internet, follow these steps:

1. Open Safari.

2. Click the Safari menu and choose Preferences (Safari ➤ Preferences). A Preferences window appears.

3. Click the General icon, as shown in Figure 27-4.

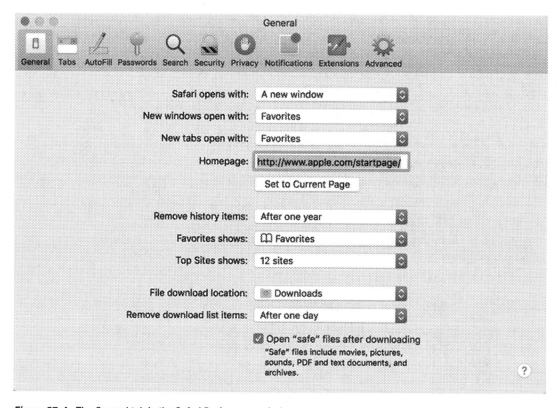

Figure 27-4. The General tab in the Safari Preferences window

4. Select (or clear) the "Open "safe" files after downloading" check box. Clearing this check box provides greater security.

5. Click the red dot (the close button) in the upper-left corner to close the Preferences window.

Defining Safari Security Settings

In the old days, browsers did relatively little, so you needed to download and install plug-ins to let them display animation or play audio. Because downloading and installing plug-ins became so popular, hackers soon started creating malware disguised as plug-ins.

Even worse, hackers also used legitimate plug-ins to break into computers. Because each plug-in needs access to your computer, each plug-in provides another potential opening for malware to break into your computer. Common plug-ins like Adobe Flash and Java are often hijacked by malware to sneak into your computer. For greater security, you don't want plug-ins, although they may be necessary on some web sites that you rely on.

To block browser plug-ins, follow these steps:

1. Open Safari.

2. Click the Safari menu and choose Preferences (Safari ➤ Preferences). A Preferences window appears.

3. Click the Security icon, as shown in Figure 27-5.

Figure 27-5. The Security tab in the Safari Preferences window

4. Select (or clear) the "Warning when visiting a fraudulent website" check box. Selecting this check box provides greater security but cannot guarantee that fraudulent web sites might still appear in Safari anyway.

5. Select (or clear) the Allow Plug-ins check box. Clearing this check box provides greater security but at the risk of not allowing certain web sites to display correctly.

6. (Optional) Click the Plug-in Settings button. A window shows you the plug-ins that are currently installed. If you click the plug-in in the left pane, you see a list of the web sites that require the use of that plug-in, as shown in Figure 27-6.

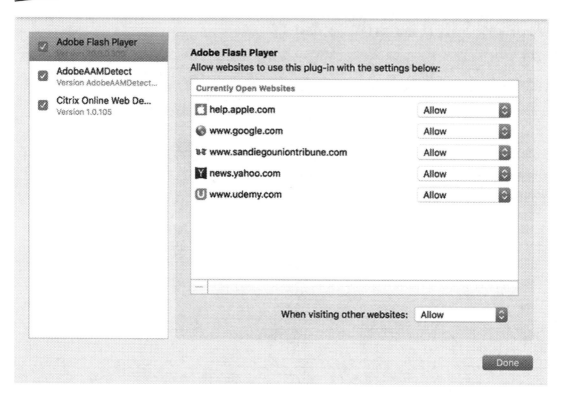

Figure 27-6. The Plug-ins option window shows all installed plug-ins and the web sites that require them to work

7.   Select (or clear) the check box to the left of each plug-in, such as Adobe Flash Player. If you don't want to completely block a plug-in, you can selectively choose which web sites can run the plug-in by clicking the pop-up menu that appears to the right of web site names, as shown in Figure 27-7.

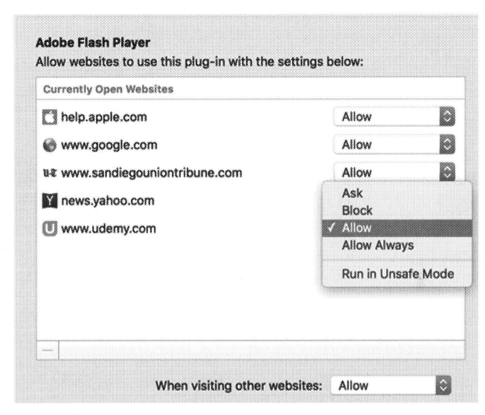

Figure 27-7. *You can selectively allow or block individual web sites from running plug-ins*

8. (Optional) Click in the "When visiting other websites" pop-up menu to select how the plug-in works with web sites other than the ones listed.

9. Click the Done button.

Summary

The best computer security starts with you. Don't visit suspicious web sites, don't open file attachments from strangers, and don't believe phony e-mail messages from seemingly legitimate organizations. In other words, trust no one on the Internet.

At the very least, turn on the firewall in OS X. This firewall may block legitimate programs from accessing the Internet, but in most cases, it prevents hackers from breaking into your computer.

To physically protect your Mac, restrict access whenever possible. Since that may not be feasible, however, password protect your Mac so that others can't access your computer without your permission.

Finally, harden Safari's security settings. Turn off unnecessary plug-ins and consider blocking access to supposedly "safe" files to download, which are not actually safe at all. Whenever you make your computer more secure, you also increase the chance of making it more inconvenient to use, so you have to carefully weigh the pros and cons of various security settings.

Ultimately, the best form of security is knowing how malware might attack your computer and then taking steps to minimize the risk. You'll never be completely free from attacks, but you can always try to make it more difficult for hackers and malware to attack your Mac.

Chapter 28

Shopping for a New Mac

Unlike other types of computers, a Mac holds its value and usefulness for years. Once you get a Mac, you won't need a new one for a long time because Apple offers free regular OS X updates.

The only problem with free OS X upgrades is that they're mostly designed to run on the latest hardware. That means over time, your Mac will simply lack the hardware necessary to take full advantage of the newest features in OS X. Eventually, the latest version of OS X stops supporting older hardware, which means you're stuck with a Mac that is unable to adopt the newest version of OS X.

That's when you need to think about getting another Mac. Eventually, you'll want to get another Mac, either as an addition or as a complete replacement.

When shopping for a Mac, you have multiple options, but you can save money by timing your purchases and shopping selectively. By doing both, you can buy a new Mac for hundreds of dollars less than the normal retail price.

Time Your Purchases with Apple's Upgrade Cycle

Apple releases new Mac models at regular intervals. Just as Apple always releases a new iPhone model every year, they also release new Mac models at fairly predictable times of the year. By timing your purchase to match Apple's release schedule, you can avoid paying top dollar for a new Mac that's outdated (although still perfectly usable) the next day.

The main web site for tracking Apple's product upgrade cycle is the *MacRumours Buyer's Guide* (`http://buyersguide.macrumors.com`), shown in Figure 28-1.

© Wallace Wang 2016
W. Wang, *Mac OS X for Absolute Beginners*, DOI 10.1007/978-1-4842-1913-3_28

MacRumors
Buyer's Guide

This page provides a product summary for each Apple model. The intent is to provide our best recommendations regarding current product cycles, and to provide a summary of currently available rumors for each model.
This page is based on rumors and speculation and we provide no guarantee to its accuracy.

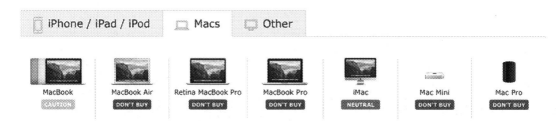

Figure 28-1. The MacRumours Buyer's Guide web site

The *MacRumours Buyer's Guide* provides estimates for when Apple will likely release a new model (such as a Mac mini or MacBook) and offers suggestions for buying a particular Mac:

- Buy Now: This means that Apple just released a new model

- Caution: This means that Apple released the latest model a while ago, so if you can afford to wait, do so to get the newest model for the same or lower price as the current-generation model

- Don't Buy: This means that Apple will likely release a new model soon, so don't buy a new Mac unless you absolutely need one now

Remember, Apple's release schedule isn't always predictable, so the *MacRumours Buyer's Guide* gives a rough estimate when a new Mac model will likely appear. By timing your purchases to the *MacRumours Buyer's Guide* recommendations, you can buy the latest model instead of paying the same amount of money to get last generation's model.

As an alternative to buying the latest Mac model on the day it arrives, you might take the opposite approach and buy last generation's model at a discount.

For example, if you purchase the latest iMac or MacBook, it might cost you the standard retail price. However, the moment that Apple releases a new model, the new model adopts the retail price while the previous generation model drops in price.

That means on the day before Apple releases a new model, an iMac might cost you $1,299, but the next day when Apple releases a newer model, that same iMac is now considered a previous generation model. As a result, the price drops, so you can buy a brand-new Mac for much less simply because a newer model just appeared.

Buy Refurbished

Even if you time your purchases to buy a new Mac the day it's released, you'll still pay full retail price. Rather than buy a new model right when it's introduced, wait a while. The reason to wait is because other people buy the latest model and then return it for whatever reason.

When that happens, Apple and other stores, such as Best Buy, take the returned products and check them to make sure that everything works correctly. Since they can't sell returned items as new, they must sell them as refurbished, which means they have to sell them at reduced prices.

By buying a refurbished computer, you can save hundreds of dollars. Refurbished models come with the same warranty as new models but at a slightly lower price.

The one drawback of refurbished models is that you can't customize them. That means you have to buy only what's available. If a particular model or configuration isn't available, you'll have to wait and hope that your desired configuration becomes available soon. If you have needs that require a specially configured computer, you may only find standard models for sale as refurbished; in which case, you would have to buy a new computer.

In exchange for waiting and taking what's available, refurbished computers offer lower prices. To purchase a refurbished computer from Apple, visit Apple's web site (www.apple.com) and look for the Refurbished link near the bottom of the home page, as shown in Figure 28-2.

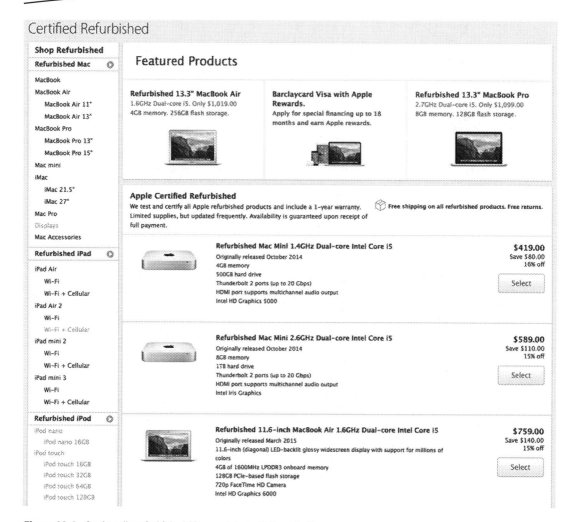

Figure 28-2. *Apple sells refurbished Mac models on their web site*

Besides Apple, other stores sell refurbished Mac models, including Best Buy and MacMall. Like Apple, these other stores give the same warranty on refurbished model as they do for new ones. Also, the variety of configurations is limited.

The next time you're in the market for a new Mac, browse refurbished Mac sites. You may find the model you want at a lower price than retail.

Shop During Holidays

You'll rarely find that the price of Mac computers differs much because Apple enforces a fixed retail price for all retailers. Yet during the holiday shopping season at the end of every year, almost every retailer—including Apple and many other electronics stores—offer discounts.

Such discounts can save you money or reward you with gift cards or other bonuses, depending on which Mac you buy. Retailers want to sell as many products as possible during each holiday season. So if you can time your purchase to wait for holiday sales, you can save yourself some money.

Do Your Own Memory Upgrade

It's no secret that Apple charges more for memory than everyone else. Unfortunately, some Mac models have soldered memory chips, which means that you cannot replace them. When you buy a Mac, make sure that it comes with enough memory, or you will never be able to increase it.

A handful of Mac models offer removable memory chips, however. For those Mac models, simply buy the model with the least amount of memory, and then buy memory chips from a third-party retailer. Then all you have to do is plug the memory chip into your Mac. You'll save money if you buy and install memory yourself rather than pay Apple to do it.

Just remember to make sure the Mac you want offers removable memory chips, because more Mac models are using soldered memory chips that can't be easily replaced.

Get an Educational Discount

If you're a teacher or a student, you can buy hardware and software at a discount. College bookstores typically offer discounts to anyone with a faculty or a student ID. Apple's own site offers a special store for educators, as shown in Figure 28-3.

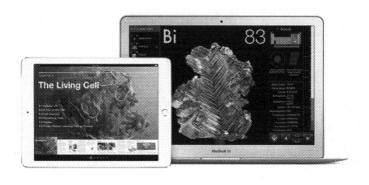

Figure 28-3. *Apple's educational site offers modest discounts on all Mac models*

Buy a Used Mac

Mac computers tend to hold their value better than ordinary PCs. That's why many people sell their used Macs so that they can use the money to buy a newer model.

If you're willing to do a little research and you don't mind getting a slightly older Mac, buying a used Mac can save you money. Just like buying a used car, buying a used computer means taking the time to understand exactly what you're getting for the price.

A used Mac may work just fine, but it will become outdated faster than a newer computer, which means that you may not be able to upgrade it to the latest version of OS X. If you are able to upgrade it to the latest version of OS X, your Mac may not be able to accept next year's version of OS X.

Just be careful when buying a used Mac. If you're wary of buying a used Mac from eBay or Craigslist (be careful that you're not buying stolen merchandise), you might feel more comfortable buying a used Mac from one of two reputable dealers.

PowerMax (www.powermax.com) sells both new and used Mac computers (see Figure 28-4). When you buy a used Mac from PowerMax, they'll give you a 120-day warranty so that you can be sure your Mac works correctly. If you're in the market for a new Mac, you can trade in your old one to PowerMax so that you don't have to sell it yourself.

USED MACS

Towers
Choose from a great selection of Mac pro and G5 towers

SHOP NOW ▶

Used iMac
27-inch through 17-inch iMac models available

SHOP NOW ▶

Used Mac mini
Many Intel and G4 Mac minis in stock

SHOP NOW ▶

Used MacBook Air
We have 11-inch and 13-inch models looking for a good home

SHOP NOW ▶

Used MacBook & MacBook Pro
Choose from 13-inch, 15-inch and 17-inch MacBook and MacBook Pros

SHOP NOW ▶

Used XServe
Need server power? Many xServes in stock and rack ready!

SHOP NOW ▶

When it comes to used Macs, nobody does it better than PowerMax!

Huge varieties of quality pre-owned Macs are constantly flowing through our warehouse, resulting in the widest range of choices available anywhere. We also have experts on staff who will answer your questions and provide unbiased advice better than anyone. We're able to say that because not only are we one of Apple's largest and longest-running Apple Specialists, we also sell both new and used Macs all day long. When you combine that with the fact that on average our Mac experts have been with us for well over ten years, it becomes pretty clear there's no one in the world like PowerMax!

Killer Warranty
All our used Macs carry a full,120-day warranty.
Extended warranties available!

Expert Advice

Figure 28-4. PowerMax sells a variety of used Mac computers

Another used Mac retailer is Mac of All Trades (www.macofalltrades.com). Like PowerMax, Mac of All Trades sells used computers with a warranty so that you can be sure that your used Mac works correctly. By buying a used Mac (or trading in your old Mac) through reputable used computer dealers, you don't have to worry about being cheated.

Carefully compare the prices of used computers, because many times you can buy refurbished computers (which are practically new) for only slightly more than an older used computer.

Buy from Apple Retailers

Apple charges the full retail price for all of their products, except during the holiday season, when they might offer discounts. On the other hand, most other retailers offer small discounts on Apple's retail price to entice you to buy from them instead of from Apple.

One prominent online dealer is MacMall (www.macmall.com), which offers small discounts on nearly every Mac model (see Figure 28-5).

Apple
21.5" iMac - 1.6GHz
1.6GHz dual-core Intel Core i5
8GB memory | 1TB Hard Drive
Turbo Boost up to 2.7GHz
Intel HD Graphics 6000
Apple Magic Keyboard | Magic Mouse 2
Usually ships the same business day

List Price: $1,099.00
You Save: $70.00(6%)
Final Price: **$1,029.00**

Select

Apple
21.5" iMac - 2.8GHz
2.8GHz quad-core Intel Core i5
8GB memory | 1TB Hard Drive
Turbo Boost up to 3.3GHz
Intel Iris Pro Graphics 6200
Apple Magic Keyboard | Magic Mouse 2
Usually ships the same business day

List Price: $1,299.00
You Save: $100.00(8%)
Final Price: **$1,199.00**

Select

Apple
21.5" iMac with Retina 4K display -
3.1GHz
3.1GHz quad-core Intel Core i5
8GB memory | 1TB Hard Drive
Turbo Boost up to 3.6GHz
Intel Iris Pro Graphics 6200
Apple Magic Keyboard | Magic Mouse 2
Usually ships the same business day

List Price: $1,499.00
You Save: $100.00(7%)
Final Price: **$1,399.00**

Select

Figure 28-5. Many retailers offer small everyday discounts below Apple's normal retail price

Other retailers, such as Best Buy, may charge full retail price on some Mac models but offer slight discounts on other models. By comparison price shopping on other retailer web sites, you can often find a brand-new Mac at a slight discount.

Summary

The most expensive option is to buy a new Mac from Apple. If you're going to buy a computer from Apple, consider buying a refurbished model. The main drawback of refurbished models is that they may not always offer the configuration that you want.

Besides refurbished computers, consider buying a used computer or a new computer using an educational discount, if you qualify as a student or teacher.

If you insist on buying a new Mac, look at other retailers besides Apple. The chances are good that you'll save a little bit of money buying from another retailer rather than directly from Apple. Whether you buy a Mac from Apple or another retailer, you'll still be able to get free technical support from your neighborhood Apple Store if necessary.

Just because the Mac is considered a premium product doesn't mean that you have to pay a premium price for it. By taking the time to research and compare all of your options, you may be surprised at how much money you can save.

Index

Get the eBook for only $5!

Why limit yourself?

Now you can take the weightless companion with you wherever you go and access your content on your PC, phone, tablet, or reader.

Since you've purchased this print book, we're happy to offer you the eBook in all 3 formats for just $5.

Convenient and fully searchable, the PDF version enables you to easily find and copy code—or perform examples by quickly toggling between instructions and applications. The MOBI format is ideal for your Kindle, while the ePUB can be utilized on a variety of mobile devices.

To learn more, go to www.apress.com/companion or contact support@apress.com.

Printed in the United States
By Bookmasters